Applied Theatre

Applied Theatre:
International Case Studies and Challenges for Practice

Edited by Monica Prendergast and Juliana Saxton

intellect Bristol, UK / Chicago, USA

First published in the UK in 2009 by Intellect,
The Mill, Parnall Road, Fishponds, Bristol, BS16 3JG, UK

First published in the USA in 2009 by Intellect, The University of Chicago Press,
1427 E. 60th Street, Chicago, IL 60637, USA

A catalogue record for this book is available from
the British Library.

Cover design: Holly Rose
Copy-editor: Jennifer Alluisi
Typesetting: John Teehan

ISBN 9781841502816

Printed and bound by Gutenberg Press, Malta.

Contents

Acknowledgements i

Preface: What is this book about? v

Part One: Theories, History and Practices of Applied Theatre

Chapter One: Theories and History of Applied Theatre
    1.1 Where do we find applied theatre? 3
    1.2 What is applied theatre?.. 6
    1.3 Why applied theatre? How did it emerge?......................................7
    1.4 What is the purpose of applied theatre? 11
        Summary 13
        Further Reading... 14
        Questions for Reflection and Discussion 14
        Suggested Activities 15

Chapter Two: Practices of Applied Theatre
    2.1 How do we make applied theatre? 17
    2.2 Who are the performers of applied theatre?.................................. 20
    2.3 Who is applied theatre for? 20
    2.4 What are the interactions between actors,
        spectators and facilitators in applied theatre? 21
    2.5 How do we assess applied theatre?...23
    2.6 What are the key areas to effective applied
        theatre practice?...25
        Summary..26
        Further Reading 26
        Questions for Reflection and Discussion 27
        Suggested Activities 27

Part Two: The Landscape of Applied Theatre

Chapter Three: Theatre in Education (TIE)

Introduction 31

3.1 **Human rights** from *Indigo* by Dukes TIE Company
(*SCYPT, 26*, 1993) 34

3.2 **Stages of development** from *Rainbows and
spiderwebs: New challenges for theatre in
a transformed system of education in South
Africa* by Michael Carklin (*RIDE: Research
in Drama Education, 2*(2), 1997) 39

3.3 **Anti-drug education** from *Drug education
through creating theatre in education* by
Joe Winston (*RIDE: Research in Drama
Education, 6*(1), 2001) 41

3.4 **Addressing LGTB biases** from *Why Devise?
Why now?: "Houston, we have a problem"*
by Norma Bowles (*Theatre Topics, 15*(1), 2005) 44

Further Reading 47

Questions for Reflection and Discussion 48

Suggested Activities 49

Chapter Four: Popular Theatre

Introduction 51

4.1 **Popular Theatre as Spectacle** from
The Welfare State Theatre by Theodore
Shank (*TDR: The Drama Review, 21*(1), 1977) 53

4.2 **Puppetry with at-risk youth** from
*Walking in both worlds: Snuff Puppets at
Barak Indigenous College* by Kate Donelan
and Angela O'Brien (*ATR: Applied Theatre
Researcher, 7*(2), 2006) 57

4.3 **Comic performance in Bangkok** from *Duen
Phen: Joker performance in the nightclubs
of Bangkok* by Mary L. Grow (*Asian Theatre
Journal, 12*(2), 1995) 62

Further Reading 65

Questions for Reflection and Discussion 67

Suggested Activities 67

Chapter Five: Theatre of the Oppressed (TO)
      Introduction 69
  5.1 **A letter from Augusto Boal** from
      INTERVIEW: *Augusto Boal, City Councillor:*
      Legislative Theatre and the Chamber in the
      Street by Richard Schechner, Sudipto
      Chatterjee and Augusto Boal
      (*TDR: The Drama Review, 42*(4),1998) 71
  5.2 **Forum theatre on sexual harassment** from
      Making bodies talk in forum theatre by
      Paul Dwyer (*RIDE: Research in Drama*
      Education, 9(2), 2004) 74
  5.3 **Eating disorders and Theatre of the**
      Oppressed from *Speaking theatre/Doing*
      pedagogy: Re-visiting theatre of the
      oppressed by Leigh Anne Howard
      (*Communication Education, 53*(3), 2004) 77
      Further Reading 81
      Questions for Reflection and Discussion 82
      Suggested Activities 82

Part Three: The Locations of Applied Theatre

Chapter Six: Theatre in Health Education (THE)
      Introduction 87
  6.1 **HIV/AIDS** from *Icons and metaphors in*
      African theatre against HIV/AIDS by
      Victor S. Dugga (*NJ: Drama Australia*
      Journal, 26(2), 2002) 89
  6.2 **HIV/AIDS & ovarian cancer** from *All the*
      world's a stage: The use of theatrical
      performance in medical education by
      Johanna Shapiro and Lynn Hunt (*Medical*
      Education, 37(10), 2003) 92
  6.3 **Child abuse and family violence** from *Making the*
      everyday extraordinary: A theatre-in-education
      project to prevent child abuse, neglect and
      family violence by Peter O'Connor, Briar O'Connor
      and Marlane Welsh-Morris (*RIDE: Research in*
      Drama Education, 11(2), 2006) 94

6.4 **Drug abuse** from *Scratchin' the surface with
Vita Nova* by Sharon Muiruri (*Drama
Magazine, 28*, 2000) 97
Further Reading..101
Questions for Reflection and Discussion 103
Suggested Activities 103

Chapter Seven: Theatre for Development (TfD)
Introduction... 105
7.1 **A Bangladesh TfD project** from *Social theatre
in Bangladesh* by Nazmul Ahsan (*TDR: The Drama
Review, 48*(3), 2004) 107
7.2 **Education for political process in Uganda**
from *A theatrical approach to the making
of a national constitution: The case of Uganda*
by Mangeni Patrick wa'Ndeda (*NJ: Drama
Australia Journal, 24*(1), 2000)... 111
7.3 **Women's rights in Pakistan** from *Fitting the bill:
Commissioned theatre projects on human rights
in Pakistan: The work of Karachi-based theatre
group Tehrik e Niswan* by Asma Mundrawala
(*RIDE: Research in Drama Education, 12*(2), 2007) 114
Further Reading..116
Questions for Reflection and Discussion 117
Suggested Activities 117

Chapter Eight: Prison Theatre
Introduction..119
8.1 **Critical citizenship in prison** from *Prose and cons:
Theatrical encounters with students and
prisoners in Ma'asiyahu, Israel* by Sonja
Kuftinec & Chen Alon (*RIDE: Research in
Drama Education, 12*(3), 2007)...121
8.2 **Fatherhood and family** from *Notes from
inside: Forum theatre in maximum security*
by Tim Mitchell (*Theater, 31*(3), 2001)..................................... 125
8.3 **Human rights in a Brazilian prison** from
Taking hostages: Staging human rights by
Paul Heritage (*TDR: The Drama Review,
48*(3), 2004) 128
Further Reading..131

Questions for Reflection and Discussion 133
Suggested Activities 133

Chapter Nine: Community-based Theatre
    Introduction.. 135
  9.1 **Large-scale community play** from
      'B-O-U-R-N-E-M-O-U-T-H! Our Town!' Effects
      on male teenagers of participation in a
      community play by Tony Horitz. (*RIDE: Research*
      in Drama Education, 6(1), 2001) 137
  9.2 **The "world of systems"/the "world of life"**
      from *Community theatre in a South Samic*
      community: The challenges in working with
      theatre in small communities by Tordis Landvik
      (*ATR: Applied Theatre Researcher, 6,* 2005) 142
  9.3 **Working with war veterans** from *Devising*
      community by Crystal Brian (*Theatre Topics, 15*(1), 2005).................... 146
    Further Reading.. 151
    Questions for Reflection and Discussion 152
    Suggested Activities 152

Chapter Ten: Museum Theatre
    Introduction 153
  10.1 **Golden school days** from *"Dear great*
      grandchildren: When I was in school there was
      only one classroom and the school was
      as big as a house. . .": Craigflower Schoolhouse,
      1860 by Juliana Saxton and Margaret Burke
      (*Drama Contact, 1*(10), 1986) 155
  10.2 **Re-examining history through museum**
      theatre from *Making history in the second*
      person: Post-touristic considerations for living
      historical interpretation by Scott Magelssen
      (*Theatre Journal, 58*(2), 2006).. 159
  10.3 **Museum-university partnership** from *Digging*
      a ditch with undergraduates: A museum theatre
      experience by Debra McLauchlan (*NJ: Drama*
      Australia Journal, 31(2), 2008)... 162
    Further Reading 165
    Questions for Reflection and Discussion.................................... 166
    Suggested Activities... 166

Chapter Eleven: Reminiscence Theatre

Introduction 169

11.1 **Memory and transgression** from *The subversive practices of reminiscence theatre in Taiwan* by Wan-Jung Wang (*RIDE: Research in Drama Education, 11*(1), 2006) 171

11.2 **Intergenerational reminiscence theatre** from *The performance of memory: Drama, reminiscence and autobiography* by Helen Nicholson (*NJ: Drama Australia Journal, 27*(2), 2003) 174

11.3 **The evolution of a piece of reminiscence theatre** from *Older people act up: Making the ordinary extraordinary* by Howard Pflanzer (*TDR: The Drama Review, 36*(1), 1992) 178

11.4 **Interrogating reminiscence** from *Reminiscence and oral history: Parallel universes or shared endeavour?* by Joanna Bornat (*Ageing and Society, 21*, 2001) 180

Further Reading 182

Questions for Reflection and Discussion 183

Suggested Activities 183

Part Four: Challenges for Practice

Chapter Twelve: Participation, Ethics, Aesthetics and Assessment 187

12.1 Participation 189

12.2 Artistry and Aesthetics 191

12.3 Ethics 193

12.4 Assessment/Evaluation 195

Summary 198

Further Reading 198

Questions for Reflection and Discussion 200

Suggested Activity 200

Afterword: Reflection 203

Bibliography 207

Index 221

ACKNOWLEDGEMENTS

The editors wish to thank the authors for permission to use their work.

Speaking theatre/Doing pedagogy: Re-visiting theatre of the oppressed by Leigh Anne Howard, *Communication Education, 53*(3), 2004. Reprinted by permission of the publisher (Taylor & Francis, Ltd, www.informaworld.com).

Rainbows and spiderwebs: New challenge for theatre in a transformed system of education in South Africa by Michael Carklin, *Research in Drama Education, 2*(2), 1997. Reprinted by permission of the publisher (Taylor & Francis, Ltd, www.informaworld.com).

Drug education through creating theatre in education by Joe Winston, *Research in Drama Education, 6*(1), 2001. Reprinted by permission of the publisher (Taylor & Francis, Ltd, www.informaworld.com).

Making bodies talk in forum theatre by Paul Dwyer, *Research in Drama Education 9*(2), 2004. Reprinted by permission of the publisher (Taylor & Francis, Ltd, www.informaworld.com).

Making the everyday extraordinary: A theatre-in-education project to prevent child abuse, neglect and family violence by Peter O'Connor, Briar O'Connor and Marlane Welsh-Morris, *Research in Drama Education 11*(2), 2006. Reprinted by permission of the publisher (Taylor & Francis, Ltd, www.informaworld.com).

Fitting the bill: Commissioned theatre projects of human rights in Pakistan: The work of Karachi-based theatre group Tehrik e Niswan by Asma Mundrawala, *Research in Drama Education 12*(2), 2007. Reprinted by permission of the publisher (Taylor & Francis, Ltd, www.informaworld.com).

Prose and cons: Theatrical encounters with students and prisoners in Ma'asiyahu, Israel by Sonja Kuftinec & Chen Alon, *Research in Drama Education 12*(3), 2007. Reprinted by permission of the publisher (Taylor & Francis, Ltd, www.informaworld.com).

The subversive practices of reminiscence theatre in Taiwan by Wan-Jung Wang, *Research in Drama Education 11*(1), 2006. Reprinted by permission of the publisher (Taylor & Francis, Ltd, www.informaworld.com).

B-O-U-R-N-E-M-O-U-T-H! Our town: Effects on male teenagers of participation in a community play by Tony Hoiwitz, *Research in Drama Education 6*(1), 2001. Reprinted by permission of the publisher (Taylor & Francis, Ltd, www.informaworld.com).

"Notes from the Inside: Forum Theatre in Maximum Security" by Tim Mitchell in *Theater*, Volume 31, no. 3, 55–61. Copyright, 2001, Yale School of Drama/Yale Repertory Theatre. All rights reserved. Reprinted with permission of the publisher.

Reminiscence and oral history: Parallel universes or shared endeavour? by Joanne Bornat, 2001. *Ageing and Society 21.* Reprinted with permission of Cambridge University Press.

"Comic performance in Bangkok from Duen Phen: Joker performance in the nightclubs of Bangkok" by Mary L. Grow, 1995, *Asian Theatre Journal* 12(2). Reprinted with permission of University of Hawaii Press.

Making History in the Second Person: Post-touristic Considerations for Living Historical Interpretation by Scott Magelssen. *Theatre Journal* 58:2 (2006), 295, 296, 298, 300. © 2006, The Johns Hopkins University Press. Reprinted with permission of The Johns Hopkins University Press.

Why devise? Why now? "Houston, we have a problem" by Norma Bowles, *Theatre Topics* 15:1 (2005), 18–20. © 2005, The Johns Hopkins University Press. Reprinted with permission of The Johns Hopkins University Press.

Devising community by Crystal Brian, *Theatre Topics* 15:1 (2005), 4–10. © 2005, The Johns Hopkins University Press. Reprinted with permission of The Johns Hopkins University Press.

"Icons and metaphors in African theatre against HIV/AIDS" by Victor S. Dugga. *NJ: Drama Australia Journal,* 26 (2). By kind permission of Drama Australia and *NJ.*

Acknowledgements

"A theatrical approach to the making of a national constitution: The case of Uganda" by Mangeni Patrick wa'Ndeda. *NJ: Drama Australia Journal*, 24(1), 2000. By kind permission of Drama Australia and *NJ*.

"The performance of memory: Drama, reminiscence and autobiography" by Helen Nicholson. *NJ : Drama Australia Journal*, 27 (2), 2003. By kind permission of Drama Australia and *NJ*.

"Digging a ditch with undergraduates: A museum theatre experience" by Debra McLauchlan. *NJ: Drama Australia Journal*, 31 (2), 2008. By kind permission of Drama Australia and *NJ*.

"Indigo" by the Dukes TIE Company. *SCYPT Journal* 26 (1993). By kind permission of the Dukes TIE Company: Ian Yeomans (Director), Danie Croft, Helen Clugston, Deb Williamson, Daley Donnelley, Lewis Frost and Chris Cooper (Actor-teachers).

"Walking in both worlds: Snuff Puppets at Barak Indigenous College" by K. Donelan and A. O'Brien. *ATR: Applied Theatre Researcher*, 7:2 (2006). By kind permission of The Applied Theatre Researcher/IDEA Journal.

"Community theatre in a South Samic community: The challenges in working with theatre in small communities" by Tordis Lanvik. *ATR: The Applied Theatre Researcher* 6 (2005). By kind permission of The Applied Theatre Researcher/IDEA Journal.

"INTERVIEW: Augusto Boal, City Councillor: Legislative Theatre and the Chamber in the Streets" by Richard Schechner and Sudipto Chatterjee, *TDR/The Drama Review*, 42:4 (T160-Winter, 1998), 75–90. © 1998 by New York University and the Massachusetts Institute of Technology.

"Social Theatre in Bangladesh" by Nasmul Ahsan, *TDR/The Drama Review*, 48:3 (Fall, 2004), 50–58. © 2004 by New York University and the Massachusetts Institute of Technology.

"Taking Hostages: Staging Human rights" by Paul Heritage, *TDR/The Drama Review*, 48:3 (Fall, 2004), 96–106. © 2004 by New York University and the Massachusetts Institute of Technology.

"Older People Act Up: Making the Ordinary Extraordinary" by Howard Pflanzer, *TDR/The Drama Review*, 36:1 (T133-Spring, 1992), 115–123. © 1998 by New York University and the Massachusetts Institute of Technology.

"The Welfare State Theatre" by Theodore Shank. *TDR: The Drama Review*, volume 21: issue 1, T73, Spring 1977.

"All the world's a stage: The use of theatrical performance in medical education" by Johanna Shapiro & Lynn Hunt, *Medical Education 37*(10), 2003. By kind permission of Wiley Blackwell.

"Scratchin' the surface with Vita Nova" by Sharon Muiruri, *Drama Magazine* 28, 2000. By kind permission of the journal of National Drama, UK.

"'Dear great grandchildren: When I was in school there was only one classroom and the school was as big as a house. . .:" Craigflower Schoolhouse, 1860' by Juliana Saxton & Margaret Burke, *Drama Contact 1*(10), 1986. By kind permission of Margaret Burke (Director).

As this book went off to the publisher for its final edit, we received the news that Augusto Boal had died. A giant in the field of applied theatre, he has left a legacy of practice that puts all practitioners, facilitators and applied theatre theorists in his debt.

> *It is not the place of the theatre to show the correct path but only to offer the means by which all paths must be examined.*
>
> *– Augusto Boal, 1985*

May 1, 2009
Victoria, British Columbia

What is this book about?

For a very new field of study, applied theatre has a significant compilation of case study and reflective theory that has appeared in an extraordinarily wide variety of journals across disciplines such as theatre studies, education, medicine, law and others. Since the beginning of this century, there has also been a growing body of texts that address this discipline (van Erven, 2001; Taylor, 2003; Thompson, 2003; Nicholson, 2005; Kuppers & Robertson, 2007; Prentki & Preston, 2008). There is, however, no text that provides an international overview for students and practitioners anxious to acquire a basic understanding of what is applied theatre and how it works. It is the intention of this text to fill that gap.

Part One offers two chapters that provide a brief historical and theoretical overview and a general analysis of the contexts and contents of practice. They serve as a background against which readers may place their own experiences as well as their reading of the case studies that illustrate the nine categories of applied theatre that this text addresses. Following the introductory chapters, Part Two maps three core practices of applied theatre that we believe to be seminal to one's understanding of the field and presents case studies in Theatre in Education, Popular Theatre and Theatre of the Oppressed. The chapters in Part Three address topics within the core practices identified in Part Two and are defined by their intention: to heal, to raise socio-political awareness and to celebrate community through history and memory. In delineating these categories of practice, we recognize overlapping boundaries that can themselves serve as points of discussion reflecting the ongoing development of the field. Each chapter includes a brief contextual overview followed by excerpted examples of case studies of applied theatre projects. Drawing on these, we offer sources for further reading and raise issues for examination and further investigation through questions for discussion. Each chapter concludes with suggestions for practical activities.

In assembling resources for this text, we have selected from the diversity of applied theatre practices so that those new to the field or seeking examples of experience may gain a broader and deeper understanding of the potential challenges and rewards of working with communities—often non-experienced communities—through theatre. A number of readers may wonder why we have left out certain practices that some may consider to be applied theatre, such as drama therapy, simulations and employment skill training (e.g., with police, military, medical personnel and business people). Our decision is based on the recognition of *applied drama* as a separate field of practice that is process-based and does not generally involve a theatrical performance to an audience (Nicholson, 2005). While much of applied theatre begins as process, working in similar ways to applied drama, the word "theatre" (*theatron*: "seeing-place") means that a public or semi-public performance is a necessary component of the work (King, 1981, pp. 6–11).

The final chapter of Part Four addresses contemporary issues about which there is a continuing discussion and upon which rests the success or failure of applied theatre work. These challenges of practice involve participation, ethics, aesthetics and assessment. The text provides an overview of examples of applied theatre work in order to open up the reader's appreciation for the breadth and depth of practice, and this final chapter begins to examine the properties that are indicative of effective facilitation and presentation.

The range of applied theatre practice is vast; it happens all over the world as part of a grassroots movement involved in social change and community reflection. While there are exceptional descriptions of that work, this text is limited to studies that have appeared in English or in English translations. It is important to note that the majority of these case studies have appeared in academic journals and are authored by scholars who may or may not be applied theatre practitioners themselves. The literature on applied theatre needs more documentation created by local facilitators and participants in their own voices. However, these voices may be found on project websites and we offer a number of these as references throughout the text.

Our selection process is focused on what we see as exemplary practices and draws on projects that have not previously appeared in book form; it is our intention to direct students of applied theatre to key journals in the field. The thirty case studies represent applied theatre practices on five continents and in fifteen countries, and this international scope points to the extraordinary power of theatre to illuminate and transform.

Invent [your] own path . . . Find your own way according to your particular personal needs, preferences, curiosities or desires.

Augusto Boal, 1998, p. ix

We have made every effort to keep words and punctuation as they appear in the original, but punctuation such as dashes, spacing and quotation

vi

marks have been standardized for ease of reading. Within the case studies, we use an ellipsis in brackets, [...], to indicate a significant cut, a regular ellipsis, ... , to indicate a small excision, and a spaced ellipsis, . . . , denotes the author's own punctuation. The methods for indicating speech have been standardized with a • before each speaker's contribution. Each one of the case studies is surrounded by a rich context of theory, other examples of practice and valuable insights that we could not include. We urge you to seek out the original articles and, following Augusto Boal's (1998) advice, invite you to select chapters of interest and not necessarily to read them in the order in which they appear in the text.

PART ONE

Theories, History and Practices of Applied Theatre

1.1 Where do we find applied theatre?

Theatre in Education (TIE): Britain's Cardboard Citizens theatre company presents a theatre in education production in schools called *Home and Away* that addresses "an issue that has been thrust to the top of the political agenda in Britain in recent years, that of refugees and asylum seekers" (Jackson, 2005, p. 114). The play weaves together a traditional Ethiopian folk tale with the story of a young Ethiopian refugee living in England. The narrator, Teri, moves from ignorance to understanding as she encounters this young man and his culture; however, her empathy comes too late and he commits suicide. Following the performance, the audience is split into four groups, each actor working with a group to seek more positive endings. The company then moves into a forum theatre session where the actors and volunteer students test these "endings" out as the scenes are re-interpreted.

Popular Theatre: A popular theatre production, facilitated by Julie Salverson and commissioned by the Canadian Red Cross, tackles the topic of land mines. The script is written as a clown show and focuses on "what it is for Canadian youth to encounter land mines" (Salverson, 2000, p. 27). "For many in the cast, tackling the problem of performing the clowns engaged the students in the conscious work of sorting out and recognizing their many and sometimes contradictory responses to the story they were telling" (pp. 70–71). The resulting play, *BOOM*, is rehearsed and performed by a group of thirteen high school students in consultation with a Toronto-based director originally from Sarajevo. At the heart of the play lies the question, "What does it mean to be a witness?"

Teacher: "What would you do if I told·you something you don't want to hear?"
Clown 1: "Is this about what happened in the news yesterday?"
Clown 2: "Which things? The horrible made up ones, or the ones that are true?"

Julie Salverson, 1999,
p. 64

The production plays to multiple community and school audiences and is published in the *Canadian Theatre Review*.

Theatre of the Oppressed (TO): Vancouver's Headlines Theatre production of *Corporation in our Heads* is performed in 2000. Using Augusto Boal's (1995) Cops in the Head—a Theatre of the Oppressed strategy that dramatizes the internal voices that oppress—the audience selects a personal story told by a woman activist who was tempted to buy her jeans at The Gap. The facilitator freezes the scene at the moment of temptation and the audience takes on the corporate voices playing in the protagonist's head. In this strategy, volunteer audience members are invited onto the stage by "The Joker" (Boal's term for facilitator) and enter into the action. After many interventions by audience members, new understandings were expressed about how corporations use various tactics to engage consumers and how gaining that knowledge disarms the power of these corporate voices to oppress (see www.headlinestheatre.com/pastwork/corp-report1.html).

Theatre for Health Education (THE): *Nobody Wants My Old Organs* is a play designed by Target Theatre to encourage organ donation. The "playwright" is the company and its director. The process first involves interviews with organ donors, transplant hopefuls, families and medical personnel. These interviews are transcribed, checked for accuracy and then shaped through improvisation into a series of scenes that address the major concerns of the topic. The company's work received major funding from the Canadian Kidney Foundation, which had asked them to take on the issue. The purpose, although expressly didactic, is mediated with a great deal of humor as the audience identifies with the variety of characters. The post performance talkback is facilitated by an organ transplant recipient who uses his own experience as an element in the discussion while the actors offer their experiences in building the play (Saxton & Miller, 2006, pp. 132–133).

Theatre for Development (TfD): A play entitled *Dukhini* (*Suffering Woman*) by Pakistan's Ajoka Theatre group exposes and explores:

> …the trafficking of women who are smuggled from poverty-stricken Bangladesh across India and into Pakistan under the false promise of a "better life," only to find themselves sold into prostitution to the highest bidder. Under such an ideology, it is never the rapist/buyer of sex who is blamed but the woman who is raped or forced into prostitution—she has to bear the burden of having "dishonoured" her family, who will never accept her back because of the "shame" she has brought them (Afzal-Khan, 2001, p. 67).

4

There are no happy endings for the women characters portrayed; they dream of returning home to their families but are trapped into forced slavery and prostitution by pimps who keep the women powerless and without hope. In 2000, the production was performed in Pakistan, India and Nepal to some 10, 000 people.

Prison Theatre: *Journey Woman* is a week-long program of theatre and drama-based work facilitated by England's Geese Theatre Company for female offenders and their caretakers. The week begins with a performance that follows the story of Ellie, a woman who has broken out of the cycle of hardship, offending and prison. Looking back on her life, Ellie revisits key episodes and moments of change: leaving home for the first time, her first involvement with offending, becoming a mother and her first prison sentence. Throughout the piece, the audience is invited to consider the different masks she has worn throughout her life, the different roles she has played and her different life stories. The audience members are enrolled as experts in Ellie's life, analyzing the crucial moments, exploring her inner feelings and emotions and contemplating how moments from her past have impacted on her present and future. This performance acts as the catalyst for the following four-and-a-half day residency: www.geese.co.uk/HTML/projects/journey-woman.html.

Community-based Theatre: The community play, *Loricum*, was written by nine teenagers in collaboration with MED Theatre's playwright/artistic director. It involves nineteen young actors working alongside adults in a cast of thirty-two, with professional input from a composer, choreographer, costume designer and visual artists. In the program, a student participant describes how the play was built:

> As a starting point…we were given the phrase: "While there is still dance and time," and were introduced to the characters of Tom and Amy…. We devised, improvised, scripted and discussed until we knew these characters as if they were old friends.

Loricum is a play that contrasts the experiences of two generations growing up on Dartmoor. The building of a reservoir divides the community and covers up a secret. Using the convention of creating a documentary film about the reservoir, the "director" begins to uncover the history that lies beneath its dark surface. This celebration of local history is performed in Dartmoor village halls throughout the month of March 2006 (see www.medtheatre.co.uk/Loricum.htm).

Museum Theatre: At Washington's Smithsonian Institute in the summer of 2006, as part of an exhibit on transportation, a pretty young blonde girl dressed in 1950s fashion is found among the cars, buses and trucks of the period. She notices an audience gathering and tells them how excited she is because her boyfriend is coming and she hopes he is going to purchase a car. The boyfriend arrives and we discover that it is his parents who are buying the car and that they are already in the manager's office signing the papers. While the two young people are waiting, their conversation gives us a picture of how transportation played a major part of life in small-town America in the 1950s. Following this historical interpretation performance, the actors come out of role and engage the audience, many of whom are anxious to share their own experiences from that period, in a talkback discussion (Saxton, 2006).

Reminiscence Theatre: A collaboration between five New York University undergraduate acting students and eight members of the JASA (Jewish Association for Services for the Aged) theatre ensemble resulted in a reminiscence piece called *I Am Acting My Age*. The project explores the relationship between two generations: "old-young, grandparent-grandchild, sage-student . . . Winter-Spring" (Pflanzer, 1992, p. 122). Some of the scenes created by this intergenerational ensemble involve rites of passage (leaving home, choosing to die), including "an elderly couple discovering their grandson has AIDS . . . [and] an elderly mother fight[ing] her two middle-aged children for the right to lead her own life" (p. 122). The learning that occurs in this playbuilding process is the realization that young and old alike share a need and "a hunger to be connected to each other" (p. 122).

1.2 What is applied theatre?

In our view, this "very capacious portmanteau term" (Giesekam, 2006, p. 91) is inclusive and does not carry any limiting fixed agendas. Instead, "the applied theatre label [is] a useful umbrella term . . . for finding links and connections for all of us committed to the power of theatre in making a difference in the human life span" (Taylor, 2006, p. 93). All of the above thumbnail narratives offer examples of a web of performance practices (Schechner, 1988/2003, pp. xvi–xix) that fall outside mainstream theatre performance and take place "in non-traditional settings and/or with marginalized communities" (Thompson & Jackson, 2006, p. 92). That is to say, they most often are played in spaces that are not usually defined as theatre buildings, with participants who may or may not be skilled in theatre arts and to audiences who have a vested interest in the issue taken up by the performance or are members of the community addressed by the performance. Alternative theatre practices, including those described above, have historically been labeled with a number of diverse terms, such as grassroots theatre,

> I have come to distrust the definitions of disciplines that we invent as our knowledge grows. These definitions are useful for the experts but can be confusing to others. And they may imply divisions and differences that don't really exist.
>
> James Zull, 2002,
> pp. xiv, xv

social theatre, political theatre, radical theatre and many other variations, but over the course of the last decade, "applied theatre" is the term that has emerged as the umbrella under which all of these prior terms and practices are embraced.

One example of how applied theatre can be different lies in the area of scripting. Whereas traditional mainstream theatre is most often centered in the interpretation of a pre-written script, applied theatre, in contrast, involves both the generation and the interpretation of a theatre piece that in performance may or may not be scripted in the traditional manner. In those cases where an applied theatre performance takes the form of a polished improvisation, a formally written script may never be recorded. There are very few complete examples of scripts although the case studies that follow will often quote excerpts. As you read through these case studies, you will note the many ways in which applied theatre differs from "theatre" as most people would think of it.

1.3 Why applied theatre? How did it emerge?

Theatre has had an historic role in society as providing a relatively safe way of talking back to power. Across many cultures and traditions over time we can trace patterns and instances of groups of people using the stage as a space and place to tell their stories and their lives. This aesthetic and emotional outlet allows for potential *catharsis*, a safe way for citizens to express their concerns, criticisms and frustration to each other and to society at large. And often that opportunity has been enough. Some examples of this kind of theatrical expression are to be found around the world in the social dramas of rituals such as carnivals, Feast of Fools, initiation rites, and through trickster figures in myths and legends— the servant figure in drama traditionally has had more power in the world of a play than his or her masters. The roots of Greek chorus, *commedia del arte*, Moliere, Shakespeare and, closer to our own time, the comedies of Shaw and Coward, for example, have always been fed by this power reversal that is sanctioned and accepted within the protected space of the fictional world of the stage.

Catharsis (*katharsis*: purgation) is a Greek medical term that Aristotle uses to argue that tragedy does not encourage the passions but in fact rids (or purges) the spectator of them. Catharsis is a "beneficial, uplifting experience whether psychological, moral, intellectual or some combination of these."

Marvin Carlson, 1993, pp. 18–19

In modern Western theatre history, playwrights like Henrik Ibsen, George Bernard Shaw and Bertolt Brecht offer a theatre of social criticism, debate and, in Brecht's case, potential revolutionary action. More contemporary playwrights, such as Caryl Churchill, Dario Fo, Wole Soyinka, Ariel Dorfman, and many others, have focused much of their theatre on exposing and exploring social and political issues in their plays. Applied

All drama is...a political event: it either reasserts or undermines the code of conduct of a given society.

Martin Esslin, 1976, p. 29

theatre is informed by these plays and playwrights to the extent that they offer clear models of how effective theatre can tackle a range of topical provocations and provide an aesthetic site for their considered examination.

Applied theatre works overtly either to reassert or to undermine socio-political norms, as its intent is to reveal more clearly the way the world is working. For example, reminiscence theatre, community-based theatre and museum theatre are most often reassertions and celebrations of memory and history. On the other hand, theatre of the oppressed, popular theatre, theatre in education, theatre for health education and theatre for development are most often focused on undermining the status quo in order to promote positive social change. Prison theatre may fall within either depending upon intention and context. Reassertions or undermining intentions are both ways by which we can re-examine the world to discover how it works and our place in it; they hold within them the potential to be educational, reflective and/or rehabilitative.

Marvin Carlson pointed out in 1993 that "[t]he continuing point of debate in modern theatre theory has been over whether the theatre should be viewed primarily as an engaged social phenomenon or as a politically indifferent aesthetic artefact" (p. 454). That debate continues. Herbert Blau criticizes theatre as aesthetic artefact (isolated and elitist), "a stronghold of non-ideas" (1965, p. 7). Theatre for Blau is a public art and one that should function at the "dead center of community" (p. 309). Like Brecht before him, Blau sees that the function of theatre lies with waking up the audience to its obligations and responsibilities through its collective imagination.

To like the theatre you have to like its transience and its immediacy: it happens in the present tense and it's fallible. There's a sense of occasion in any theatre performance and of participation in a communal act: you go into a theatre as an individual and you emerge as an audience.

Richard Eyre & Nicholas Wright, 2001, p. 11

Using Bertolt Brecht's lehrstücke (short, severe and instructive works performed for audiences of students, workers and children [see Eyre & Wright, p. 204]) as the first indication in the 20th century of a "new aesthetic" for theatre, we can begin to trace the threads of change through the work of Michael Kirby (1965) and Jerzy Grotowski (1968). Kirby wanted to rid theatre of the constraints of its conventional structure of plot (rising action, climax and dénouement) and replace it with something he called "compartmental structure" akin to collage (Carlson, 1993, p.

Alfred Jarry (1873–1907) and Vsevolod Meyerhold (1874–1940) could be regarded as early fathers of applied theatre in that they (out of their time) created theatre that challenged received ideas of performance.

For a survey of changing theatre practices in the UK, see Eyre & Wright's *Changing Stages* (2001, pp. 284–288).

457). Compartmental structure foreshadows the often episodic nature of applied theatre presentations where scenes are linked by theme rather than plot development. Grotowski sought to create "archetypical images and actions that would force the spectator into an emotional involvement" (p. 455). He was interested in his highly trained actors addressing the needs of a small group of individuals in a totally open way (p. 457). Even such a theatrical anchor as intention or purpose was questioned by French theorist practitioners like Fernando Arrabal (1973). Arrabal and his circle prefigured chaos theory by their abandonment of structure and the invitation to include "the widest possible elements" that embraced such opposites as "the sacred and the profane, executions and celebrations of·life, the sordid and the sublime" (Arrabal, 1973, p. 98).

Richard Kostelanetz in 1968 drew attention to other significant shifts, of which two are important for our study here. "Staged performances" were much like traditional theatre but *without the reliance on words*. They were strongly movement-oriented and the actors *performed without masks as themselves* or as a kind of "neutral sign", the emphasis being on the experience itself and the *process of creation* rather than the *product of creative acts* (Carlson, 1993, p. 461, italics ours).

As Tarlington and Michaels (1995) explain, an applied theatre piece can be "linked logically, rather than temporally, to those [scenes] before and after it" (p. 20).

Audiences, too, began to be recognized by theatre makers as integral to the wholeness of a performance. But after a couple of centuries of being quiet and in the dark, audiences did not always take kindly to this new attention; even today, being "recognized by the stage" can make people embarrassed or uneasy. The playwright Peter Handke attempted to revitalize the audience by making them conscious that "they are there, that they exist" (cited in Carlson, p. 462). Richard Foreman (1976) took this idea further by creating theatre pieces that were deliberately intended to lead the audience to become more self-aware and self-reflexive. Many of these "new" ideas came together in the work of Peter Brook (1968), whose theatre-making was designed to join spectators, actors and performance in a "communal celebration of experience" (Carlson, p. 464).

It was clear by the middle of the 20th century, notable for the dazzling pace of its change, that the relationship between actors, audiences and performance structures was undergoing significant shifts in aesthetic understanding. Indeed, 1968 has become for theatre historians, theorists and practitioners the dividing line between the traditional and the new theatre. The Avignon Manifesto, an open letter from young theatre radicals inspired by the student and worker uprising in Paris in 1968, makes the shift clear. It called for a theatre of " 'collective creation' with no schism between artistic activities and 'political, social, and everyday events'," a theatre of 'political and psychological liberation' of 'direct rather than represented

The relationship between the actor and the audience is the only theatre reality.

Peter Brook in
Croyden, 2003, p. 28

action,' which would place the spectator no longer in an 'alienated and underdeveloped situation' " (Copfermann, 1972, cited in Carlson, 1993, p. 471).

There are three writers whose theory and practice are of particular interest as we explore the antecedents of applied theatre: Armand Gatti, John O'Toole and Augusto Boal. Director Armand Gatti, like Kirby, was intent on freeing theatre from its reliance on sequential time: theatrical action for Gatti was most generative when it allowed spectators/participants to see the same thing from a number of different viewpoints, where endings remained open and available to questions. He was a forerunner of the popular theatre movement—a people's theatre, a theatre engaged with the popular culture of the society and belonging to it (Prentki & Selman, 2000). For this revolutionary theatre artist, the function of theatre was to enable "the disinherited classes" to create a theatre that reflected their concerns—not through performances *for* them but *with* them. He did this through a series of what he called *mini-pièces*—short scenes encouraging reflection, which might lead later to further action that could perhaps alleviate those concerns to some degree. Gatti saw himself as a "catalyst of the creative powers of the people of the community" (Knowles, 1989, p. 202), not as a playwright, and he saw the theatre as the means of giving language to those who lacked the words to describe their social situations.

The second practitioner/theorist was John O'Toole, whose 1976 text, *Theatre in Education: New objectives for theatre—new techniques for education*, describes and analyzes a number of UK-based case studies of school performances. In this seminal text, O'Toole lays the foundations that resulted in a vigorous two decades of TIE practice in England and still informs effective applied theatre practice today. In Chapter 5, "The perils and pleasure of participation," O'Toole draws our attention to a number of strategies and techniques used by various teams of actors to engage the audiences through what he calls "integral" participation in which the audience "acts as well as being acted upon" (p. 88). One of the most effective ways, he notes, is when:

> [O]ne or two brave teams have taken [the technique of hot seating] further and stopped the action for the children to discuss the situation with the characters, who then carried on the play according to the advice the children gave them (p. 97).

This is, he suggests, a "technique worth exploring in more depth and more frequently" (p. 97).

This responsive, improvisatory strategy was taken up by Brazilian director Augusto Boal—founder of Theatre of the Oppressed—and became a key concept in his Forum Theatre. Boal himself was deeply influenced by Paolo Freire's *Pedagogy of the Oppressed* (1970/2000) that aims to empower learners as active agents in their own education. Indeed, the practice of engaging the audience interactively with the performance (before, during or after the performance—and sometimes all three), as seen in the work of Gatti, O'Toole and Boal, is a consistent characteristic of all forms of applied theatre.

This brief historical overview enables us to identify the strands that are integral to the fabric of applied theatre as an engaged, social, artistic phenomenon and some of the characteristics of its practices:

- focus on multiple perspectives
- disregard for sequence as fundamental to effective structure
- endings that remain open for questioning
- less reliance on words; more exploration of movement and image as theatre language
- greater reliance on polished improvisation
- theatre as a close, direct reflection of actual life with an overt political intent to raise awareness and to generate change
- a collective approach to creating theatre pieces in which the makers themselves become aware and capable of change
- issues of local importance that may or may not be transferable to other communities
- audience as an important and active participant in the creation of understanding and, often, of the action

All of these shifts occurred inside a wider socio-political and economic context. The last half of the 20th century boiled with new thought and was influenced by such things as the fall of the Berlin wall, feminism, globalism, the space race, chaos and complexity theory, and the rise of the individual ready to question authority and ask "Who holds the power?" and "By what right?" Theatre, like all art, both reflected this new awareness and had foretold it in the practice and theory of earlier playwrights, actors and directors who were already laying the foundations for a more public art that truly functions at the living center of its communities.

1.4 What is the purpose of applied theatre?

Theatre artists have always turned to their art form as a means of finding their way through crises and challenges: for example, Jean Anouilh's subversive adaptation of *Antigone* (1942/1951) was performed in Paris under the Nazi regime or Tony Kushner's *Angels in America* (1993) that challenged audiences to address the reality of HIV/AIDS. This is theatre as activism, enfolded in the "safety" of entertainment, which rises "spontaneously from within situations of war, insurgency, political and civil crisis" and has long been a part of theatre tradition (McDonnell, 2006, p. 2). Another impetus for applied theatre involves "self-conscious attempts to influence political reality" (p. 2), using theatre as a facilitated intervention from the outside with communities for whom theatricality is not intrinsic. This interventionist theatre is the primary focus of this text.

James Thompson (2003) writes about the nature of intervention in applied theatre. He says:

> Much applied theatre in its 'intentional' form creates a practice that seeks to debate vital issues and see those concerns transformed into new stories or within unfamiliar settings. . . . [It is a way] to provide people with a means to work their way through difficult transitory periods [as an] aid in seeing them safely into a new place or time (pp. 200–202).

Interventionist theatre may be generated in three ways:

1. An outside organization, generally a theatre group or individual facilitator, is aware of or is invited into a site that is struggling with socio-political issues. The needs expressed by the community become the themes explored through theatre processes and presented back to the community as a theatre piece;
2. An outside agency commissions a theatre production for or with a target group to tackle a specific topic or issue for various purposes, most often educational; or
3. A facilitator or theatre company instigates a community-based theatre project that aims to celebrate some aspect of the community for the psychological/emotional health of that group.

What is most helpful in guiding our understanding of these interventionist models is the distinction between *presentational* and *representational* forms of theatre. *Representational* theatre has as its organizing principle the creation of another fictional and hypothetical onstage world performed by actors who are intentionally hidden behind the mask of character from those who sit and observe in the audience. This theatre form clearly represents people, times and places that are "other" from our contemporary reality and functions under the rubric of "the willing suspension of disbelief" (Coleridge, 1817). *Presentational* theatre, in contrast, is more interested in presenting non-fictional material within thinly-disguised fictions of authentic contemporary reality. The actor in presentational theatre is less hidden behind the mask of character and is closer to being him or

In *believed-in performances* people are who they perform, playing their social and/or personal identities: judges, accused, rabbis, lawyers, teachers, activists, bus drivers, lovers, whoever.
Richard Schechner, 1998, p. 77.

herself—although still protected by the safety of the role—thus enabling the actor to present a character who lives in the world of the audience as well as the world of the play. It is this latter presentational form that most often manifests in applied theatre practice. Bernard Beckerman (1990) summarizes the difference between representational and presentational theatre:

Simon Shepherd and Mick Wallis discuss presentation and representation from a theoretical perspective in their book *Drama/ Theatre /Performance*, 2004, pp. 225–235.

What is normally called dramatic presentation is actually a form of *direct* presentation. The performer acknowledges the presence of the audience and presents the show making that acknowledgement explicit. This type of playing differs from the *indirect* form of presentation where the performer supposedly does not "admit" the presence of the audience and acts as though the activity performed has an autonomous existence (pp. 110–111).

Whereas in representational theatre a fourth wall is in place much of the time, in presentational theatre the fourth wall is permeable, transparent, and often breached by audience members who directly participate in the action of the play.

Applied theatre is not only local in its attention to the everyday world; it is also contemporaneously concerned with the greater issues of active citizenship and democratic practice (Nicholson, 2005) framed in the aesthetic structures of theatre, the most social of art forms. It is the negotiation of the aesthetic with the everyday through the medium of theatre that results in the variety of forms of applied theatre.

Summary

We hope that this overview of the history and aspects of theatre theory that are applicable will stand as useful background for the applied theatre practices that we now begin to examine. Remember that most contemporary theatre strategies and techniques you will read about in the case studies are based on the experiences of people whose own practice served as the playing space from which their theoretical understandings grew. As you develop your own practice, we urge you to write about it in ways that will enable those who follow you to learn from your experiences. Applied theatre is a multifaceted field and all of us who work in it (and on it) have a responsibility not just to those who come after us but also to those with whom—and for whom—we create the work. You will note that there would be little for you to read without the commitment and contributions of theatre practitioners and, especially, of applied theatre participants.

Further Reading

Ackroyd, J. (2001). Applied theatre: Problems and possibilities. *Applied Theatre Reseacher,* *1*(1), unpaginated. www.griffith.edu.au/centre/cpci/atr/journal/article1_number1.htm. Ackroyd raises some important questions and concerns for anyone interested in applied theatre to consider. This accessible online journal is one to keep your eye on for new issues. You might also be interested in Ackroyd, J. (2007). Applied theatre: An exclusionary discourse? *Applied Theatre Researcher/IDEA Journal,* 8 (unpaginated) in which she examines what is happening in the field today and revisits her earlier comments.

Balfour, M. & Somers, J. (Eds.) (2006). *Drama as social intervention.* Concord, ON: Captus. This collection of keynote speeches, papers and abstracts from the Research in Drama Education triennial conference of 2005 offers up-to-date examples of current practice in applied theatre.

Bradby, D. & McCormick, J. (1978). *People's theatre.* Totowa, NJ: Rowman & Littlefield. This text offers an historic overview of the development of a "people's" theatre.

Prentki, T. & Preston, S. (Eds.). (2008). *The applied theatre reader.* London, UK: Routledge. This text provides an indispensable collection of writings by theorists and practitioners that will deepen your knowledge of the field.

Taylor, P. (2002). *Applied theatre: Creating transformative encounters in the community.* Portsmouth, NH: Heinemann. This is a good introduction that employs theory in practice and practice in theory as Taylor reflects on his own and other applied theatre practitioners' work.

Thompson, J. (2003). *Applied theatre: Bewilderment and beyond.* New York, NY: Peter Lang. Thompson writes a wide-ranging analysis and description of work and practice in the UK and other countries. He interrogates many of the ethical and practical issues that arise in applied theatre.

Questions for Reflection and Discussion

1. In what ways do any theatre experiences you have had, either as artist or audience, resonate with any of the examples given in this introduction?

2. What can we learn from the history of applied theatre? How could we use this knowledge in our practice?

Suggested Activities

1. How would you describe applied theatre to someone who has not read this introduction or experienced applied theatre in other ways? Working with a partner or a group of three, take turns role-playing this conversation.

2. Re-read the thumbnail descriptions of applied theatre practices (pp. 1–6). Which of these types of applied theatre most draws your interest? What is it that attracts you to this particular form? Write a reflection that begins with, "I could see myself working in this particular area of applied theatre because…"

2.1 How do we make applied theatre?

Facilitation

As in so much of applied theatre, there are a number of terms for those who work in theatre with communities—teaching artist, director, co-creator, artistic assistant, Joker (Boal's term) and so on—but "facilitator" seems to be the most common and, in terms of its original meaning ("to make easy"), the most appropriate. The applied theatre facilitator is a multidisciplinarian who must know about theatre and how it works as well as being equipped with an understanding of teaching and learning. It is this knowledge and these skills that make the work easier for those for whom theatre is unknown territory. In addition, a facilitator should be familiar with the social structures and community contexts within which he or she may be working. There are all-too-common instances of applied theatre projects being led by facilitators with insufficient knowledge and experience that result in experiences of little impact or value for anyone, either for those involved or those attending. Sullivan (2004), in delineating the skills of the Joker in Forum Theatre, describes the skills that all effective facilitators need as they function as the "conductor of the energies, intentions and desires released" (p. 23) during the devising and rehearsal process as well as (when appropriate) during performances:

A dramaturg is "the literary adviser associated with a theatre company" who may carry out documentary research, adapt the text, determine how meanings are linked, identify ambiguities, put forth possible interpretations and integrate the perspective and reception of the spectator.

> Patrice Pavis, 1998,
> pp. 122–123

[The facilitator]…must be able to sense and serve the needs of the audience, and create a safe container for individual self-expression as well as manage the segues among performance of scenes, spect-actor interventions, processing the results of dramatic ideas from the audience, and direct communication with the audience.

> Effective [facilitators] must combine the skill of dramaturg, director, improvisational actor, drama therapist, political philosopher, rhetorician, talk show host and stand-up comic (p. 23).

We see applied theatre facilitation as essentially grounded in drama and theatre and in education strategies and techniques, having close kinship with good pedagogical praxis. That is to say, a facilitator knows how to do something, knows why it is appropriate, when it needs to be done and how to do it in the most effective way. These are skills that require training and experience. In addition, participants benefit from a facilitator who is a communicator and a listener who possesses both social and empathic intelligence (Arnold, 2005; Goleman, 1995, 2006) in order to work with people in groups and help them arrive at decisions. Facilitation requires skills of diplomacy as this kind of work is fraught with difficulties around what is left in and what is taken out and how an aesthetic product is shaped out of dramatic process. Also key to applied theatre facilitation is the recognition that the community participants—both actors and spectators—hold the knowledge of the subject under investigation, whereas the facilitator holds the aesthetic knowledge of the theatre form.

Scripting

An applied theatre process is a collaborative and negotiated dance choreographed between people for whom the content is significant and applied theatre facilitators, dramaturgs and/or playwrights who have both competencies and experience. In certain models of applied theatre practice, a playwright will be commissioned to write a play based on research, interviews and other primary sources. The playwright will often be involved in the rehearsal process to rewrite and restructure the play. In the case of a dramaturg, it is the participants who are doing the interviewing, retelling their stories, improvising and researching. Those contributions are then assembled and shaped by the dramaturg, who is involved in an ongoing way in the process. The facilitator, in many cases, may take on the role of dramaturg because he or she knows the discipline and theory of aesthetic strategies and understands how to use them within a pedagogy of practice. Most often, however, performances in applied theatre are playbuilt.

Playbuilding

Playbuilding is the root theatre activity of applied theatre practice and is a constant process of negotiated meaning-making. Playbuilding is also called "collective creation" or "devising." Collective creation emerges from late 20th century theatre practice and describes the creation of an original play based on documents or living research by a group of skilled performers often working with a director and/or dramaturg. Some examples in a Canadian context are *The Farm Show* (Theatre Passe Muraille) and *Paper Wheat* (25th Street Theatre), both created by urban professional theatre companies

For an interview with Peter Cheeseman, an exemplar of early documentary theatre, see Gabriella Giannachi and Mary Luckhurst's *On directing.*
    (1999, pp.13–20)

interested in exploring rural issues of farming in socio-political contexts (see Filewod, 1987). Devising is a British/European term referring to the gestation phase of the theatre-making process; the first of a number of stages leading to some kind of performance outcome. Alison Oddey (1996) describes devising as:

> [A] process of making theatre that enables a group of performers to be physically and practically creative in the sharing and shaping of an original product that directly emanates from assembling, editing, and re-shaping individuals' contradictory experiences of the world. ... Devising is about thinking, conceiving, and forming ideas, being imaginative and spontaneous, as well as planning. It is about inventing, adapting, and creating what you do as a group (p. 1).

When we talk about a piece of theatre that has been devised, it suggests that the work was originally created through democratic processes of exploration utilizing many forms of improvisation. We choose to use the term "playbuilding," a name which implies not just the process of building through devising/collective creation, but also the intended outcome—that is, the development of some kind of theatre performance. These performances are generally not "plays" in the traditional sense but rather a series of monologues and scenarios built around a particular theme. Errol Bray (1991) writes that playbuilding:

> ...enables a participant to come to grips with the pleasures and problems of every aspect of drama and theatre; to be playwright, performer, director, composer, technician, designer, critic. It introduces participants to the creative discipline and co-operation required in theatre .... The process involves rehearsing the play as it is created, thus developing a strong presentation that comes to belong to the group in a very personal and committed way (p. 1).

It is the presentation that then becomes the stimulus for engagement with a larger community (the audience) about the issues and themes under investigation. This conversation itself leads to the broader possibility of potential socio-political revelation and/or change. Even an applied theatre project intended primarily as a community celebration holds within its presentation the possibility of communal reflection and fresh envisioning.

2.2 Who are the performers of applied theatre?

Performance is always a component of applied theatre. There are different kinds of performers in applied theatre projects, ranging from highly skilled professionals to community participants with little or no experience. In certain types of applied theatre, such as theatre in education, reminiscence theatre and prison theatre, it is general practice to use professional actors. For professional actors who choose to work in applied theatre, there are particular skills required. Professional actors are, of course, used to touring and are adaptable to ever-changing conditions. They should also be able to both sing and dance (skills very important in performances for children and senior citizens) and be comfortable working in non-theatre spaces where there is no fourth wall. The ability of performers to engage directly with audiences—before, during and after a performance—is key.

> [A] devising group working creatively under pressure is a particularly delicate species, with a fragile and volatile membership. It needs to be nurtured.
> Gil Lamden, 2000, p. 88

When non-professional actors form a company, as in the case of some companies of senior actors in reminiscence theatre or university or high school students, it is essential that the facilitator pay attention to the social and emotional health of the group in addition to teaching necessary performance skills. In a community-based model, facilitation involves enabling unskilled participants to function collaboratively within a dramatic process and to develop the skills that will allow them to move confidently out of the process into presentation. Often, one of the goals will be to enable participants to continue the work of development and facilitation after the facilitator has left. This highlights the importance of time spent in rehearsal on the development of acting skills through improvisation, role play, characterization, movement and voice. The most important process in group development focuses on trust and safety so that unskilled performers become comfortable risking themselves in performance. The job of the facilitator is to then negotiate, post-performance, between the performers and the audience as they reflect together upon issues that have been raised. There are, however, some circumstances where the facilitation may be undertaken by the actors or mediated by a non-theatre professional. For example, Somers and Roberts discuss a play on schizophrenia in which the post-performance discussion was led by an experienced psychiatric nurse (Somers & Roberts, 2006, p. 32).

2.3 Who is applied theatre for?

Inherent within these models of applied theatre is the participatory element that carries forward from the rehearsal process into the performance and beyond through the interaction between performers, audience and facilitators. Simply put, like all good theatre, applied

Integral participation occurs when "individual or small group contributions [are] registered, considered and…acted upon."
John O'Toole, 1976, p.104

theatre is for an audience. In mainstream theatre performances, the interaction between audiences and performers is in most cases minimal and limited to reactions within the performance that do not alter the performance. In applied theatre the opposite is true. Audiences are invited to engage both verbally and, in some cases, physically with the performance and their presence may be acknowledged by the performers before, during and/or afterwards. O'Toole (1976) calls this kind of audience participation "integral" in that this participation has the power to effect changes to the performance itself in a number of ways (p. 104). At the very least, an applied theatre piece will generally include a carefully facilitated post-show discussion that gives spectators the space needed to process and respond to what they have seen—what O'Toole calls "extrinsic" participation (p. 88). In other cases, a pre-show interaction with the audience may be necessary, especially when an audience is relatively inexperienced in spectatorship. This preparatory interaction invites the audience into the dramatic process and gives them guidelines as to their role in the performance. At other times, the audiences may be invited to a follow-up workshop in skills exhibited in the performance or used in making the performance. But, for O'Toole, this "peripheral" participation gives the audience little power because whatever it may do or say, the structure of the play is "unalterable." Integral audience participation is directly opposite as it can involve speaking directly to characters as they engage with problems that need to be addressed, calling out suggestions for possible improvised responses to dramatic situations or, as in Boal's Theatre of the Oppressed, actually taking the place of a character and performing alternative solutions to a dilemma. An applied theatre facilitator needs to be very sensitive to the particular culture of the community for which the applied theatre piece is to be played, as there are many culturally diverse practices of audience response.

2.4 What are the interactions between actors, spectators and facilitators in applied theatre?

Play, games, sports and sacred and secular rituals are all forms of performance (Schechner, 1988/2003, 2002/2006). In all of these, the audience is expected and encouraged to participate, either verbally, physically or both. In his analysis of these performance forms, Richard Schechner distinguishes between an *integral* and an *accidental* audience:

> An accidental audience is a group of people who, individually or in small clusters, go to the theater—the performances are publicly advertised and open to all. On opening nights of commercial shows, the attendance of

the critics and friends constitutes an integral rather than an accidental audience. An integral audience is one where people come because they have to or because the event is of special significance to them. Integral audiences include the relatives of the bride and groom at a wedding, the tribe assembled for initiation rites, dignitaries on the podium for an inauguration (1988/2003, p. 220).

Schechner goes on to suggest that "an accidental audience comes 'to see the show' while, in applied theatre, an integral audience is 'necessary to accomplish the work of the show'" (p. 220).

We see four distinct models of actor/participant/spectator/facilitator interaction in applied theatre. An applied theatre project may draw upon one or more of these models, depending upon its intentions. It is useful to note that the first two models below are generally engaged with integral audiences while the last two can move from integral to accidental audience engagement. In some applied theatre models, a script is generated with and for a particular community group but is then transferred to and performed by a troupe of skilled actors. This is seen most clearly in reminiscence theatre where interviews with seniors become the basis for making an applied theatre piece that is subsequently performed by professional actors for the seniors and their community. These models often involve the audience working after the performance with facilitators and actors (who may remain in role) and/or with drama-based activities to unpack the content of the performance.

In community conversations, "the focus is not on understanding theatrical craft or appreciating the skill of directors and designers, but rather on the potential for communities to express their own anxieties and hopes"
Anne Ellis, 2000, pp. 91–92

These four models, illustrated throughout the book, are:

1. **Community-based model:** A piece of theatre is created for, with and by community participants primarily for an integral audience. This process is usually facilitated by one or more outside applied theatre facilitators. Their responsibilities carry beyond their facilitation of the process into the "community conversations" (Ellis, 2000, p. 91) that follow the presentations.

2. **Curriculum model:** A skilled group selects or is contracted to engage with a topical issue and generates a theatre piece for performance in the community, primarily for the purposes of education. As in the community-based model (above), the audience is generally integral.

3. **Transfer model:** A community-based applied theatre project and presentation is transferred to and adapted by a skilled acting troupe to be performed for a more accidental audience. For example, a local presentation may prove so successful that it is invited to tour outside the context of its origins.

4. **Interview model:** Interviews become the basis for an applied theatre piece that is subsequently performed for the interviewees and their community by a group of skilled actors. This model ideally involves inviting interviewees into the rehearsal process to evaluate the authenticity of the transcribed interviews into dramatic forms, as well as the usual post-show responses through community conversations.

Those who create and spectate in applied theatre have a concern for the issue or issues under consideration and are interested in collectively reflecting upon them. This process does not necessarily apply to mainstream theatre, where actors and audiences may have considerably less personal investment in the content of the play. The potential success of any applied theatre piece relies on the fact that the concerns, issues or ideas are available to an audience—that is, that the drama portrayed has relevance and resonance with the lives of those who witness it. Reflecting with an audience on how and why a performance works in terms of the meanings it makes, or fails to make, is a key component in gauging the impact of applied theatre.

2.5 How do we assess applied theatre?

Assessment depends upon which model of applied theatre is being evaluated. When external agencies are involved in the evaluative process, their interests will generally be around questions of efficiency and effectiveness. The financial commitment of an outside agency dictates that the measures of success will be primarily attached to the outcomes of the original purposes of the project. For example, in an applied theatre project intended to increase human organ donation, the number of organ donation cards signed by audience members became an indicator of success (Saxton & Miller, 2006, p. 132–133). On the other hand, a presentation to raise audience awareness of patient issues with breast cancer did not have outcomes that could be assessed beyond the anecdotal or secondhand accounts (Gray & Sinding, 2002). In a third case, the question of what is to be valued and voiced publicly becomes even more complicated

Drama cannot instruct. It confronts, perplexes and intrigues imagination into recreating reality.

Edward Bond, 1996,
p. xxxxiv

when the applied theatre company's purpose is to generate a community conversation on, for example, the societal challenges faced by lesbian, gay, bisexual and transgendered (LGBT) students (Freire, 2007). Assessment in cases such as this can be very "murky" as Paul Newman (2008) has pointed out.

A key question for any applied theatre company is, *How do we balance privacy and protection with the need to prove worth?* Outside agencies are very likely going to employ evaluative language and terms concerned with efficiency and effectiveness that are not necessarily consonant with aesthetic performance practices. This is because they are interested, as performance theorist Jon McKenzie (2001) puts it, " in the bottom line: maximizing outputs and minimizing inputs" (p. 81).

To help us sort out these problems, McKenzie (2001) traces the use of the word *performance* in three distinct fields of contemporary society: culture, economics and technology. He suggests that cultural performance is centrally concerned with issues of *social efficacy*, or social justice—that is to say, how performance positively assists us in understanding ourselves, seeing ourselves, re-forming ourselves in relation to the culture that surrounds us and/or transforming the culture itself through performative actions (pp. 29–54). McKenzie sees the notion of *challenge* to be at the core of performance, however and wherever it may it may be used and found.

Efficacy (*n*): Power to produce a desired affect or result.
> Clarence Barnhart, 1965, p. 264

McKenzie's theory of performance as *social efficacy* allows us to limit assessment language in applied theatre to the realm of the efficacy of a process, not the efficiency and/or effectiveness of an intervention. Efficacy has the etymological root meaning "power" and is therefore an appropriate location for assessment rather than in realms of economic efficiency and technological effectiveness (pp. 55–81, 106–130).

One of the most appropriate assessment strategies, given this philosophical position in regard to social efficacy, is "contemplative assessment" (Morgan & Saxton, 1987, p. 198). "The nature of contemplative assessment is that it occurs outside the drama and thus outside the timeframe of drama . . . [I]t cannot change the nature of the dramatic experience itself but is a result of it" (p. 198). This approach is concerned more with asking better questions than in finding the "right" answers (Morgan & Saxton, 1995/2006). Jackson and Lev-Aladgem (2004) follow this principle as they document audience involvement and responses and what is remembered over the long term of a theatre in education piece about teen-age pregnancy (pp. 225–230). Prendergast (2008) offers a question series for audiences and performers to share as a guide for processing theatre experiences, amongst which are:

- What new questions has this performance generated in me?
- How do they shift my being in the world? (p. 143)

Assessment strategies in applied theatre should be context-driven and centrally concerned with giving voice to the participants: actors and spectators alike. Thus, assessment in applied theatre is primarily focused on "*what* is being interpreted rather

24

than *how* it is being done [in the recognition that] it is not possible to prove the success of applied theatre performances quantitatively" (Saxton & Miller, 2006, p. 134–135). Qualitative approaches to assessing move away from measuring how a presentation has succeeded or failed and toward considering its broader effect and affect on individuals and communities.

2.6 What are the key areas to effective applied theatre practice?

We invite you to consider keeping a self-reflective response journal as an extremely useful way to trace your journeys of discovery as you read. We also invite you to create an "operations manual" by logging those techniques and strategies in applied theatre practice that you find resonate with your own interests and learning experiences. In addition, you will find that many of the following case studies address four areas key to effective practice. The final chapter of this text examines these areas in more detail. We offer here some guiding questions in these four areas for you to consider as you reflect upon your reading of these case studies:

1. **Participation:** How key to effective practice are interactive collaborative processes that engage performers and their audiences with the material? How do we ensure that the quality of participation between facilitators and community players is as important a consideration as the quality of participation with audiences at the performance stage? How central are power relations to all participatory elements of an applied theatre process? How can these relations be made evident and kept in continuous negotiation?

2. **Aesthetics:** These are the qualities of an artistic work that we can identify and value. For example, how does a performance engage our multiple senses (hearing, sight, touch, smell and taste), exhibit moments of beauty, harmony, metaphor/symbol, recognition and surprise and use the elements of theatre (focus, tension, sight/sound, dark/light, movement/stillness [Wagner, 1976, p. 148–158])? In what ways do the contexts of any given applied theatre project directly affect the aesthetic/artistic choices made by participants and the values generated from the work by audiences?

3. **Ethics/Safety:** Applied theatre takes as its first principle, "Do no harm." How can we better understand the cultural and socio-political boundaries through which we cross back and forth to do our work? How do we begin to generate our work in communities that do not know nor care to know our work? How do we establish a way of working that helps communities or groups of individuals to

create events that are self-determining and structured on principles agreed-upon by the group? What is being left behind after an applied theatre intervention that allows for and generates further community thought and action?

4. **Assessment:** This is a huge problem for the arts and for applied theatre workers, as you may have gathered from your reading so far. How can we lay out a program that is emergent in nature and cannot be pre-determined? How can we guarantee a product? How can we measure the learning? What timelines can we realistically envision?

As you read through the examples in each chapter, you will become aware of the extraordinary range of strategies that promote the efficacy rather than the efficiency of an applied theatre project. You may also become aware of how little attention has been paid to the challenges presented by the four key areas we have outlined—particularly of assessment and exit strategies in applied theatre. Your reading and practice together should help you to begin to understand why and how you might address these issues.

Summary

What it means to be a good citizen in pluralist societies is fraught with ambiguities and contradictions, requiring a revitalized political vocabulary and a renewed concept of radical citizenship.

> Helen Nicholson, 2005,
> p. 20

This overview of the practice of applied theatre will have given you some understanding of the complexities and range of practices that make up the field. It has introduced you to a background against which to place the case studies that follow. You will also be aware of those things that make applied theatre a particularly rewarding discipline in which to practice.

Further Reading

Bray, E. (1991). *Playbuilding: A guide for group creation of plays with young people.* Paddington, NSW: Currency. This is a seminal text on building plays from the bottom up. Full of examples of various types of playbuilt scripts.

Lamden, G. (2000). *Devising: A handbook for drama and theatre students.* Abingdon, UK: Hodder & Stoughton. A well-organized and accessible practical manual focused on the development of devising skills.

Rohd, M. (1998). *Theatre for community, conflict & dialogue: The Hope is Vital training manual*. Portsmouth, NH: Heinemann. An excellent manual for working with groups, particularly for building trust and generating story.

Sternberg, P. (1998). *Theatre for conflict resolution: In the classroom and beyond*. Portsmouth, NH: Heinemann. Activities and games designed to teach effective communication skills, problem-solving, negotiation techniques and to celebrate difference.

Weigler, W. (2001). *Strategies for playbuilding: Helping groups translate issues into theatre*. Portsmouth, NH: Heinemann. Full of ideas for working with groups based on Weigler's extensive practice in community-based theatre. Includes checklists and handouts to help facilitators guide participants in their decision-making processes.

Questions for Reflection and Discussion

1. In looking at your own community, where is applied theatre happening? Where might it happen and with whom? What community groups would benefit from an applied theatre project?

2. When have you experienced applied drama (as in schools, summer camps, churches and so on)? How do you make a distinction between applied drama and applied theatre?

Suggested Activities

1. Choose a possible place in your community where you could imagine initiating an applied theatre project. Who would it serve? Who would participate? Who would make up the audience? What sort of awareness might be raised? In a paragraph, write a summary of the project including this information. Attach any relevant pamphlets, brochures, etc.

2. What sorts of knowledge and experience would best prepare an applied theatre practitioner? Examine a university or college calendar and list those courses that you (and your group) would consider to be essential or useful.

PART TWO

The Landscape of Applied Theatre

CHAPTER THREE
THEATRE IN EDUCATION

Introduction

Theatre in education (TIE) is one of the two historic roots of applied theatre practice, together with political/popular theatre. TIE developed as a new theatre form in England in the 1960s. At that time, progressive government policies regarding funding for the arts meant that many theatre companies were able to create new programs for community outreach. In fact, funding was tied to companies engaging in these kinds of community-based projects, and working with local schools was an obvious site for partnerships. These theatre companies were beginning to work in school settings (as opposed to schools coming to the theatre), so it was imperative that curriculum content became part of the challenge in creating theatre for these new audiences. For professional actors who were very often members of the resident company, the typical way of working in a traditional proscenium theatre was called into question because they were working in classrooms, with very little in the way of production support, and audiences that were deliberately small in number. In addition, this close relationship with the student audience invited a higher level of participation and a different kind of audience participation than was in use in contemporary children's theatre, of which Brian Way's London Theatre Centre (established in 1953) was the most reputable example. Because they were dealing with audience participation *and* curriculum, the actors who worked at and toured into the schools were required to gain an understanding of and ability to achieve effective

> TIE at its best has shown, in perhaps the most complete way yet, that theatre and learning need not be incompatible bedfellows.
>
> Anthony Jackson, 1993, p. 34

> [The children] do not dispassionately watch, as they might a chemical experiment or a vaulting demonstration; their emotions are actively engaged, willing and desiring and responding to the tensions and the humours of the action.
>
> John O'Toole, 1976, p. 33

teaching. The result of these developments was a new genre of theatre—theatre in education—and a new kind of actor, called an *actor-teacher*.

Conversely, for teachers in schools, this new practice became an opportunity for professional development and training in drama/theatre education. Teacher workshops, and the direct involvement of teachers in developing and implementing materials that prepared and followed-up each performance, became of central importance in delivering and assessing the success of TIE projects.

The scripts created by TIE companies were most often devised collaboratively by the members of the "team" with teacher input, and they often addressed issues of local relevance as well as curriculum content for specific age groups. The devising process demanded that actors also be capable of working collaboratively, researching and holding broad critical perspectives on socio-political and educational issues. Central to an effective process was the ability to keep the needs of the audience and the needs of the curriculum contained in an aesthetic framework. The resulting theatre performances, as best practiced, held intellectual and emotional resonances for their audiences through universalizing the particular local and authentic references that with post-performance reflection and opened wider relevant applications for the issues.

James Hennessy (1998) answers the question, "What is TIE?" in the following points (which he does not claim as absolute terms):

- TIE, like all forms of theatre, is a socially-oriented activity usually taking place in a defined space and requiring the willing and tacit agreement of all involved to be bound by conventions necessary to sustain an awareness of fiction.
- TIE is performed before captive audiences; the choice by young people to attend a performance or not is restricted.
- TIE's prime intention is to teach; it is a mediated learning experience (usually) initiated by the actors through characters which are integral to the dramatic narrative.
- TIE, like other forms of theatre, is dependent on the physical, emotional and intellectual involvement of the participants.
- TIE's praxis has evolved through work in schools and colleges. Productions (usually) target age-specific, but mixed ability and gender, students from one class or group. [...]
- "Central to the (TIE) work...are the twin convictions that human behaviour and institutions are formed through social activity and can therefore be changed, and that audiences, as potential agents of change, should be active participants in their own learning" (Vine, 1993, p. 109).
- The essential difference between TIE and conventional theatre is the quality of the relationship the actors share with the audience.... TIE directly engages its audiences by encouraging them to participate within the art form; to be

actively—and interactively—responsive to and responsible for the dramatic narrative (Hennessy, 1998, pp. 86–87).

In summary, Hennessy's last point is that what distinguishes TIE from traditional theatre are "the ways and means of its creation [and] that the central activity of most TIE companies has been devising" (p. 87).

In the forty years since its inception, TIE companies have flourished and the practice has spread to countries like Canada, Australia and some European countries. As governmental policies in England became more conservative in the 1980s, centralized funding for TIE companies, many of which were openly critical of certain political stances and decisions, was threatened and in a number of cases, withdrawn. Many TIE companies survived by maintaining their educative thrust while adapting their programs to become more attractive to local school boards. Companies learned to devise work that could be played to larger audiences in bigger venues like gymnasia or auditoria. The principle of participation was still central to the practice, but was necessarily—because of timetable strictures—moved into preparatory and follow-up activities. The content of programs had to become more general with a growing reliance on study guides rather than active partnerships with teachers. TIE companies did not vanish; there are still a number of vital TIE companies, particularly in England. More recently, an interest in TIE has revived as part of the interventionist mandate of applied theatre in educational contexts. Throughout this text, you will note that there are a number of case studies that "fly" under other names but are very much rooted in the original intentions and practices of TIE.

The first case study in this chapter offers an example of a TIE project from England that models the early development of the genre in the 1960s and '70s and reflects the interest in and commitment to socio-political issues. The South African work that follows shows the transition from a school-based to a community-based TIE project that draws on traditional African performance forms. In the Winston case study on drug education through TIE, we are able to hear the voices of teachers and students assessing the value of the theatre experience. The final case study addresses issues of discrimination and diversity in a devised TIE production with and about lesbian, gay, bisexual and transgendered (LGBT) young people.

3.1 Human Rights

from *Indigo*

Dukes TIE Company. (1993). *SCYPT Journal, 26,* 21–26.

For much of the last year the television images of the devastation and suffering in the former Yugoslavia have been relentless. Have they been powerful? Perhaps we remember the news item which "exposed" the existence of the concentration camps: [p]erhaps we remember the broken and burned bodies of the entire population of the village carried from the cellars by the UN troops. We may look at the broken buildings in Sarajevo and remember a few short years ago the entire world's media gathered for the winter Olympics in one of Europe's most beautiful and cosmopolitan of cities. Perhaps initially we followed the development of this apparent madness quite closely. Remember the questions: Do we understand it? How can we come to understand it...this world seemingly gone mad?

In the end though, do we become inured; do the images continue to flash across our TV screens while we begin to accept that it is mad[?] There is no logic. Another small war rages.

The television reports are watched by our children. Are they powerful? Our children have an enormous capacity to understand. They have a vast capacity to empathise with the experience of their fellow human beings who struggle to survive in the midst of the hellish violence unleashed by neighbour on neighbour. Every fibre of their being[s] knows the suffering. They are not reliant on the television reports. As young people[,] they are intuitively so much closer than we are to the knowledge that civil war rages in every part of the world. As children, they are in its front line, and given the opportunity, will give powerful expression to their empathy and drive themselves tirelessly towards understanding.

Indigo is a Theatre in Education programme for lower secondary students which each day [seeks] to develop the collective understandings of all those taking part about the forces of nationalism. [...]

We develop a fiction. A class of children become[s] a delegation from the International Council of Nations—ICON. Their task [is] to undertake a study of the social/economic situation, and to draw up a charter of human rights for the small nation of Borovia.

How this fictional context for our drama is made available to the children[,] how they meet it and what of themselves they bring to it, is crucial.

The actor-teacher framing the children has an extremely delicate job to do. She welcomes the children, allows them to "stare" briefly at the company and at the design elements that will assist the drama as it develops. She then poses a simple question:

"When I say the words 'Human Rights' what do you immediately think about?"

This question is placed as simply and as directly as possible. The actor places as little of herself as possible between the words and the children. There is usually a moment of silence before the first tentative responses are offered. This silence is allowed to sit as a natural and unthreatening silence. It is not often that we are asked such a question.

"People"....

Very gently, and giving due weight and respect to each and every meaning offered[,] the actor moves the group toward sharing socially with those next to them and eventually into sharing their more developed responses with the whole group. At a given point another actor, unannounced, records what is offered[,] finding a simple and direct language and drawing the connections that are being established. The record is as true a reflection of the social understanding of the group as is possible. This opening to the work is concluded when the actor leading the session reads through (again, in [a] direct and uncluttered manner) our conclusions.

This process, of developing from an individual[']s courageous first response to a highly developed social statement[,] very often (for all involved[:] children, company and teachers) made available a profound and moving content.

"Every Human Being has the right to live in peace; to have health care, education, a shelter and justice. People have the right to their own beliefs. Every Human Being has the right to have help, and the responsibility to give help. The right to love and be loved. Human Beings have the right to believe in whatever gods they wish to believe in. We have the right to move about freely without fear. Human Beings have the right to work, and holiday and celebrate. Every Human Being has the right to their own name."

This statement . . . is not, in the moment regarded as fixed, complete all embracing . . . it is an embodiment of what the enquiry is opening up for us. It is a trail.

As the actor facilitating begins to twilight the children into frame[,] they already have a strongly felt sense of the significance of their present enquiry; they know that the world they inhabit does not guarantee these rights. The contradiction is socially present in the room.

As the ICON Delegates, experts in the field of Human Rights, receive their official identification, Borovia stands in the centre of the school hall. The Nation is embodied in the form of a small Tailors workroom; there are no walls; there are portals[:]

A window

A door

A portrait frame: [e]mpty, full length

A full length mirror: [n]o glass, again only the frame

Each of these portals is connected, the whole room/nation girdled and embraced by rich swathes of brilliant Indigo cloth. This girdle denotes an interior and an exterior.

Inside, some simple workmanlike furniture, the tools of the tailoring trade, and a tailor's dummy upon which rests the recently completed ceremonial jacket with its brilliant Indigo Sash. In another corner a second tailor's dummy, holding work in progress. Outside nothing.

As the framing proceeds, the actors move into place and Borovia becomes peopled. The object of enquiry begins to live. The children are aware. It is an indeterminate beginning: things are sensed but not yet known.

An old tailor and his young apprentice enter the room and begin to cut and sew. Focussed and comfortable with each other. Outside the room in the "street," a man sits curled beneath the window; alone. Also outside, a woman sits on bulky bags of laundry.

The delegation is informed they have been invited to Borovia by The Prince: [h]e is recently returned from a life in exile, ready to grasp and weld the future of his beloved Borovia[,] a nation newly re-emerged into independence after the collapse of the "Old Empire." They learn that the Prince is the recognised leader of the emerging INDIGO party.

"INDIGO the colour of my Nation's Flag, the colour of the very blood that runs in Borovian veins."

The Prince greets the delegation and invites them on an initial tour of his country. Other than those of the ICON Delegates, should they choose to ask questions, his is the only voice. He speaks warmly and sincerely of his fears, hopes and aspirations. He requests their help. Borovia needs the assistance and recognition of the international community. The delegation pauses by the window:

> "A window on my Nation. For so long the window has been boarded up. No light has spilled through to warm the hearts or guide the footsteps of my people. INDIGO will tear down the shutters...the light and air will enter Borovia again...."

The drama is now fully underway. The tailor's room, the five actors, and the delegates with the secretary/facilitator constitute the whole that is Borovia. Though highly selective and sparse, it is a complex whole, not easy to discern in its totality. Each of its parts offer the delegation fleeting and contradictory impressions.

Indigo is a fully participatory programme. As it develops[,] the delegation meet[s] and interact[s] with the roles: sensations registered during their first "tour" are shared in the hotel room; perceptions are developed. As each part of the whole is probed and becomes revealed to them, they develop a sense of the quality of Borovia. The portals begin to offer a way of seeing. Borovia is gradually discerned as a sum and unity of opposites:

The Tailor: A man who is highly skilled, and proud to make the jacket for the Prince. He came to Borovia many, many years ago. (The actor knows him to be Jewish and feels that in many ways the man's life embodies the history of our century.) He is overjoyed that once again there is independence for Borovia and has a vast optimism for the future. There is little cloth left in his shop. He awaits payment from the Prince.

The Apprentice: Young, Borovian. He loves his master and is a good pupil. He welcomes the return of the Prince and longs to learn the stories and the songs that for all his short life have been denied him. (The actor knows that the future direction of his developing ideas is necessarily uncertain. He embodies potential.)

The Laundry Woman: One of the mountain people; Borovian, but with a distinct ethnic identity. Her people came from the mountains long before the days of the Empire. She works hard. She does the laundry for the tailor and has done so for many years. There is an almost perceptible unease about her and she is loathe to enter discussion with the visitors from abroad. (The actor knows that for this woman the return of the Prince is an indeterminate beginning...she senses its impact on the community.)

The Man In the Street: He has no work. Under the Empire he had work. The return of the Prince has had no material [e]ffect on the quality of life. (The actor knows he represents an entire disenfranchised layer.) Waiting. Through the window, he catches the eyes of the other young Borovian.

The Company [players] understand the economic position of the roles. In many senses[,] they are archetypes. They embody the joint and conflicting aspirations of the society. There is little pre-determined dialogue or action. The development of the action of the drama is very much dependent on what the children bring. The actors interact directly with the delegates and listen closely as they reflect "privately" in the hotel room. Each development in the analysis they are making of the situation provides the stimulus for the actors to intuitively develop the forms to drive the children closer to the essence of the Borovian predicament. At no point does life in Borovia cease to go on. As the children debate with each other, the signing is still on offer, confirming, contradicting, confounding.

The facilitator is the only member of the company operating overtly at the teacher end of the actor/teacher spectrum. She can stop the drama and use any of the available conventions to peel back the layers of appearance.

The children's sense of a society poised on the verge of communal violence grows. However, from within the stricture of the frame, they cannot intervene directly into the fabric of Borovian society and devise alternative narrative solutions to the developing economic and social problems.

On many occasions, attempting to explain to the Prince and/or the other protagonists the likely outcome of a position held or of a course of action, they would draw on their knowledge of the real world. ...Their knowledge of the world driving their meaning making within the drama[,] and the drama (their very real subjective relationship to the people) driving them....

"Look, you have to understand...."

... to push that [a] bit further, by necessity, their grasp of events witnessed through the television news images.

As the situation inexorably builds, they struggle to create their charter for Human Rights. It cannot remain simply a statement of principle; it begins to have the quality of a programme of action. They are naming the phenomena they are witness and party to.

- At the end of the programme, the actors hold the image the facilitator has chosen to arrest[:]
- The apprentice sings the Borovian National Anthem as the tailor stares confusedly at his image in the mirror.
- The man from the street is measured for a new suit, an Indigo tie with a new white collar.

In the street, the Mountain Woman, "cleansed," lies face down in a pile of dirty laundry. In the room the tailor is covering the windows.

These are moments. Each performance of the programme would ideally "live" its own truthful development and would offer different aspects. The children, now twilighting back out of role, are invited to let the image work on them and then to place the charter they have made in it. They and the Company know that this is not a resolution.

[...]

This has been an attempt to offer the objectives and intentions of *Indigo* as an example of work conceived and created for and with young people in this period. [...] The practice of the programme[,] our experience of the integrity of the children and their determination to remain truly human in the world, was a rich and enabling learning experience.

He stands so proudly
an image of darkness
looking up
into the future.
A man of Borovia!
A rabble of thoughts
churn inside him,
a strained weary expression
on his face
which is a diary of secrets.
A Prince of Borovia,
A Prince of thoughts.
Borovia was his wife.
He was father
to the children of Borovia.
He wanted to be Borovia.

He tried to be Borovia.
He murdered himself inside.
His mad watchful eyes
swerve towards me.
—Rowan Taylor, Yr. 6, Whalley C. E. Primary School

3.2 Stages of development
from *Rainbows and spider webs: New challenges for theatre in a transformed system of education in South Africa*
Michael Carklin. (1997). *RIDE: Research in Drama Education, 2*(2), 203–213.

[...]
South Africa has a long history of Theatre in Education (TIE)[;] [often] "one-off" interventions that have characterised TIE in the past need to be reconsidered. Much more effective intervention is needed in which a sustained impact can be made. I would like to look at the DramAidE project as one example of this kind of theatrical intervention, which uses multiphased interventions, and, very significantly, begins to link directly to the syllabus in terms of the lifeskills development that forms such a core part of the new Guidance curriculum.

DramAidE was initiated in Kwazulu/Natal province nearly 5 years ago under the leadership of Professor Lynn Dalrymple, and has now spread across that province . . . . It is concerned with HIV/AIDS and lifeskills education in secondary schools using drama and theatre methodologies. I would like to use the Eastern Cape project as an example of the kinds of interventions that are taking place.

This project has had four phases of intervention: on the first visit to the school, the team conducts a needs analysis workshop with each standard separately. They use Image Theatre techniques to catalyse and facilitate group debate. Images used focus on specific research questions that differ according to standard and developmental factors. For example, images may depict scenes of peer pressure, or various attitudes to sex. The important thing is that they remain open to interpretation and become good indicators of pupils' own perceptions, experiences and understandings. At this phase the team also runs a workshop with teachers to introduce them to the project and to the idea of interactive learning techniques.

The second phase is a lifeskills workshop, again with each separate standard. Here a series of catalyst scenes are presented multilingually by the team in roles as members of a youth club. Issues from the needs analysis workshop are problematised and Forum Theatre is used to examine various potential solutions. Some of the scenes used here will form part of the storyline of phase 3, the play.

The play is performed for the whole school, and the team has made a conscious commitment to work for theatrically exciting work. Clearly, educational efficacy relies on polished and innovative theatricality. It is this phase in particular that interests me in terms of theatrical intervention. The play developed by the Eastern Cape team has been of some controversy within DramAidE more broadly. When performed at an "all-teams forum" in Durban, there was a degree of criticism from some members of other teams as to the symbolic, metaphorical nature of the work, with many arguing that the message needed to be clearly spelled out for pupils in what I understood to mean pure didactic theatre.

The Eastern Cape team, however, defended their theatrical decisions, which are aimed at meeting the changed context of life in South Africa head-on. It not only sees the world of multiplicity and intertextuality out there, but consciously employs these concepts in designing and executing the work. The play is multilingual and the team is very conscious of the importance of physical expression. Gesture, for example, becomes a crucial part of the communication process. A mixture of puppetry, drama, Image Theatre, Forum Theatre, dance, physical theatre, song, and praise poetry make an eclectic piece which both challenges the audience and provides multiple layers of meaning. It acknowledges that each pupil faces different experiences and will relate differently to the work.

An interesting influence on the development of the play has been the composition [of] "community theatre practitioners" who have no tertiary training. This team is unique within DramAidE in terms of its composition. In developing the play, the work has included a strong staff development component in which each team member has been responsible for running workshops with the rest of the group. These might include facilitation skills, gumboot dancing, *mapantsula,* Forum Theatre, physical theatre and mime, for example.

This does not mean that in developing the play one is left with a mishmash of Rainbow Nation aesthetics in which ballerinas in gumboots become the order of the day. Rather, it is a conscious transformation of the collective performance resources of the group into work that is visually exciting, challenging, and that sees the need for expression beyond the limitations of the spoken word. It also draws on notions of Theatre for Development in using cultural forms with which pupils might be familiar, but then goes further in challenging them with possibly new theatrical experiences. Team leader for the pilot project, Nan Hamilton, describes the process of creating the play as: "finding a modern ritual response to the [AIDS] crisis."

The fourth phase of the project is an open day, hosted by the school, for which pupils have prepared their own plays, or songs, or poems, thus needing to really come to terms with the issues. The project also included a poster competition with the theme "HIV/AIDS in my African Dream . . . mind, body and soul." At present, this model is being developed to include interventions into clinics and with parents and teachers.

3.3 Anti-drug education
from *Drug education through creating theatre in education*
Joe Winston. (2001). *RIDE: Research in Drama Education,* 6(1), 39–54.

[...]

The Project and Its Aims

The *Drugs Education: Theatre in Education Project* was a Grants for Education Support and Training (GEST) funded initiative . . . . The main aim of the project was to increase the range and strategies that teachers use for drugs education. The foci of this development were stated as follows: ·

1. To increase teachers' confidence and competence when using drama and role play to enable pupils to explore their own attitudes and values and the moral issues that are raised through effective drugs education. . . .

2. For each secondary school involved to provide a Theatre in Education experience. . . .

An important aspect of the project was to involve two teachers from each school, one with an English/drama background, the other with responsibilities for PSE/health education.
[...]
The presence locally of Catalyst, one of the foremost companies in Britain to specialize in Theatre in Health Education (THE), provided a good opportunity to show teachers the potential of THE in the area of drug education and to provide them with the resources to create it themselves with their students.
[...]
All 11 schools which began the project saw it through to its conclusion, apart from one. . . . The remaining 10 schools presented a total of 23 performances in 19 different primary schools and two special schools. In addition, five of the schools presented performances to their Year 7 pupils, one to Year 8 pupils and one to an audience of parents and governors. Overall, approximately 125 Year 10 students successfully completed the project and approximately 800 younger children saw the results.

The initial training days were organised to provide teachers with background information on drugs and the nature of effective drugs education and to give practical experience of how drama can be devised to help children explore drugs-related issues...
.Both sets of teachers strongly affirmed the usefulness and value of these 2 days in giving them the ideas they needed to pursue the work. Comments like[,] "We couldn't have done it without the two initial training days[,]" were common from English and PSE specialists. Interestingly, both sets of specialists learned in both areas; drama staff found

the drama input very valuable as well as the drugs information, and some of the PSE teachers remarked how they had learned valuable information about drugs and drugs education.

[...]

Teachers' increased confidence can be detected in their willingness to try similar projects in the future. Some teachers stated that they were already planning to run a similar project again in the following year. All teachers were able to state clear and precise ways that they would do things either similarly or differently in the future. As one drama specialist wrote:

> Next time I'll split the class and use smaller groups, have them visit the feeder school first to develop relationships and find out what the children know—and I won't coincide with the school production!

The educational aims for the Year 10 students were intended clearly to enable them to clarify their own attitudes and feelings while exploring moral issues related to drugs and their social and personal effects . . . . Some students were able to articulate this as an aim for their own pieces of theatre:

> "We were trying to tell the children about the bad effects drugs can have on you and your family/ friends. How they can destroy friendships and relationships."
> "Our aim was to get the message into the children's heads that drugs can be harmful to the human body."

Many also articulated that they wanted to help the KS2 children clarify their own values, to help them make their own, informed decisions. The following quotations are typical:

> "We hope our play will make children aware of the consequences of drug taking but still let them make up their own mind."
> "We hope it will not only grab their attention but also make them experience some of the happiness and sadness of the character to make them think what if it was them."

Just as typical, and often in the same groups as those who expressed more liberal intentions, were students who held to a strong, morally didactic agenda:

> "Many primary students don't know a lot about the subject and definitely know nothing of the experience or situations. Our play, I hope, will deter

them from getting into these situations."
"I hope to make them realise that drugs are bad for you and can kill."

How the tension between these two attitudes could be resolved was clearly articulated in the words of one student, as follows:

> We are trying to show Year 6 pupils that drugs are wrong without telling them not to do drugs.

The pieces of theatre the students produced strove to present underlying social or moral messages whilst avoiding an overtly didactic manner.

The majority of the students were evidently stimulated by the project into exploring and articulating their own values, and many were able to voice them with great clarity and passion:

> "My attitudes towards drugs have changed. Before, I would have got embarrassed and looked stupid but now I know a bit more I can know what risks there are and just say no."
> "My attitude has remained against drugs and has perhaps been strengthened by what I have learned."

A small minority of students had their stances clarified in ways that some might find problematic:

> I don't know if my attitude has changed towards drugs but now I would feel safer taking drugs as I know more about them and their effects.

[...]

The moral issues associated with drug use and its effects were explored in a number of ways by the plays that the students devised. The model of theatre with which the teachers were initially presented clearly had a very influential effect on the various TIE pieces that emerged. The play *Sorted* was performed by Catalyst and dealt with issues of family stress, parent-child relationships, the problems of being an adolescent, peer pressure and society's contradictory attitudes to drugs, some of which are legal, some of which are not. It raised questions as to why some people, young and adult, come to take drugs; how poor relationships between parents and children can exacerbate problems associated with drug abuse; and whether adult attitudes to drugs are inconsistent and hypocritical.

All students had a large say in the choice of drugs they chose to place at the centre of their plays. Five schools chose to focus on alcohol and cigarettes, two on solvent abuse and four on illegal "soft" drugs such as cannabis and ecstasy. Some of the schools that chose to focus on legal drugs did so for fear of adverse reaction from primary school parents. In each case, however, the issue was placed firmly in a social milieu and the students explored how particular young people came to be involved in legal or illegal drug abuse and the consequences of this involvement. These consequences ranged from being caught by one's parents, to stealing to buy the drug, to death while under the influence. As with the play *Sorted*, the social and moral issues were at the heart of the stories created and explored similar areas of family relationships, adult hypocrisy and peer group pressure.

Sorted employed a participatory model of theatre, allowing the audience to question the characters directly, to speculate upon gaps in the narrative and to influence how events in the story might develop if the characters acted differently. The form of many of the students' pieces was similarly participatory in nature, using techniques such as hot-seating, where the audience had the opportunity to ask questions of the characters; Forum Theatre, where they took on roles themselves in situations related to the plot; or involving the children in role as the audience of a chat show. Such structures clearly made the students think carefully about the information they were giving and the moral impact of their work:

> "We had to do a lot of research to make sure that when the children asked the characters questions the information we gave in our answers would be accurate."
> "During the chat show, the questions they asked were very thoughtful. We made them feel good about themselves, treating them as adults, a lot older than they really were."

3.4 Addressing LGTB biases
from *Why devise? Why now?: "Houston, we have a problem"*
Norma Bowles. (2005). *Theatre Topics, 15*(1), 15–21.

[...]

Reaching the Audience: 90210 GOES QUEER!
When we were developing our high school tour show, *90210 Goes Queer!*, to address anti-LGBT bias in schools, we worked with over two hundred students, teachers and parents, mostly from lesbian, gay, bisexual and/or transgendered (LGBT) or LGBT-friendly organizations. At first we gathered in homes, youth shelters and schools *to discuss the problem and share stories.* There were stories of teachers taking class time to rail against homosexuality and parents trying to get teachers fired for including LGBT-related curricula. One young woman was called "Dyke" by the coach during football tryouts; another was elected "Homecoming Princess" as a joke. A transgender girl's

administrators counseled her to[,] "Just lay low and dress like a man." A young man showed us scars from when he had to jump over a barbed-wire fence to escape the group of gangbangers chasing him, yelling "F**king [f]aggot!" A girl told us that she'd swallowed bleach when her family kicked her out, and then found a "family" that would accept her, the local Crips unit. One boy found his friend dead, hanging in a stall in the boys' bathroom.

After sharing the horror stories, we began discussing *whom we needed to reach to begin to transform the situation*, at the very least, to stop the anti-LGBT slurs, jokes, exclusion, and physical bashing. Well, everyone . . . but . . . for now? We decided to begin with the students. I suggested we consider the old rule of thumb for persuasive speaking: 20% of your audience ("The Choir") probably already agrees with you; 20% of your audience may well be unreachable; the remaining 60% are the "Moveable Middle." I then recommended that, as we made dramaturgical decisions, we think about reaching the students in the harder to reach section of the Moveable Middle. The group came up with a description of John Q. Tough-but-Moveable Middle: an 11th [g]rade guy, probably into sports, someone who regularly peppers his conversations with[,] "Fag!" and "That is so gay!" The group also felt that Latino and/or African-American young men might be a more difficult audience to reach about these issues because there is generally less discussion about and/or acceptance of LGBT people in their communities, and because of the still pervasive stereotype that all gay guys are white.

Once we had a clear image in mind of whom we were trying to reach, we set about determining *how to reach this audience*. We all agreed that it would be good for our play to be as realistic as possible, funny but also hard-hitting, and for it to include a diverse, multidimensional, stereotype-busting, and likeable cast of lesbian, gay, bisexual, transgendered, and straight characters (and actors!). We had numerous group discussions about the central characters. Who is friends with whom and how honest are they with each other? Is the bisexual Homecoming Queen/Captain of the cheerleading team into a [g]oth, [g]lam [g]oth or punk aesthetic? Would it be more of a stereotype-buster for her to invite the dyke quarterback to the Homecoming Dance, or vice versa? And what if CJ, the Homecoming King/Captain of the football team is in the closet? We made each decision with "John Q. Tough-but-Moveable Middle" in mind.

Working with a diverse and knowledgeable group was crucial, as it enabled us to grasp the complexity of the issues and to navigate the institutional and attitudinal minefield we needed to traverse in order to reach the audience. Lawyers and Gay, Lesbian, Straight Education Network (GLSEN) members helped us identify laws that characters might invoke at moments of crisis in the drama, as well as laws we needed to be aware of in cases when our right to present the play might be challenged. LGBT studies experts advised us about how to portray the characters and situations and how to define key terms. Administrators advised us regarding what kinds of supporting materials and references would be needed, and what compromises needed to be made when representing the discriminatory slurs and jokes, etc. Teachers showed us various strategies they use to proactively address LGBT issues and to respond effectively as problems arise in the classroom or hallways. They also gave us historical information that we were able to use both in the script and in the study guides. Some teachers also gave us access to swabs of (often toxic bacterial) culture from faculty lounge gossip. Parents joined in improvisations to develop the pre-Homecoming Game dinner, helping us flesh out how a supportive, inclusive family versus how a more rigid and patriarchal family might discuss the news that two girls planned to attend Homecoming as a couple. The youth were fiercely committed to keeping the characters, situations, and dialogue realistic: "Oh, he would never say that to his mother! Are you kidding!?"

In many instances, when Fringe Benefits gets to the point in a collaboration when we ask the group, "What's the best way to reach our audience?" we arrive at some delicious decisions regarding the genre, style, and/or format of the play. A group of Latina mothers asked us to help them devise a Spanish-language play to help their husbands understand the negative impact of gender bias and homophobia on their children. When it came time for them to decide what kind of play would reach their husbands . . . they started to laugh. "Our husbands won't come see a play!" "Yes! We'll have to do something on TV to reach them!" And so we did. Families to Amend California's Three Strikes decided they could best reach their target audience, African-American mothers and grandmothers, if their piece could be woven into a church service. The Los Angeles Youth Justice Coalition needed to reach legislators, so they created a piece of Forum Theatre and performed it for a group of activists, educators, artists, and legislators. Another group decided to do Invisible Theatre during lunch in the cafeteria; another, a piece the marching band worked into a halftime routine; another, a puppet show. For *90210 Goes Queer!*, the format the group selected was pretty traditional: a one-act play, with the unities more or less intact.

One of the most interesting Dramaturgical Quilting Bee discussions concerned how (or if) to address the high rate of LGBT teen suicide in *90210 Goes Queer!* Should we address it or shouldn't we? Who would try to commit suicide and why? Would it be a successful attempt, and if not, who or what might stop it? When in the play might it happen? As we debated each question, we kept "John Q." in the front of our minds. "Oh, that's way too melodramatic for him." "If the dyke, the tranny girl or the openly gay guy commit suicide, he'd be, like, 'Good, one less queer!'" Ultimately, we decided it would be most effective if the character most like John Q., CJ (the Captain of the football team), were the one who would attempt suicide. John Q. could laugh along with CJ's gay jokes at the beginning, but gradually start to find him more difficult to side with as his jokes become more vicious. John Q. might begin to identify with CJ again when his good friend, Maya, won't go to Homecoming with him; and John Q. might perhaps even sympathize with CJ as he struggles to accept his sexual orientation, while being constantly bombarded with his mother's and father's virulent condemnations of homosexuality. We worked slowly and carefully, trying to construct a believable series of events that might lead such a young man to try to kill himself, situations "John Q." might be able to identify with.

The result of our collaborative devising process was complex, rich, and effective. We felt and heard the audience move with us from laughter to understanding. The tone and content of the post[-]show discussions and audience surveys also indicated that the audience, including some "John Q."s, had taken the ride with us and had gleaned that, although it may seem like no big deal at the time . . . and may be totally fun to do . . . it can be incredibly destructive to use anti-gay slurs and tell gay jokes. After each show, many in the audience pushed up to the front of the auditorium to meet the openly LGBT and straight actors. Many wrote us that they thought the LGBT characters were believable and likeable, and that they could identify with the problems they faced.

[...]

Further Reading

Cassidy, H. & Watts, V. (2002). 'Burn an image in their head': Evaluating the effectiveness of a play on bullying. *NJ: Drama Australia Journal, 26*(2), 5–19. Anti-bullying is a "hot topic" for TIE work (see O'Toole, below). This article describes the development and assessment of an Australian TIE project in useful ways.

Jackson, A. (2005). The dialogic and the aesthetic: Some reflections on theatre as a learning medium. *Journal of Aesthetic Education, 39*(4), 104–118. While largely theoretical, this essay contains a description of a TIE project on immigration and refugees in England (114–116).

Jackson, A. (Ed.) (1993). *Learning through theatre: New perspectives on theatre in education.* London, UK and New York, NY: Routledge. An anthology on theatre in education with international contributions that also looks at the historic development of TIE, ways of working, case studies and discussions.

O'Toole, J. (1976). *Theatre in education: New objectives for theatre—new techniques in education.* London, UK: Hodder and Stoughton. This seminal text on TIE is widely available in libraries and is a must-read for anyone interested in this area of applied theatre. Also very valuable for facilitators in all genres.

O'Toole, J., Burton, B. & Plunkett, A. (2005). *Cooling conflict: A new approach to managing bullying and conflict in schools.* Frenchs Forest, NSW: Pearson/Longman. These authors present a long-term anti-bullying TIE project in Australia that was delivered in a pyramid model where senior students devised and performed a play to younger students.

Schweitzer, P. (1980). *Theatre-in-education: Five infant programmes*. London, UK: Methuen.

Schweitzer, P. (1980). *Theatre-in-education: Four junior programmes*. London: Methuen.

Schweitzer, P. (1980). *Theatre-in-education: Four secondary programmes*. London, UK: Methuen. The three collections of British TIE companies' scripts above are an invaluable resource. Difficult to find but well worth the effort.

Smillie, R. & Randall, J. (1989). Zeke and the indoor plants. *Canadian Theatre Review, 60*, 46–64. An early Canadian TIE script that includes participatory elements as part of the performance and where student choices change the outcome of the play.

Tan, J. (2005). "One island": A theatre-in-education approach in Singapore. *NJ: Drama Australia Journal, 29*(1), 45–50. This TIE project deals with citizenship and cultural identity in a South Asian context.

Questions for Discussion and Reflection

1. What strategies can you find in the four case studies presented in this chapter that address ways of creating, performing, reflecting upon and assessing a TIE project?

2. What do you perceive to be the skills required by an effective actor-teacher? What are the most important acting skills needed? Teaching skills?

3. What different kinds of participation are involved in each of these case studies? Why might you use any or all of these participatory strategies in your own TIE projects?

4. How does TIE compare to children's theatre or Theatre for Young Audiences (TYA)? Consider the theatre-based versus school-based contexts of these two forms of theatre for young people.

5. Some suggest that "good theatre" is antithetical to educational needs. What is your opinion about the possibilities of creating engaging theatre while conforming to curricular contexts?

Suggested Activities

1. With a small group, select a grade range and take a look at the government-mandated curriculum guides in various subject areas. Find a curriculum area that you and your group agree opens itself up for dramatic exploration. Write three or four drama-based activities that promote a learning outcome and share these with other groups in a practical workshop.

   An excellent reference for curriculum-based drama is Larry Swartz' *The New Dramathemes* (2002).

2. Choose a real person who is involved in environmental issues. Research this person and create a monologue either as that person or as another character talking about that person. With a partner, take turns introducing each other in-role to the larger group. After the monologue, your partner facilitates an in-role conversation between you as the character and the audience.

3. With a partner or small group, create a teacher workshop that introduces the concept and practice of TIE and that includes a number of drama-based activities.

4. Select a fairy or folk tale and adapt it as a piece of story theatre (see Text Box) that includes integral participation and also has a clear and well-defined learning outcome. If possible, perform this adaptation in a local elementary school.

   Story theatre involves narration and characterization, direct address and simple theatrical devices. See Paul Sills' (1971, 2000) books on story theatre.

Chapter Four
Popular Theatre

Introduction

In our introductory chapters, we suggest that the roots of applied theatre are doubly-formed, found in the history and development of both theatre in education and popular theatre. Popular theatre has the longer history of the two and, because it was created to address the concerns and lives of ordinary people, is often referred to as grassroots theatre. Popular theatre that draws on mythologies and folk tales flourishes in many parts of the world (for example, *pongsan t'alch'um*, masked dramas still performed today in South Korea), but in the Western world, its roots are clearly traceable to the Dionysian rituals of Ancient Greece. In these rituals, as in all popular theatre, social norms were subverted, and it became possible for performers to satirize the all-powerful religious and political leaders of the day. Regarded by those in authority as a sanctioned way for "the masses" to "let off steam," in popular theatre there has always been the question of risk and boundaries: What happens if a theatre performance goes too far? What price is there to be paid in talking back to power? These questions are as politically and socially appropriate today as they ever were.

> Art is not merely contemplation, it is also action, and all action changes the world, at least a little.
>
> Tony Kushner, 2001, p. 62

Over time, popular theatre has never lost that early impulse toward socially conscious theatre that takes on indigenous and accessible forms such as song and dance, circus and sideshow acts, puppetry, mask and mime—entertainment forms that clothe subversion with wonderment at the skills and delights of high theatricality. Examples of popular theatre forms that emerged include Italian *commedia dell'arte* with its stock characters of clever servants who triumph over their foolish masters; the circus and sideshow traditions along with their grotesque, comic and dexterous elements; animal acts such as bear-baiting and bull-fighting; and the traditions of spectacle, pageants and parades. Joel Schechter (2003) defines contemporary popular theatre as a "democratic, proletarian and

51

politically progressive theatre" (p. 3), and borrowing from Peter Schumann's definition of puppet theatre (p. 6), Schechter also calls it "illegitimate." Placing this "illegitimate theatre" up against the "legitimate theatre"—mainstream literary theatre that is usually performed in purpose-built spaces—sets up popular theatre as a theatre of subversion and celebration, and one that is highly participatory in nature.

Prentki and Selman (2000) place the roots of contemporary popular theatre with Paolo Freire's principles of education that embrace "the notions of exchange, participant ownership, reflection and action" (p. 8). Following Freire's notion of "conscientization," (p. 39) popular theatre aims to raise the critical consciousness of its participants and audiences toward the taking of action. In this way, the intentions of popular theatre begin to mesh with Bertolt Brecht's political theatre and Augusto Boal's theatre of the oppressed in offering performers and spectators a language that can lead to transformation. The name "popular theatre" has now become an umbrella term for this kind of politically and collaboratively-created theatre.

For Brecht (1938) "popular" was writing that is "intelligible to the broad masses, taking over their forms of expression and enriching them/adopting and consolidating their standpoint/representing the most progressive section of the people. . . ."
In John Willett, 1964, p. 108

"Popular theatre [is a] creative approach to analyzing, naming, and acting on problems and working creatively with conflict," write Butterwick and Selman in 2003 (p. 8). While this definition could apply to all applied theatre practices, it is the socio-political element that helps us to distinguish the purposes and practices of popular theatre. To be considered truly "popular," there is an implication that the project is free of outside influence (for example, free of curriculum in theatre in education or funding agencies in theatre for development) and that the participants hold the ownership of the piece. Even though the carnivalesque frames of the early popular theatre have almost disappeared, popular performance forms such as music, dance, song and mythic figures (as in Bread and Puppet theatre) are still being used within the popular theatre-making process (Enderby Community Play, 1999, www.assemblybcartscouncils.ca).

The tension between authorship and ownership throughout the history of popular theatre is one that allows us to see how popular theatre has developed toward more collaborative forms over the past decades. While there are still playwrights who write politically and in sometimes popular forms (as with Dario Fo and Tony Kushner), true popular theatre privileges improvisation over the written text. In this context, we are more interested in the collective authorship and ownership of popular theatre processes that clearly belong to the world of applied theatre.

It is the way popular forms combine their festive and revolutionary impulses that make popular traditions useful for creating theatre for social change.
Claudia Orenstein, 1998, p. 6

Although today it is less common to find a popular theatre project that involves the use of puppets, mask, mime and/or spectacle, it is our intention to focus the case studies we have selected on the more traditional and historic roots of this genre.

> *The first case study takes us back to the 1970s when alternative theatre practices were flourishing all over the world. Welfare State was a leading popular theatre company in England and this case study is a synthesis of the kind of politically implicit work company members did and the ways in which they worked. The Australian case study documents one part of a larger statewide education project, Risky Business, on anti-bullying. Here, puppets are used as a "way of looking at the dark underbelly of things" and as a means of connecting with students' aboriginal culture. So too with the third case study, in which cultural traditions are woven into a satirical performance by a comedy troupe that plays in the bars and massage parlors of Bangkok.*

4.1 Popular theatre as spectacle
from *The Welfare State Theatre*
Theodore Shank. (1977). *TDR: The Drama Review* 21(1), 3–16.

[...]

There are revolutionary socialist theatre groups, often comprised of Marxists, who play almost exclusively for trade Union members at meetings and workingmen's clubs, attempting to raise political awareness with respect to the worker in a capitalist society and to stimulate discussion about political problems. And there are theatre groups that do not consider their work overtly political who make plays dealing with the problems of certain constituencies such as teachers, children, old people, prisoners, women, or gays, sometimes involving them in theatrical activities as a kind of therapy.

In 1976–77 the largest Arts Council subsidy received by a "fringe" or "experimental" group went to the Welfare State Theatre, which refuses to be placed in any of these categories. ...They refuse to condescend or patronize by adapting their work to specific audiences. They present the same work for children and adults, for well-educated artistic sophisticates at art festivals, often on the continent, and for those in small towns and the ghettos of large cities with little education who may never have attended live theatre or an art gallery. The reactions of their spectators range from adulation to stoning.

John Fox [artistic director] considers much of what is done by groups with "social" aims as "baby minding, to keep children off the streets, but it has nothing to do with art or theatre or poetry."

[...]

Welfare State has made two kinds of performances. They have made large outdoor environmental spectacles incorporating regional mythology and invented myth-like images, for audiences of 3,000 or more, and they have presented small performances intended for no more than forty spectators.

[...]

The great majority of Welfare State performances are for people who live in small towns or in the ghettos of large cities—people who have had little, i[f] any, experience with the arts. Often the performances are sponsored by local community centers, and under these circumstances most of those who attend the performances are of school age. The attitude of these children at the outset is often aggressive and sometimes violent.

[...]

In September 1976, performances of plays from *The Island of the Lost World* cycle were sponsored by a community center in Halewood, a town of about 25,000 in the north of England where a Ford factory is the principal employer. On Tuesday (September 7)[,] Welfare State set up the white canvas enclosure in an open area of the town and were immediately troubled by children. The first performance was scheduled for Wednesday evening, but on Wednesday morning rocks were already being thrown and there was danger the canvas would be ripped and children hurt. They took down the enclosure and decided to do only processions in the streets, beginning at 5:00 that afternoon. By the time they had done three processions with breaks between them, the children were becoming dangerous. Rock[-]throwing became more frequent, they were clinging to the back of moving vehicles, there was an attempt to steal a Welfare State bicycle, one of the children was hit by a frustrated member of Welfare State and an argument ensued with the child's mother. It was decided that processions were not a good idea as they were raising energy and giving the kids expectations that would not be fulfilled by performances. So they decided to perform away from Halewood and bring the children to the performances by bus, sixty at a time.

On Thursday it was beginning to rain. The group dispersed to find a new site.

Near Burtonwood, ten miles away, they discovered a nearly deserted U.S. Army base, where they set up the white canvas enclosure inside a warehouse. Their first performance took place on Friday evening, and three more were given on Saturday afternoon and evening.

Welfare State audiences are always greeted in some fashion at the entrance to the area. For some productions, the Welfare State band, including most of the company, meets the arriving spectators at the entrance gate. At the U.S. Army base, the bus loads of spectators from Halewood were met outside the warehouse by a member of the group dressed in a seedy old-fashioned black tuxedo. The audiences consisted predominately of children between the ages of six and fourteen, but there were also some babies and adults. They were led into the warehouse where a labyrinth had been set up leading into the white space.

A Guide, with a craggy green-and-white face that looks as if the makeup had been applied with a palette knife, gestures silently with his bamboo hand for the spectators to follow him through the labyrinth. In the semidarkness, they are confronted by a series of grotesque figures and sculptures. Later a four-year-old girl was asked what she thought of the experience. She replied, "It was lovely. There was a man with a funny hand." When asked i[f] she had been frightened, she said, "Oh no. It was lovely, he was all gooey in the face. He told me where to come." A three-year-old, holding tightly to her mother's neck, sobbed quietly during most of the first play, looking only briefly at the performance. A woman, sitting some distance from one of her charges, called instructions to him throughout the performance. In one performance, a man of about thirty-five who was there for the second time felt compelled to share his pre-knowledge with his friends, telling them what was about to happen, warning them and making jokes.

From the time the spectators enter the labyrinth they hear live music being played on saxophone and strung piano frames that have been removed from their cases. When the audience is seated, a woman dressed as a mythological bird appears in the window-like opening in the canvas wall and sings the song that is used at the beginning and end of the performances:

> *As the wind ties skeins*　　　　　*As the wind fold petals*
> *In the heart of a tree*　　　　　*In the Lattice of bone*
> *So the wind*　　　　　*So the wind*
> *Blows seeds in the air*　　　　　*Blows men to the stars*
>
> 　　　　*As the wind drives smoke*
> 　　　　*To the edge of a field*
> 　　　　*So the wind*
> 　　　　*Finds fire in the sky.*

The purpose of the song, says the director, is to charge the space, to define it with music at the beginning of the performance and, at the end, to defuse the space and return it to what it was.

In each of the forty-minute Halewood performances, the song was followed by the same three plays from the cycle, separated only by the entrance of a "Blue Priest" wearing a cowl, who set up or removed props. The first two plays, *King of the Ditches I* and *II*, are based on Ghelderode, but the story probably goes back to the Middle Ages. In the first, the King of the Ditches with white face, skull cap, costume of coarse brown material, and feet wrapped in rags, enters carrying a two-foot wooden boat in which there are three pilgrim dolls made of brown burlap. The entire play is a monolog by the King of the Ditches, who also speaks for the Pilgrims who are on their way to Rome. The King taunts them and tortures them with a knife, making them sing and dance. He pulls them around on their boat and finally makes "a miracle" by burning one of them at a stake. A five-year-old in the audience, sitting on the lap of a man, kept asking, rather calmly, "Is he going to cut us with the knife?" A thirteen-year-old relieved his fear by making a joke about buying a pair of "shoes" like the King's.

In *King of the Ditches II*, all of the characters are played by human performers. Two blind pilgrims enter, clinging to each other. Their costumes seem to have been collected from medieval castoffs and their makeup is grotesque. The brightly costumed King of the Ditches (John Fox), with bones and feathers for a headdress and a dried beet root for a nose, gives them advice. None of the roads leads to Rome; they are in the ditch country not having left their native land. He offers them shelter, but the pilgrims mistrust him, first thinking he is an echo[,] then, thinking he intends to harm them, they swing at him blindly with their sticks, hitting each other. Finally, the pilgrims step in a hoop representing a ditch.

> *I can do nothing*
> *The ditches are deep.*
> *The blind will not sing*
> *They have come to the end of the road.*

[...]

At the conclusion of the final play at each performance [t]he strings of the piano frames are plucked several times; then the song that opened the entire performance is sung off[-]stage.

When the song is finished, music from the Welfare State band is heard coming from the entrance to the warehouse, and the spectators get up from their seats and go toward it. The band, playing, leads them out of the warehouse to the bus that brought them. The band continues to play as the bus departs for Halewood. As the bus drove away following one of the performances, a twelve-year-old boy shouted, "Rubbish!"

[...]

The esthetic objectives of Welfare State precede their social objectives. They are not making plays in order to accomplish a social end. However, having made the best work they can, they are determined to perform it not only for those who are already predisposed to their kind of work but for people who have little or no experience with the arts. They are not taking culture to the provinces, they live in the provinces; and they do not condescend to their audiences by thinking that Halewood will accept work that is inferior to that acceptable in London. They do not have an intentional political objective, but a political attitude is implicit in their work.

> **John Fox:** *If you choose to read it as such, there is a very clear political statement in the energy of our performances, the fact that we show ourselves open in making them, and that we are committed to our art and our lives*

*being together. We are showing that although we are intellectuals, we work
with our hands and discover that every moment of the day is different from
every moment of the previous day, so we are learning and growing all the
time. That is an enormously important political message in a death culture.
But we do not use the techniques of a death culture, which are to make a
lecture or a didactic statement about something, canonizing and fossilizing
it. Instead, we are actually doing it.*

4.2 Puppetry with at-risk youth

from *Walking in both worlds: Snuff Puppets at Barak Indigenous College*
Kate Donelan & Angela O'Brien. (2006). *Applied Theatre Researcher, 7*(2), 1–14. Retrieved
February 29, 2008 from: www.griffith.edu.au/centre/cpci/atr/content_journal_2006.html.

[...]

This paper focuses on the Snuff Puppets case study, a performing arts project conducted
at Barak College, a residential secondary school for [i]ndigenous students ([n]ote:
pseudonyms have been used for both the name of the college and for the students). The
Snuff Puppet artists worked intensively with the young people for two weeks, writing a
story, designing and building giant puppets, developing music and dance, and creating
a performance. The participants performed *Singing the Land* at a community event
at the conclusion of the project. The following account of this performance project,
in its unique, culturally complex site, explores the serendipitous application of theatre
involving giant puppets. It highlights the challenges of engaging the young [i]ndigenous
people and negotiating cultural differences.

Although it was not the intention of either the Snuff Puppets or the Risky Business
team, the focus on giant puppets in performance process and product exemplified
Edward Gordon Craig's theory that theatre is more inspirational when it rejects
"impersonation and the reproduction of nature" in favour of representing the
spiritual: "beautiful things from the imaginary world...strange, fierce and solemn
figures...impelled to some wondrous harmony of
movement" (Craig, 1911, p. 74). Craig argues that
the human actor should be replaced by "god-like"
puppets, Ubermarionettes (p. 81). In the Snuff
Puppet project, the involvement of the huge animal puppets not only illustrated Craig's
theory that the use of Ubermarionettes can offer a transformative theatre experience, it
also supported Barak's cultural curriculum and allowed the young people to create a
liminal theatre space which connected them to their Aboriginal Dreaming and the
mythical Land that existed before human time.

Craig, E.G. (1911). *On the art of the theatre.* London, UK: Methuen.

[...]

Phase one: Meeting the puppets

On the first day of the project, the Snuff Puppets artists met with the students in the conference centre, a beautiful building overlooking the valley and housing the school's collection of Aboriginal paintings and art[i]facts. This space, used only for "special occasions," contrasted with the old and poorly maintained portable buildings normally used for classes. The artists laid out two large puppets from their "Nyet-Nyet" project. One of the students, Scott, was drawn to the giant blue-green Bunyip puppet with its pendulous breasts and huge webbed feet. With the support of puppeteer Nick, he climbed inside it and worked out how to manipulate its outsize limbs.

As researchers, we watched from the window as the Bunyip lumbered across the basketball courts where boys who had ignored the bell were still playing. He continued onwards through the school grounds and emerged from the side of the portable classrooms like a giant Pied Piper with 20 students trailing behind. A female student manoeuvred herself into the other huge "Nyet-Nyet" puppet and joined the Bunyip in gambolling around the space. The first session could now begin.

Andy, the puppet designer, explained the project to the 24 young people:

> We're going to make a performance together by the end of the two weeks. We're going to build puppets like these two after we've got together some stories from you guys. We're looking for people who are into dancing and singing and performance-making. Today we'll play some theatre games together, get thinking about some ideas for stories, and do some drawings and designs for the puppet.

The session of theatre games, led by Sarah, the artistic director, began awkwardly when the deputy principal intervened to remove a thick rope that had been laid out in the space. She explained to us: "Rope has bad associations for one of our kids." After three games, many students drifted away. The task was to create the story of the play, but discussion with the remaining students was stilted and unproductive.

Tony Briggs worked with a group of boys who covered a large whiteboard with lurid drawings. They talked about how logging was destroying native flora and fauna and began to develop some characters. Their ideas were constructed into the plot outline of the performance:

> Bush animals are living in harmony. A logging truck crashes in the bush, killing a kangaroo but not its Joey. Poisonous oil is spilt into the environment. Creatures emerge from the poisoned lagoon. Eagle watches the disaster from above. Orphaned Joey appeals for help and Eagle transforms into a young woman who eventually sings the land back to health. (artistic director's notes)

Phase two: Building the puppets

> We use cane and bamboo and fabric and hot glues to hold them together. We use a range of materials that are often about how puppets move and operate. But the most basic one is making three-dimensional cane shapes, a sphere a head a body or starting from a backpack frame which means you carry the puppet on your back, which means you can have a long frame above your head, or it's like making humans or animals from the bones up. (Andy, puppet designer)

...Students were expected to participate in the process of building the puppets alongside the puppeteers. However, by the second day it became clear that the involvement by most of the young people was sporadic and many seemed reluctant to persist at the technical tasks despite the encouragement of adults.

[...]

> *By 11.30 only one student, Brodie, is still in the hall working alongside the puppeteers. The other kids are scattered around the school grounds, kicking footballs or hanging around the residential houses. Sarah rounds up a group and, with the assistance of Tony Briggs, they set to work cutting out the fabric for the eagle's wings, gluing with the glue gun and pushing in the stuffing. In half an hour they are all gone again, leaving their tools, the glue and bits of puppet in a tumbled heap. Brodie remains. He has worked out a way of opening and closing the emu puppet's mouth and he demonstrates this to Nick. Tony Briggs comments approvingly on the huge size of the evolving emu puppet and explains: "[T]his is the size of animals before men came." Brodie turns to us and says: "That's true, that's a fact!"* (field notes, day five)

Phase three: Creating dance and music

Dance was an important component of the preparation period and the final performance. Sarah discovered that dance provided opportunities for expression that were not otherwise available for the girls.... For Tony Briggs, the students' affinity with dance was not surprising:

> *There was nothing special in working on the dance with the boys: it's something they have all been a part of at some stage or another during their stay at Barak. It's their culture. This was one of the main reasons the school was started in the first place, to preserve our culture. Dance and storytelling are fundamental to this.*

The young people engaged with the music activities more readily than with designing and building puppets. Many of the young people demonstrated considerable ability with drums and guitars. A small group of boys, including the boys from the remote community, were proficient with [i]ndigenous instruments and played clap sticks and the didgeridoo for the traditional dances. A small group worked intensively with James, the musician, on the creation of a digitalised soundtrack.

Phase four: The performance of Singing the Land

The performance took place on a sunny Saturday morning in the grounds of Barak College, in a natural outdoor meeting place between the school buildings and the main road. Sarah had selected the performance space in front of and around a large tree-trunk painted with Aboriginal symbols.

[...]

> *The artists and the students are still working on a last dress rehearsal even as the audience is arriving. There are families and friends with children and babies, and older non-[i]ndigenous people who are "friends" of the college. There is palpable excitement, even amongst the young people who are not involved in the performance. Behind the audience, under trees, the two mothers from the Northern Territory have set up a table with their bark paintings and shell necklaces.*

> *The performance begins about half an hour after the scheduled time as Sarah, the director, introduces the play: "The students have designed and helped build the puppets. They have written the story and composed the music and written the lyrics." To one side, a small group of young artists with drum kit, synthesiser, guitars and traditional instruments are warming up.*

> *Four girls enter and perform their version of a traditional dance. It is a subdued performance—the girls move forward with repetitive movements, waving branches of gum leaves; their heads are bowed. They perform to clap sticks and didgeridoo, played by the musicians. This is followed by a more confident and vigorous dance by three of the boys, representing kangaroos and emus. The music speeds up and Scott ends the dance with a showy leg-kick.*

> *At this point, the music changes to a simple digitalised piano piece on loop. The Emu enters slowly; his movements are deliberate as he leans forward to simulate eating. The effect is quite powerful and we are surprised the young person inside the puppet is managing so well, although he is having*

problems with the huge feet. Wombat enters from behind the audience. A young female student is manipulating this puppet; again, the movements are slow and theatrically powerful. The Kangaroo enters from behind the tree, the largest of the puppets at around ten feet. The animals meet and commune.

There is a dramatic change in the music from the simple piano to a raucous rap song, "My Big Black Truck." Five boys enter running from the road, carrying giant logs to represent a logging truck. The "truck" crashes into the Kangaroo.

Tony Briggs begins his narration of the story, explaining the accident and the consequence: "The Joey, finding himself alone, searched through the bush looking for his mother." The youngest boy from the Northern Territory emerges as the orphaned kangaroo and moves around the performance space. A tall blue Creature appears, somewhat like a misshapen man but faceless and spotted as though with a terrible disease. Tony explains how the petrol has poisoned the lagoon and the Swamp Creature has been disturbed. The Joey asks the creature how the land might be repaired. A huge Eagle appears, the most spectacular of the Ubermarionettes. The performer moves across the space, displaying the great bird—a significant symbol for the school—with its wings outstretched. The narrator explains how the Eagle transforms into a beautiful young girl (who emerges from behind the tree). The Joey asks her if she will sing the country back to life. At first she refuses, too ashamed to sing by herself. After the Joey begs her to sing, the girl agrees and as she sings the animals return to the land and the play ends.

It has been quite a spectacular and moving performance, despite the lack of rehearsals. . . . (field notes, performance day)

[...]

Outcomes for the students

In spite of what we perceived as disengagement from the project by many of the young people, senior staff at the school were extremely positive in their responses. They argued that the impact of the project for the school community and for many of the young people had been significant.

The deputy principal spoke passionately about the impact of the project beyond the immediate school community. . . . Another senior staff member recognised the benefits for young people who became involved. . . . One of the themes that emerged from the data was the importance of the mentoring relationships that developed between the artists and some of the young people as they engaged in the puppetry construction, music and dance workshops, performance-making and rehearsals.

[...]

The deputy principal of the college outlined the positive effects on many individual young people with histories of family breakdown, violence, substance abuse and depression.

[...]

Tony Briggs identified considerable personal achievements for the young people:

> *I think the entire group of students who participated managed to discover more about what they are capable of when they step out of their comfort zone. I saw a visible change in attitude and demeanour with some of the students after the event; they seemed to carry themselves with a little more pride.*

4.3 Comic performance in Bangkok
from *Duen Phen: Joker performance in the nightclubs of Bangkok*
Mary L. Grow. (1995). *Asian Theatre Journal, 12* (2), 326–352.

[...]

The Joker Performance

The joker performance is a form of urban entertainment popular in Bangkok Clubs frequented by the working class. The genre derives its inspiration from traditional and popular Thai culture, and its routines rely heavily on comic improvisation and audience interaction. Scenarios typically feature familiar folktales composed of seemingly incongruous and surprising elements that subvert the audience's expectations. In an evening's entertainment comedians portray Thai mythic heroes tethering their elephants to pursue villains on a Kawasaki[,] or Han Solo rescuing a princess from the Chao Phraya River moments after she is seduced and betrayed by Mohamar Kadaffi. By lacing scenarios with current events and situations—and, moreover, by encouraging audience members to participate—comedians explore new ways of performing stories that have been a part of Thai cultural heritage for centuries.

Like most forms of improvised comedy, the joker performance is at the forefront of popular Thai culture. The genre's very survival demands that comedians keep pace with the moment. . . . Comedians who play the Thai joker performance skil[l]fully combine themes and images belonging to both the emergent and the residual culture, and they often juxtapose one against the other, thereby creating ridiculous and imaginative scenarios. This style of nightclub comedy not only provides insight into those structures of thought and belief that remain constant through time, but it also highlights change in the Thai sociocultural system.

[...]

I was continually impressed by Duen Phen's creative attempt to reflect upon and ridicule social, economic, and political issues in Thailand and the international community. During the two years I accompanied the troupe in and out of clubs like the Gold Sweet Café, the Can Can Palace, and the Tick Toc Shop, I watched them cultivate a loyal following among audience members and club owners. Their fans repeatedly told me that Duen Phen's comic material gave voice to their everyday concerns. Their comedy often involved issues of class conflict, broken love, economic hardship, and the hope for something better to come. I realized that here in the nightlife of Bangkok was an emergent social commentary inspired and framed by the traditional performance genres I had observed in the countryside, yet it was also shaped and reshaped by the influences of an ever-changing and increasingly global urban lifestyle characteristic of Bangkok.

[...]

"Saiyasaat": A Typical Routine

The routine known as "Saiyasaat" was performed at the Phop Suk (Meet Happiness) Café on November 4, 1987. It featured four characters: an Announcer, a Spirit Medium, a Country Bumpkin, and a Child, each played by members of Duen Phen. A drummer and *ranat* player provided musical accompaniment.

The action begins when the Spirit Medium, costumed in a flowing cape, enters through the audience and joins the Announcer onstage. The Medium then begins to speak, rattling off an impressive list of his accomplishments, including levitation, fire eating, and mental telepathy. Accompanying this monologue Duen Phen's musicians play melodies that suggest the arrival of an Indian snake charmer. The Medium is soon visited by a Country Bumpkin who wants to win the lottery. This new character wears a checkered *phakhaoma* and a pair of rubber thongs, typical attire of an upcountry peasant. His bare chest appears hollow as the performer sucks in his breath and hunches his shoulders. In an effort to impress this client, the Medium chants mantras of gibberish while grandly striding to and fro. Finally he turns to the audience and shouts:

> I am a great master, a practiced ascetic, an indestructible force in the universe. All people love me, all people venerate me, all people come to me for advice. Stop your drinking! Stop your romancing! Watch my powers unfold.

Several of the audience members respond with applause, while others jeer and hiss.

The Medium then challenges everyone to witness his skill in mental telepathy, adding that his expertise far surpasses the monetary fee humbly offered by his ignorant client. He selects a Child seated in the audience to assist in his demonstration. After fussing a bit, the Child is dragged to center stage by the Announcer, where he stands staring blankly at the audience and picking his nose. Finally he steals a fearful glance at the Medium and begins to whine. The Medium orders the boy to stop, pushes him into a chair, and then drapes an enormous cloth over him. Muffled sniffles and sighs can be heard as the Child resigns himself to the task at [h]and.

The Medium then walks among the audience members and stops at a patron's table. He selects a glass of beer, holds it up for everyone to see, and asks the Child to identify the object. Onstage the Child, still covered by the cloth, responds with the correct answer. Overwhelmed by the Medium's impressive display of power, the Country Bumpkin falls to his knees and gestures with a *wai*. Triumphantly the Medium moves to several other tables where the "miracle" is successfully repeated with a variety of items. Audience members who initially expressed scepticism at the Medium's skill now shout words of praise. Turning to the Announcer, the Country Bumpkin remarks:

> This man is a great master! He has great power. With his help I am sure to win
> the lottery. I will stake my entire life savings on whatever number he selects.

Gloating with pride over his success, the Medium continues the demonstration, but this time he capitalizes on his fame and solicits money from converted audience members. Suddenly the room is filled with people waving banknotes and urging the Medium to come to their tables. Calculating the situation, he goes to a group offering a large reward. The Medium quickly selects an item from their table, holds it up, and asks the Child onstage to identify it. After a few moments of silence the Child blurts out a response. It is incorrect. Grabbing another item, the Medium demands a repeat. But again the Child's response is wrong. The Country Bumpkin, now suspicious of a scam, quickly runs to the chair and snatches away the cloth covering the Child—exposing the Medium's planted accomplice, the Child, who is puzzling over a sheet of paper that apparently does not list the last items held by the Medium. Realizing the jig is up, the Medium dashes for an exit. A drum roll accents the punchline and the show is over.

Behind all these shenanigans lies trenchant social commentary directed at Thai spirit mediums. In October 1987 the State Lottery Bureau faced a serious crisis of credibility when it was discovered that six of the seven wheels used in the previous month's drawing were rigged. . . . As this scandal hit the Thai news media it created an uproar throughout the country, for many people had invested fortunes in the lottery hoping to beat the odds with a lucky number. Not only was the nation's confidence in the State Lottery Bureau shaken; so too was the reputation of spirit mediums who claimed to assist their patrons in selecting winning numbers.

[...]

While members of Duen Phen jokingly refer to the lottery as "Thailand's national pastime," they too are eager to purchase lottery tickets in hopes of winning substantial cash. They are sceptical of spirit mediums who claim supernatural powers, however, and openly resent those who extort money from the poor and naive. Kii Simakok of Duen Phen explains: "Spirit mediums are only playing a clever performance. They often take advantage of people in desperate circumstances by taking money from those who need answers to their problems. Our performance demonstrates how cunning these practitioners are."

Duen Phen's role as critic and social commentator is best understood in relation to audience members seeking this form of comic entertainment. The joker performance is popular in the notorious nightlife sector of Bangkok, where it is enjoyed by a variety of people, primarily Thai, who work [h]ard for a daily wage yet are never quite able to improve their standard of living. Construction workers, taxi drivers, blue-collar employees, hustlers, and call girls typically frequent the joker performance. Many audience members, as well as the comedians themselves, have come to the urban center of Bangkok from the rural countryside in search of new economic opportunities. Compared to the low wages or even underemployment of the rural areas, most workers have in fact increased their financial earnings. At the same time, however, these people are also compelled to spend most of their wages just to keep pace with the high cost of urban living. Moreover, some of them are seduced by the consumerism that is now part of Bangkok life and gamble or spend their meager earnings on a wide variety of luxury goods.

[...]

Thus comic inspiration for Duen Phen's "Saiyasaat" performance was drawn from current events—in particular, the scandal that shook conventional faith in the legitimacy of the lottery and the relationship between spirit mediums and their clients. Furthermore, the comedians explored the struggle between existing and emerging value systems, as well as the vulnerability of people experiencing social, economic, and political change. In "Saiyasaat" Duen Phen exposes the internal conflicts of Thai society for its themes and social commentary. Events that shape and reflect a dynamic Thai worldview are the target of comedic exposé.

Further Reading

Bates, R. A. (1996). Popular theatre: A useful process for adult educators. *Adult Education Quarterly*, *46*(4), 224–236. From an adult education perspective, Bates outlines both terms and processes for popular theatre.

Butterwick, S. & Selman, J. (2003). Deep listening in a feminist popular theatre project: Upsetting the position of audience in participatory education. *Adult Education Quarterly, 54*(1), 7–22. This essay looks at facilitation skills needed when working with challenging material and promotes the notion of "deep listening" as part of the reflective process.

Coult, T. & Kershaw, B. (Eds.) (1983). *Engineers of the imagination: The Welfare State handbook*. London, UK: Methuen. More reading about the UK company Welfare State.

Drennan, B. (1995). *Performed negotiations: The historical significance of the second wave alternate theatre in English Canada and its relationship to the popular tradition*. Unpublished dissertation, University of Victoria, British Columbia, Canada. An examination of alternative theatre practices in Canada, including useful diagrams showing the contrast between mainstream and alternative theatre.

Filewod, A. (1989). Forum: The marginalization of the Canadian popular theatre alliance in the discourse of Canadian theatre history. *Theatre Research in Canada, 10*(2), unpaginated. www.lib.unb.ca/Texts/TRIC/bin/get.cgi?directory=vol10_2/&filename=Forum.htm. A concise overview of the history of Canadian popular theatre and its relationship to mainstream theatre.

Kidd, R. (1984). Popular theatre and nonformal education in the Third World: Five strands of experience. *International Review of Education, XXX*, 265–287. Kidd, a Canadian who worked in Africa for many years, offers useful definitions of key terms as they applied in the 1980s.

Prentki, T. & Selman, J. (2000). *Popular theatre in political culture: Britain and Canada in focus*. Bristol, UK: Intellect Books. This text has an excellent collection of case studies with particular emphasis on process and facilitation.

Riccio, T. (2001). Tanzanian theatre from Marx to the marketplace. *TDR: The Drama Review, 45*(1), 128–152. A very thorough survey of popular theatre, TfD and other cultural performance practices in Tanzania.

Salverson, J. (2001). Questioning an aesthetic of injury: Notes from the development of BOOM. *CTR: Canadian Theatre Review, 106*, 66–69. Salverson was commissioned by the Canadian Red Cross to develop a play on land mines and made use of clowning in its inception. This issue of CTR also includes the script of *BOOM*.

Questions for Reflection and Discussion

1. Who are the audience members for each of the three case studies in this chapter? What do they hold in common and how are they different?

2. Looking at your own theatre experience, where have you seen the use of mask, puppet and/or spectacle? How are those experiences of that kind of performance different from other kinds of theatre you have seen?

3. Popular theatre uses practices that are often outside of our traditional understanding of theatre, including the absence of written text. What criteria might we use to assess its effectiveness?

4. What is the difference between *popular* and *populist* theatre?

Suggested Activities

1. As a class project, invite a skilled practitioner of mask, puppetry or circus techniques to offer a workshop. Next, identify an audience, location and locally-relevant topic that you would like to explore through theatre. Incorporate some of the new performance skills into the project.

2. "Comedy makes the subversion of the existing state of affairs possible." —Dario Fo (n.d.) Nobel prize-winning actor, director and playwright Dario Fo has drawn on clown traditions throughout his distinguished career to create highly political and activist theatre in Italy and around the world. In small groups, create and perform a clown-based piece of theatre that has a satirical and subversive intent.

3. Create a short piece of politically-based theatre that tackles an issue of shared concern. Recreate the piece using puppets you have built, bought or borrowed. These puppets could be as simple as children's toys or dolls, even kitchen utensils endowed with character. After presenting both versions of your piece in class, facilitate a conversation that considers the different qualities seen in the two versions of the same scenario.

Introduction

Theatre of the Oppressed (TO) is a genre of applied theatre developed by Brazilian director Augusto Boal and codified in his text of the same name (1979), partly in response to the groundbreaking work of educator Paolo Freire and his book *Pedagogy of the Oppressed* (1970/2000) and also in response to the social and political turmoil present in Brazil at that time. Boal's theatre practice underwent a revolutionary shift during a performance when a spectator spontaneously stepped onto the stage and intervened in the action of the play. Boal realized that it was this breaking down of the fourth wall between actor and audience that is demanded in politically conscious theatre. He and his theatre company began to train themselves to work more directly with disenfranchised communities and developed an "arsenal" of games and activities that allowed unskilled participants to explore their own lives and socio-political oppressions (see *Games for actors and non-actors*, 1992). His plans were to transform the spectator into an actor—called the "spect-actor"—through games that allowed for more self-expression before moving into theatre as process and language. Theatre became a method for communities to generate discussion and rehearse action toward real social change. Boal's theatre of the oppressed involves a number of important strategies, the foremost known as Forum Theatre.

> [The spectator] assumes the protagonic role, changes the dramatic action, tries out solutions, discusses plans for change—in short, trains himself for real action.
> Augusto Boal, 1979, p. 122

> Forum Theatre consists, in essence, of proposing to a group of spectators, after a first improvisation of a scene, that they replace the protagonist [the Oppressed] and try to improvise variation on his actions. The real protagonist should, ultimately, improvise the variation that has motivated him the most (Boal, 1995, p. 184).

In Forum Theatre, the play is presented twice—the first time straight through. During the second time around, the audience of spect-actors has an opportunity to identify any scene of oppression with a negative outcome for the oppressed protagonist and have it re-played. During the re-playing, the spect-actor can stop the scene at any time he or she feels that things could be done differently, replace the protagonist and lead the scene toward a different solution. The scene can be repeated with a number of spect-actor interventions until an agreeable solution is reached or a variety of other perspectives on the action have been explored.

Key ingredients of Forum Theatre are the role of the facilitator, known as the Joker, the concept of *metaxis* and the importance of *praxis*. The Joker plays the key role of bridging the two worlds of the play (the fictional world) and the audience (the real world) by directly addressing both spectators and characters and facilitating their interactions. The Joker is a kind of trickster figure who is charged with keeping the dramatic process open, steering participants away from easy or simplistic solutions (Boal refers to the Joker as "the difficultator" rather than a "facilitator" [Jackson, in Boal, 1995, p. xix]) and, at times, educating the audience about the issues at hand. This interchange between the world of the play and the world of the audience is known as *metaxis* and the Joker is the all-important door-opener between these two worlds. The notion of *praxis* lies in the process of action that emanates from "reflection which in turn produces a new set of reflections, leading to the next action, and so on, in an ongoing dialectic" (Mutnick, 2006, p. 42). This is the intention of Forum Theatre, to provide a space not only for discussion and reflection but also as a rehearsal for real action toward change.

> **Metaxis**: The state of belonging completely and simultaneously to two different, autonomous worlds: the image of reality and the reality of the image. The participant shares and belongs to these two autonomous worlds...
>
> Augusto Boal, 1995, p. 43

Political upheavals in Brazil led to Boal and some of his followers being imprisoned and to Boal's subsequent exile in Argentina and Europe. During those years through the 1980s, Boal shifted his practice from the exploration of overt political oppressions experienced in South American settings to more internal psychological oppressions seen in the developed world. This adaptation of his work was published in a book called *The rainbow of desire: The Boal method of theatre and therapy* (1995) and centered around physical and dramatic strategies that brought out the "cops in the head" of Western participants, primarily the oppressions wrought by capitalism, materialism and individualism at the expense of community.

When Boal returned to Brazil after a decade overseas, he was elected to the city council of Rio de Janeiro in 1992. In his new role as politician, Boal became interested in using his theatre methods to provide a way for citizens to engage in a democratic and dramatic process focused on the creation of new laws, published in a book called

Legislative theatre: Using performance to make politics (1998). Some issues, including anti-racism, child prostitution, geriatric care and mental health, tackled through Boal's theatre strategies by Boal and his actors, led directly to the implementation of new city statutes.

It is clear in looking at the history of Boal's practices that he has continuously adapted his work for different settings and communities. Today, we find TO and Forum Theatre being used in many parts of the world by theatre workers assisting communities that want to take action around an agreed issue.

Our first reading is a description by Boal of a Legislative Theatre workshop he conducted in Germany. Although this is a very condensed version of the full process, we can see how effective theatre can be as a way to envision new laws. The second case study describes the work of Vancouver's Headlines Theatre in a college setting that involved students in a Safer Campuses program addressing problems of sexual harassment of female students. The author raises interesting issues around the training of the Joker as a process that should resist standardization. The third example again takes place with university students and is about body image and eating habits. The author's interest is in the effect of the work on student actors who express a shift in understanding these internal oppressions.

5.1 A letter from Augusto Boal
from *INTERVIEW: Augusto Boal, City Councillor: Legislative Theatre and the Chamber in the Streets*
Richard Schechner, Sudipto Chatterjee, and Augusto Boal. (1998). *TDR: The Drama Review, 42*(4), pp. 75–90.

Symbolism in Munich (letter from Augusto Boal, pp. 86–87)
The Paulo Freire Society, so named in honor of the great Brazilian educator, invited me to show some examples of Legislative Theatre in the city of Munich [in 1997]. I explained that our experience in Rio had taken us four whole years to approve 13 new laws, and that the most we could do in only four days would be a pale and symbolic event, a hint of what might be that theatre form in the future, in the city of Munich or elsewhere.

We started our work and, over four days, prepared five small scenes about situations of oppression revealed by the 35 participants of the workshop. One of the scenes prepared by the group dealt with a very common problem in Germany—and, as far as I know, in many other European countries: [s]ome men choose a wife in matrimonial agencies, looking at their photos, CVs, and other information. Those women are recruited from countries like Romania, Thailand, and even in my own country, Brazil. Once the bridegroom has chosen his wife, she is imported by the agency with promises of marriage and a wonderful European-style princess life. Of course, those young women are very poor and full of hope—also very naive. Once the women arrive in the country, part of the agency's promise is fulfilled: they marry. Once married, the husbands—in most cases, not always—behave as though they bought a slave, and treat their wives as such, in the kitchen and in the bed. More often than not, those women don't speak a word of German and have difficulties learning the language. They don't have friends and sometimes are forbidden to go out without their men. The husbands keep strict control over them. If the wife decides to leave her husband—it is not easy but it is possible—she automatically loses her German citizenship and is sent back to her country by the police. She is punished, not him!

During the Forum that we did inside the group, the participants revealed their opinion: [i]f a crime was committed—namely, a marriage of convenience for the purpose of getting German nationality for the woman and a slave for the man—both persons are responsible for that crime, and not only the woman.

The proposition of a Project of Law became clear: the woman should be punished with the loss of citizenship, yes, but not with deportation from Germany[.] [M]ost of those women had not only economic problems back home, but political ones; in some cases, their lives would be endangered should they be deported. And the husband, considering that he was also responsible for faking a marriage, should be punished with a short term in prison, to discourage this practice. Other short scenes were made about social security, marriage of gay partners, use of public space for private activities, etc.

On the fifth day, Fritz Letsch (from the Paulo Freire Society) obtained permission to do the Forum Theatre inside the city hall (the Rathaus), and invited many politicians, including the mayor of Munich, who did not come because it was his birthday but sent his vice-mayor. The vice-mayor attended the session at the side of the secretary of the Green Party for Bavaria: those two persons were the only authorities present. Of course, we had invited everybody else but, understandably, they had more urgent things to do. The information released about the starting time for the session was wrong and some people came to the Rathaus at 11 in the morning when we were rehearsing for the presentation at 1:30 P.M. Among those persons came an old lady with totally white hair, using a cane to move around. She had been at the public lecture that I delivered on the first day of the workshop, during which I explained the functioning of the Legislative Theatre.

I remember that, during the dialogue after my lecture, another woman said that this process could have worked well in Brazil, because in Brazil we are Brazilians (meaning that we dance and sing, which is not necessarily true for some of us. . .) and that we are extroverted people. But—according to her—this could not work at all in a country like Germany, where people are more introverted, less expansive. She totally ignored the

Oktoberfest! I replied that when I introduced the Theatre of the Oppressed (TO) in Europe, I frequently heard the same opinion. And yet today, the TO is practiced very intensely in almost all European countries. Of course, in each country, people have to adapt the method to their own culture, their own language, their own desires and needs. TO is not a Bible, not a recipe book: it is a method to be used by people, and people are more important than the method.

The same can happen with the Legislative Theatre: in each country, it has to find its own form for application to real situations in that country. But the woman that night held to her opinion. And the old lady with white hair and a beautiful cane at her side did not say anything. When we started the show at the Rathaus, I explained that what we were going to do had only a symbolic value: we had not done the whole procedure of the Legislative Theatre; we had not done many shows for many different kinds of audiences; we had not done the Chamber in the Street about the problems presented in the scenes; we had not done the Interactive Mailing List to consult people whose opinions might be useful in preparing a law, and whose knowledge could enlighten us. On the contrary, we wrote the Projects of Law ourselves, which positively is not the right thing to do. So, if any, the presentation at the Rathaus would have only a symbolic value.

After my introduction, we did the scenes. The audience chose three of them, including the slave-wife scene, and we did a Forum Theatre session on those three. Many people intervened, even the secretary of the vice-mayor! On the slave scene, most of the interventions were similar to ours. To close the event, we delivered our Projects of Law—someone had painted beautiful letters on a beautiful paper—to make a good impression to the Secretary of the Bavarian Greens. She was very nice to us, and said that she understood the symbolic nature of the event but, even so, she would really take those Projects of Law to the Green Legislators for consideration.

We were very happy. On her way out, the old lady with the cane and white hair approached me—she was one of the first to come in, and one of the last to leave. She called me and said:

> It is very entertaining what you have done. I agree with you and I know that this is just a symbolic action. But it was very important for me: you have shown that this is possible. And it had never crossed my mind to imagine that people, common people, people like us, could get together, make theatre about our own problems, discuss them on the stage, and then sit down and propose a new law. [...] I agree with you: we have to make our desire become law!

I must say: I was happy.

5.2 Forum theatre on sexual harassment
from *Making bodies talk in Forum Theatre*
Paul Dwyer. (2004). *RIDE: Research in Drama Education, 9*(2), 199–210.

[...]

Observing Forum Theatre

In 1995, I observed a two-week workshop/rehearsal process and four preview performances of "Boundaries," a Forum Theatre project presented on the campus of Langara College in Vancouver, Canada. The project was directed by two facilitators from *Headlines Theatre Company* (one of the major disseminators of TO methods in North America) and developed with students from the actor-training programme at Studio 58, a part of Langara College and one of Canada's leading theatre schools. The development of "Boundaries" was funded under a provincial government campaign which aimed to "reduce the incidence of [physical and psychological] violence against women" at colleges and universities throughout British Columbia (Ministry of Skills, Training and Labour, 1994). In line with this campaign objective, the *Headlines* facilitators worked with the *Studio 58* actors to devise two Forum Theatre scenarios on the theme of sexual harassment which could later be performed in lecture halls and classrooms. Of particular interest for my purposes here is the opportunity which this project afforded of seeing four young performers being trained to take over the role of joker for the rest of the "Boundaries" season.

[...]

Forum Theatre dramaturgy (or "boys will be girls")

Forum Theatre is based on a deceptively simple dramaturgical formula. The audience is invited to watch "with a critical eye" (as the *Headlines* facilitators would say) the struggle between an oppressed protagonist and his or her antagonist. The scenario is played through once, uninterrupted, until it reaches some kind of catastrophe. The actors then begin to play the scenario a second time, stopping whenever an audience member wishes to improvise some alternative tactic that he or she feels may help the cause of the oppressed protagonist.

For a Forum Theatre piece on the theme of sexual harassment, there is no great difficulty in guessing the likely gender of the oppressed and oppressor characters. Thus, on the first morning of "Boundaries" workshop/rehearsal process, some of the male actors involved confessed to feeling somewhat defensive: "I don't want to be typecast as an oppressor;" "I don't think all men are ogres;" "I feel like the issues are quite sticky." In response, the *Headlines* facilitators explained that since funding for the project had been obtained from the "Safer Campuses for Women" programme, the forum scenarios would focus on the oppression of women by men (in fact, the programme was simply called

"Safer Campuses" but the intent—as noted above—was to support women's participation in post-secondary study). The facilitators also flagged, however, the role of what they called the "powerless observer" as an important part of the dramaturgical model: where the issues are "sticky," there can be characters (male and female) who are momentarily unaligned, capable of supporting either the oppressed or the oppressor depending on the particular tactics which intervening audience members choose to pursue.

The two forum scenarios which the group devised covered a broad range of oppressive behaviours—from the mundane (but by no means insignificant) experience of a female student struggling to get a word in edgeways as her male colleagues bulldoze their way through a group assignment, through to the more extreme (but by no means uncommon) experience of a young woman who is raped by a male acquaintance at an off-campus party. With both scenarios, the various catastrophes facing the protagonists clearly had the desired effect of stimulating a large number of audience members to intervene on stage. These interventions ranged from relatively playful attempts to deflect the unwanted attentions of a male harasser to strong confrontation and (mimed) physical violence. Situations which, in the model forum scenario, seemed quite black and white quickly turned to some much more interesting shades of grey as soon as spectators intervened.

Boal, A. (1992). *Games for actors and non-actors.* (A. Jackson, Trans.). London, UK: Routledge.

Perhaps surprisingly, given that the focus of the scenarios was on female protagonists, a very large proportion of these interventions were made by male audience members— 48 out of a total of 92 (or 52%) over the course of the four preview performances. A much more striking statistic, however, is the difference between the interventions of male and female spectators regarding the gender of the characters they played: when women intervened, they nearly always took the part of the oppressed female characters (that is, women played women); yet when the men intervened, it was also nearly always to play a female character (men played women on 41 out of 48 occasions). Boal would generally advise against the joker allowing such a high number of cross-gender interventions on the basis that only the women in the audience could truly identify with the oppressed female protagonists (Boal, 1992, pp. 240–242). In this instance, neither the trainee *Studio 58* jokers nor the *Headlines* facilitators ever invited the audience to question the relevance of the spect-actors' gender to the interventions proposed (to be fair, neither was the issue raised by any member of the audience).

[...]

The substantial amount of debriefing within the overall performance structure of "Boundaries" (together with the fact that the trainee jokers and *Headlines* facilitators seemed unaware of this fact) is certainly one reason why Forum Theatre may be thought of as enacting an "invisible pedagogy." However, when one looks more closely at the pattern which the *Studio 58* trainee jokers were taught to follow during debriefing talk, there is no mistaking the joker's role as teacher. In rehearsals, the trainee jokers were encouraged to work from the following basic structure:

- interview the spect-actor (e.g.[,] "Did you get what you wanted?");
- interview the actors (e.g.[,] "What changed for your character? Could your character take that kind of action?"); and
- make a brief summary for the audience (e.g.[,] "So what we learn from this intervention seems to be . . .").

Taken together, these summary evaluations amount to a compendium of recommendations for the audience to consider and thus point to the broader discourses which are being reproduced and/or challenged in this Forum Theatre event. With this in mind, here is a selection of some typical comments which cropped up during the "Boundaries" performances:

- So we can learn that by expressing your opinions right from the start then you can sort of maybe get a better perspective on what's really going on.
- I think we're seeing a lot of people stand up for themselves[.]
- So I guess what we learn from your intervention is that we can't—we shouldn't always follow our friends or give in to peer pressure. We sometimes have to go with how we feel.
- So in effect by being very conscious and open about your consciousness you can . . . educate people around you and . . . get out of situations that you don't want to be in.
- By hitting things at a very human level instead of a "man versus woman" nonsense level . . . just cutting right under it, caring . . . you managed to open things up and stop the nonsense[.]
- By insisting on your space and … really being honest about what it is that you're comfortable with, you can avoid conflict and that's something that everybody needs to do in their life.

I should stress that my point here is not to damn the "Boundaries" jokers for lacking a more sophisticated analytical language.... Like anyone else, these students are prone to fall back on the clichés and common sense understandings of the dominant discourses into which they have been apprenticed. . . . At best, out of this mix comes a discourse in which the oppressors are never named as such and their actions rarely scrutinised; at worst, comes a discourse in which those who are oppressed, if only they could get in touch with their true feelings, would learn to stand up for their rights. . . . Given the generic features of the debriefing routine adopted here, it takes a linguistically dextrous and committed spect-actor to make this challenge public.

Forum Theatre may or may not be a "safe space" in which to investigate "alternative scenarios" and social interventions. It is certainly not a value-neutral space, despite the way Boal at times portrays it as a theatre of free expression, automatically empowering by virtue of the fact that spectators can transgress the "sacred" space of the stage. Against such rhetorical claims, the "Boundaries" project offers instead a salutary reminder that Forum theatre always occurs in a precise context, wherein the participants—including individuals and organizations participating as sponsors/supporters—are engaged in multiple (sometimes contradictory) forms of ideological struggles.

5.3 Eating disorders and Theatre of the Oppressed
from *Speaking theatre/Doing pedagogy: Re-visiting theatre of the oppressed*
Leigh Anne Howard. (2004). *Communication Education, 53*(3), 217–233.

[...]
Beauty and the Feast: Stories of Eating and Body Image
My introduction to Augusto Boal's techniques involved using performance as a way to generate understanding about eating habits and body image. Combining my interests in performance and ethnography, I conducted ethnographic interviews . . . with groups of men and women about their eating habits and how they felt about their bodies. In order to volunteer for the group interviews, participants needed to be interested in discussing body image and eating practices, and they needed to attend each of the five 90[-]minute sessions. In return, participants would receive one hour of elective credit in speech communication. I led five groups (four groups of females, one group of males); each had five or six participants ranging from 17 to 29 years old. None of the participants claimed to have an eating disorder, nor were they diagnosed with such disorders, since this project was about their *perceptions* of body image and eating practices, not about eating disorders *per se*.

Six female participants (ages 17–25) chose to continue with the project after the end of the school term by forming a performance troupe. For their continued work, they received another hour of elective credit. Over the next ten weeks (nearly twice the rehearsal time for other performances), troupe members generated over 60 hours of rehearsal, in addition to their independent "homework" related to writing scenes and journal writing, and their later work memorizing and assisting with the production. Our troupe goal was to create a public performance that would give voice to the experiences reflected in the earlier group interviews.

Reason, P. (1994). *Participation in human inquiry.* London, UK: Sage.

At our first meeting, I explained that we would create a collaborative performance that would reflect the ideas from the group discussions, as well as any changes they noted in their own attitudes. Although the group determined all of the decisions during the rehearsal phases, I made two initial decisions. First, we would adapt Boal's techniques, and second, we would all keep personal journals about the process and our reflections about body image. The journals served to track our observations about our own behavior and also served as a place to record performance ideas or themes from the group interviews. The overall process of the observation and reflection that generated the performance script resembled what Reason (1994) called "co-operative inquiry" (p. 324), because all participants were so dedicated and respectful of the process and other troupe members. To be sure, this degree of collaborative decision-making generated some frustration for the one participant accustomed to a more traditional theatre process with a director in control. And the process was a time-consuming one; two weeks prior to the public performance, we still had not determined the order of the scenes or the set design, but troupe members at every point were fully engaged. None missed a rehearsal. All came prepared each time. They freely offered (and sought) suggestions to improve scenes.

In addition to the group goal of giving voice to the interviews, I had a secondary goal that entailed documenting and assessing what happened to the performers as a result of engaging in this type of interactive performance project.

[...]

This performance project was a space for the performers to declare what had not been heard—or in many cases what they could not say in any other way. Many student performers said that the performance enabled them to talk to their parents or partners about their eating habits, because the performance created a safe frame for the discussion.

Furthermore, students determined what they would say and do based upon their ideas and improvisation work during rehearsal; these women were not "vessels" who enacted my vision. . . . During rehearsal, our troupe would watch the group interviews I conducted and videotaped prior to the troupe's formation, and troupe members would use the ideas and experiences as the foundation for the movement exercises characteristic of Boal's (1992) first set of games and exercises. The troupe's goal was to develop a public performance that could communicate the ideas, attitudes, and beliefs suggested by the group interviews. This particular activity represents my second adaptation of TO as the exercises were used to generate material for a *public* performance, entitled *Beauty and the Feast*. More often, TO and RD (Rainbow of Desire) performances resemble a stylized improvisation, an intense form of role[-]playing primarily for the purpose of helping participants themselves. Generally with TO, there is no script, memorization, rehearsal schedule, or production.

In contrast, as we moved through rehearsal in this adaptation of TO, performers used Boal's techniques to shape ideas into specific scenes about beauty pageants, diet plans, and food cravings. Some scenes were more traditional performances of original poetry, while others were performance art pieces. In one scene, by way of illustration, a prim and proper persona meticulously set the breakfast table. After painstakingly lining up the utensils and determining the exact location of the milk carton, the performer sat at the table, placed her napkin in her lap, glanced over her shoulders, and attacked her food. She "chugged" the milk from its carton and scooped grits into her mouth with her hands.

Toward the end of the rehearsal sessions—after we had generated scenes and determined which the public performance would comprise—we used the techniques to solidify performance choices and character personae. Using TO as a way to strengthen a performer's ability to develop characters stands as my third adaptation of TO. The games and exercises provided troupe members with a way to develop complex, multi-dimensioned speakers. The public performance, which ran two nights on campus and was revived for a third show at a regional communication conference, consisted of nine scenes. One scene became the impetus for the Forum Theatre portion of the public performance.

Boal, A. (1995). *The rainbow of desire: The Boal method of theatre and therapy* (A. Jackson, Trans.). London, UK: Routledge.

During a Forum Theatre (Boal, 1992) session, performers improvise a scene based upon a social problem. This problem, according to Boal, must be a concrete problem... that causes oppression for the gathered collective. As the improvisation occurs, audience members are encouraged to approach the playing area to intervene directly in the action; audience members become spect-actors who are no longer content merely to watch what happens. They must determine what is happening, discover alternatives to the events, decide how to intervene, and then enact the intervention; otherwise, the troupe members repeat the same problem/script, and the scene ends in the same oppressive manner as [it] did the first time. In our Forum scene, a performer (antagonist) would surreptitiously wrap food from her plate in a napkin that she would then drop on the floor. Later in the scene while she was offstage, her dining companions (one antagonist, one protagonist) noticed the napkins and began to discuss their courses of action. They had not determined a strategy when the antagonist returned, and after a few more lines, the scene ended, and the rest of the public performance continued.

At the conclusion of the public performance, the players re-entered the performance space and explained that they wanted to create a more satisfactory ending for the restaurant scene. They invited audience members to replace the protagonist and create a modification that would end the dramatic tension featured in the first run. At both campus performances, audience members first wanted to discuss the show, rather than act in it. They offered the explanation that the performer dropping food was in denial or that her friends should show compassion. When pressed to take the stage, audience members were less eager to participate. Even one seasoned performer refrained from taking the stage to rehearse her suggestion. Later at each performance, an audience member broke the wall and entered the scene to perform. After a few interventions at each show, the event concluded, and audience members approached us with questions and comments. Audience reactions at the performance given at the professional conference differed from the campus audiences. While the conference audience did not wish to discuss the content of the show, they were interested in the content as it related to performance choices and performance theory.

If the goal of this particular performance project had been to generate audience participation by enticing audience members to come on stage, then it would have been only moderately successful, as each campus performance generated only four or five interventions in the Forum scene. What is important to note, though, is what the performance did to the collective in the entire space. As Boal (1995) wrote, "The centre of gravity is in the auditorium, not on the stage" (p. 40). While only a few audience members actively participated in the performance, several expressed to me later that they wanted the Forum to continue and that they had talked about it for hours after the show concluded. Audience members were engaged at each performance and responded in a manner consistent with the performance context. At the campus performance, audience members engaged the ideas and experiences; they entered the stage and co-created a supportive place for the performers to speak. At the conference, audience members engaged the work on a theoretical level and then discussed the practicality of using this rehearsal format.

[...]

In a debriefing session after the Forum, audience members from one campus performance disdained the comedy and parody that underscored the performer's choices; these audience members wanted a serious show that positioned the characters as victims. However, since the performers did not see themselves as such, they made deliberate and consistent choices not to present their stories in such a way.

[...]

Beauty and the Feast developed self-awareness or a better understanding of others in every performer. Moreover, the awareness spurred change. Even those who did not change their own eating practices remarked that they had thought about their behaviors in a different way and/or would alter their reactions to others. While the experience did not generate a new community agency to address body oppression, the experience did enable the performers to share and resolve what Boal would call internal oppressors. By enacting—and declaring publicly—their fears, observations, and insights, the performers learned that they could promote change by starting with their own behaviors and by communicating their understandings to others. Moreover, performers learned to incorporate the actions rehearsed/learned via the performance project into their social behaviors.

Further Reading

In addition to his own texts, there is a great deal of writing about Boal's work in many settings, across many cultures and a variety of applied theatre genres. You will have already met some of them in this text. In addition, we suggest:

Burton, B. & O'Toole, J. (2005). Enhanced Forum Theatre: Where Boal's Theatre of the Oppressed meets process drama in the classroom. *NJ: Drama Australia Journal, 29*(2), 49–57. Presenting the project "Cooling Conflict" that led to the development of these ways of using Forum Theatre, the authors then go on to analyze the four "enhancements" (three scenes, not one; multiple interventions; the fourth scene; and process drama additions) and the reasons for their use. Much helpful information here about structuring and presenting this adaptation of Forum Theatre.

Cohen-Cruz, J. & Schutzman, M. (Eds.). (2006). *A Boal companion: Dialogues on theatre and cultural politics.* London, UK: Routledge. A wide-ranging collection of essays, case studies and critical discussions on the work of Boal that address the impact and implications of Boal's work by American practitioners and theoreticians with rich experience of using his strategies and techniques.

Headlines Theatre/Theatre for Living, www.headlinestheatre.com. This is an excellent website. Click on "past work" to learn about the work that engages this company and its artistic director, David Diamond. There is an invaluable description under "2000–present" of "Practicing Democracy" (2004) Legislative theatre by people experiencing chronic poverty.

International Theatre of the Oppressed Organization, www.theatreoftheoppressed.org. This website contains a rich variety of project reports, facilitator handbooks, evaluations, photos and videos from many countries.

Schutzman, M. (1990). Activism, therapy, or nostalgia? Theatre of the Oppressed in NYC. *TDR, 34*(3), 77–83. An interesting historical article that provides examples of the concerns Schutzman has about the value of using Boal's Theatre of the Oppressed in North American settings so different from those of political suppression. *Rainbow of Desire* (1995) could be seen, in part, as Boal's answer to her dilemmas.

Questions for Reflection and Discussion

1. Consider the implications of cross-gender role taking in Forum Theatre. In replacing the protagonist, how important do you consider it to be that the spect-actor is the same gender as the protagonist and for what reasons?

2. Boal talks about adapting his work for various cultures and communities. Based on your reading and understanding of TO, what elements of Boal's practice need to remain consistent wherever it is done? What elements do you see as more changeable?

3. In a group, discuss the implications of Boal's desire to transform theatre into a democratic arena that gives equal space to all opinions, voices and political perspectives. How possible would this be? Consider how open each member of the group would be to hearing ideas expressed by spect-actors that are contrary to their own beliefs and ethical/moral standards.

Suggested Activities

1. In groups of four, discuss a political oppression that you see in your community (racism, sexism, power imbalance, etc.). Create a scene that illustrates this oppression at work on the protagonist and also reveals the wider social implications of that oppression.

2. Share these scenes with the class and look at each to see how successfully it holds the personal story within the more general social implications.

3. Conduct research in your local newspapers to discover the issues that are relevant to your community (e.g., sewage treatment, private use of public space, homelessness, etc.). Choose an issue. What law does your group envision that could improve the problem at hand? Create a scene that presents the problem and supports the need for the new law. Present it in a community setting to an invited audience interested in the issue, including local activists and politicians. What written documentation of this performance can be passed on to lawmakers to take to the next level of implementation?

4. In a group, decide upon a shared internal psychological oppression that you all face, such as procrastination, ambition, pressure, etc. Using Image Theatre, the

person who suffers that oppression creates, without using words, a tableau of that oppression with other members of the group and finds his/her place in the frozen image. The other figures in the image may be oppressors or allies. Share these images with the rest of the class and the facilitator, and encourage them to express what they see in the images, what they think and feel in response. On the basis of the position each actor is in, and in response to the shared discussion, on a slow count of five the images re-shape themselves into a more positive image. Discussion is then around what actions were suggested in that re-shaping that could be taken into the real world to deal with that oppression.

PART THREE

The Locations of Applied Theatre

CHAPTER SIX
THEATRE IN HEALTH EDUCATION (THE)

Introduction

Theatre in health education (THE) is a fairly recent initiative that combines the principles and practices of theatre in education and health education to address issues of health, safety and well-being (Bury, Popple & Barker, 1998, p. 13). THE emerged as a form of theatre in education largely in response to the HIV/AIDS crisis in the late '80s and early '90s. Traditional ways of informing people of the dangers of unsafe sex were not working (often because they were counter-cultural) and the enactive and entertaining possibilities of THE were seen to be a more engaging way of educating audiences in safe sex practices. Consider, too, the Aboriginal view of what is health; effective theatre always addresses the whole being.

Australian aboriginal people generally define health thus: "...Health does not just mean the physical well-being of the individual but refers to the social, emotional, spiritual and cultural well-being of the whole community. This is a whole of life view and includes the cyclical concept of life-death-life."
National Health and Medical Research Council (Australia), 1996, Part 2, p. 4

Since the last two decades of the twentieth century, due in part to the growing focus on prevention and personal responsibility for health, THE is now practiced internationally as a means of education on a variety of health issues. Some of these issues include: disability awareness (visible and invisible), drug abuse, child abuse, effective parenting, mental health, elder abuse, safe driving, sex education, safe/clean water, head injuries awareness, workplace safety and organ donation. At the same time, THE offers a new means of presenting research and models of best practice to health care workers and medical workers in the field and in training. There are also instances of mainstream theatre addressing health issues that have been performed for medical personnel as stimuli for discussion. *The Doctor's Dilemma* (1906) by Shaw and *Wit* by Margaret Edson (1999), which follows an ovarian cancer patient's journey from diagnosis to death (*Times Colonist*, 2000, D2), are two examples that have been used extensively for this purpose. The work of oncologist and THE practitioner Ross Gray (2003) has led to remarkable shifts in health care providers' understanding of the power of artistic and narrative forms to communicate vital information: "They are the way of the future for educational and dissemination practices" (Gray, Fitch, LaBrecque & Greenberg, 2003, p. 223).

THE practitioner Steve Ball (1994) sees a united philosophical basis between THE and theatre in education consisting of seven characteristics or threads held in common:

1. Both demand affective as well as cognitive involvement

2. Both utilize active learning

3. Both are concerned with an exploration of attitudes and values

4. Both involve role-taking

5. Both emphasize self-empowerment

6. Both are concerned with what it is to be human

7. Both involve a community dimension (pp. 222–224)

THE's community-based process reminds us that health is not limited to individual choices and behaviors, but is a larger social responsibility. Health is contextualized by the culture, values and social, political and economic conditions of a community. As you read through the following examples of THE projects, watch how these threads are woven into the fabric of each applied theatre performance.

When I interviewed health professionals about their responses... many noted that seeing situations unfold on stage gave them the possibility of distance that they were denied in their everyday working lives.... They were far from passive, engaging actively with the drama through reflection and meaning making.... [I]t is important to consider the vulnerabilities and qualities of each audience before deciding how far to go in seeking participation.

Ross Gray, 2004,
p. 247

THE often addresses difficult topics—"We don't talk about those things in public"— therefore the element of ethics and safety become of paramount importance in theatre in health education projects. Note, too, how these applied theatre projects involve a freeing of suppressed voices, as in cultural taboos in various African cultures around public discussion of sexuality or, in almost all cultures, around child abuse. The careful aesthetic use of symbol and metaphor through a range of theatrical devices (puppetry, mask, simulated video game, traditional cultural entertainment forms) offer audiences a greater protection and at the same time a heightened accessibility to challenging material. THE is about raising awareness and changing behavior, and this is enormously difficult to assess. Consider carefully and log the techniques used by the researchers/ practitioners in these excerpts.

As HIV/AIDS is seen to be the progenitor of Theatre in Health Education, we begin with two examples of THE projects that, in very different contexts, address issues around HIV/AIDS education. "Icons and metaphors" shows how traditional African dramatic and storytelling forms can be adapted effectively into two different THE projects. "All the World's a Stage" offers a THE model in medical education. Medical students learn greater sensitivity towards patients through live dramatic encounters with an HIV/AIDS patient (who is also a professional actor) and, in a second example, with an ovarian cancer survivor. One of the major challenges today in education and social work is the issue of abuse in a variety of forms. "Making the everyday extraordinary" is valuable because it looks at an applied theatre program developed on a national scale in conjunction with government ministries and local social agencies. The final case study deals with drug addiction incorporating performers who are dealing with these issues in their own lives and who are taking the opportunity to express themselves to the larger community through the medium of theatre. "Scratchin' the surface" is remarkable for its direct telling of the project by the facilitator, performers and a range of audience members who have participated in post-show strategies.

6.1 HIV/AIDS

from *Icons and metaphors in African theatre against HIV/AIDS*
Victor. S. Dugga. (2002). *NJ: Drama Australia Journal, 26*(2), 63–72.

[...]

The task for the theatre is first of all to remove the issue from the private premises of human life to a public platform. In many societies in Africa, the topic of sex is not publicly discussed and, where it is, certain spectrums of the society—like children and women—may not be expected by social convention to participate in the discussion.

[...]

[T]heatre creators like C. J. Odhiambo [use] narratives of old and familiar forms . . . to re-construct pressing and immediate health concerns. Usually, one or more storytellers tell the story and a somewhat "harmless" story gets encoded with issues of the HIV-AIDS scourge in ways that are identifiable to the listening public. Sometimes, the audiences of these narrative performances are incorporated into the performance as direct participants in the story or merely as chorus singers. Within this structure, certain stock qualities have been emerging including the lead character, Bodi (euphemism for "body"), who personifies the typical victim of AIDS.

[...]

The use of the narrative techniques [are] re-captured in the following example:

> *Bodi was born as a prince in a little town where everyone was given books at birth. At the time of his birth, the village diviner had prophesied that in all Prince Bodi's lifetime, he would require a book of only two hundred pages. Bodi was quite happy with his allotted pages until one day, he overused his pages and began to desire more pages. Finding none in his village, the prince abandons his right to the throne and travels to the city where he stumbles into books in a public library. He was so excited seeing so many volumes of books under the same roof and began to read ferociously. One day, Prince Bodi walked into a bookshop and found that, instead of borrowing the books as he did in the library, he could actually buy as many books as he wanted without restrictions. He bought as many books as he wanted and kept reading until one day a strange [thing] happened to him. He could neither read nor write with the same zeal and pace that he was used to.*

At this point, the story-telling facilitators interrupt the story. The audience is divided into groups and designated as village people awaiting the news of the arrival of Bodi, the library staff, the bookshop owners, etc. and asked to play-act their groups to Bodi's predicament. All the while, a pre-arranged song is sung at intervals to whet people's appetite or foreclose the immediate past or coming action in the story.

In this example, Bodi's character is used as a poetic license that frees the creative spirit of the artist. While he is an identifiable stock character in true universal concept of folk theatres, Bodi is additionally an interactive proposition that engenders dialogue and challenges the audience to expose their knowledge of HIV/AIDS. That way, wrong mindsets can be addressed, new techniques revealed and new information passed on in post-performance discussion. The story utilizes many symbols in the process of communication. The most evident is the symbol of absence—nothing about HIV/AIDS is mentioned. Instead, there are repeated references to [an] insatiable quest and hunger for books. When one follows the logic of a number of pages being allotted to the prince, one discovers that it is not a book of printed pages but a representation of life that is regulated by forces outside one's self. As the story follows Bodi's insatiable search to the point of his physical incapacitation to read, demand is placed on the audience to apply the story to the issue of HIV. It is arguable that the audience would already be aware of the theme of the story even before it starts and would therefore instantly know that the story is metaphoric. Whatever imagery is created is juxtaposed with the known facts about HIV/AIDS. Books then translate to one's partners from whom the virus could be contracted and this story can be well-received when taken to youths of school age, for whom books are daily stuff.

Like all good theatre that re-enacts and calls for the willing suspension of disbelief, no one looks at the illogicality of being given a limited number of pages at birth. Indeed, the illogic makes the story more forceful as one is ushered into the realm of the abnormal where actions contrary to one's current lifestyle are introduced. Where this technique hits the mark is its ballooning into seeking the views of the audience. The story is no longer about Bodi, but about what audiences think should or ought to happen to that character. Suggestions then end up with him being taken to the village and used as an example of how not to indiscriminately "read books."

[...]

Among the Tiv of Central Nigeria, ...is a rich tradition of performances called Kwagh-Hir theatre. These performances are made up of animation of carved images manipulated by puppeteers through rhythmic movement of songs and instrumentation. Kwagh-Hir has since developed to a state festival [on the] last week of the year . . . prizes are awarded to the most outstanding groups. Participation is usually very high.

Themes of the performances are enlarged to cover every issue that draws the practitioners' attention. At [a] different point in the history of the Tivs, Kwagh-Hir was used for anti-colonial protests, for inter-ethnic or political squabbles and for social criticism. . . . A larger-than-life wooden carving of a human figure was brought onto the performance arena. It was a skinny body, smoothly carved and polished in glossy brown paint. The ribs were exposed to amplify the fact that it was the body of an emaciated AIDS patient probably at full-blown level. Three animators held the body using long wooden poles that suspended it a few feet from the ground. While music was played, they walked this body around the theatre as if to get it to speak to the audience. First it seemed lifeless but soon became intimidating as the animators simulated movements into the crowds. Then the body began to falter, displaying frailty and inability to walk properly. Soon, it was stumbling and threatening to collapse on the audience, causing them to raise alarm and shout helpful advice to the "body."

Without a word being said, the wooden carving animated the truth of devastation of HIV/AIDS. It began by projecting a super-human figure, only to bring it to a fragile less[-]than[-]human strength. It did not convey the message all by itself but built on the previous knowledge of the subject by the audience. Hence, they were able to identify the stages of deterioration that the emaciated body presented. The latent messages received about the devastation of the virus suddenly came alive in the inanimate figure as it tries to interact with the audience. Much of the credit however lay in the artistic quality of the wooden carving, its manipulators and the atmosphere generated by the music. However, the imagination and the skill of the creators and the players elicit the involvement of the audience to fully realize the communication intended. As the wooden figure was raised as an icon of AIDS, individual understanding and experience of the AIDS scourge generated other personal interpretations.

[...]

Why circumvent the "real" issues with symbols? One instance of the covert presentation of facts in family reproductive [issues] . . . where a female nurse used a bottle of Coca[-]Cola to demonstrate how a condom is used. . . . Months later a man showed up with a complaint—he used the condom on a bottle as demonstrated and his wife still took ill.

6.2 HIV/AIDS & ovarian cancer

from *All the world's a stage: The use of theatrical performance in medical education*
Johanna Shapiro and Lynn Hunt. (2003). *Medical Education, 37*(10), 922–927.

Student exposure to theatrical performances holds intriguing educational possibilities. This project explored uses of drama within the context of medical education. Two one-person shows addressing AIDS and ovarian cancer were presented to audiences totalling approximately 150 medical students, faculty members, community doctors, staff and patients.

[...]

The presence of live actors means that theatre has a uniquely compelling emotional quality, making it difficult to avoid or intellectualise the struggles and suffering portrayed. In a live performance, the audience experiences emotional engagement in a visceral way that becomes especially intense when the actors are also actual patients. . . .

Projects and participants

Two theatrical programmes were presented on separate occasions roughly eight months apart to a mixed audience of medical students, university and community doctors, patients, family members and caregivers. Both programmes were one-person shows created by individuals who were professional actors as well as patients. The first, *Living in the Bonus Round: A Perspective on HIV and AIDS* commenced with a 1-hour entertainment by songwriter/playwright Steve Schalchlin in which he chronicled, through songs and stories, his experiences as a person living with AIDS. A half-hour panel discussion followed in which two physician experts and a humanities scholar commented on the performance and engaged in discussion with the audience and the performer. This show was linked thematically and chronologically to a second[-]year patient/doctor course module on HIV and AIDS.

The second show, *Deep Canyon*, consisted of a one[-]hour performance by Annan Paterson, in which she chronicled her diagnosis, medical treatment, and psychological and spiritual journey as an ovarian cancer survivor. Similar to the first performance, an audience discussion followed, facilitated by the chair of the UCI Cancer Center Psychosocial Oncology Task Force. This event was scheduled to coincide with the end of the third and fourth years of clinical training as a reminder and reinforcement of teaching themes throughout the years that emphasised the importance of empathising with the patient's perspective and treating the whole person.

Both performances were followed by a reception in which performer, panellists and audience mingled informally and exchanged ideas. There were lively contributions and questions from the audience both during the discussion and at the informal reception, which provided the artists with the opportunity for continued interaction with audience members. The performances were offered at no charge to participants, although advance registration was required, and [they] were held at locations considered convenient for the target audiences.

[...]

On-site discussions and informal follow-up feedback
REACTION TO THEATRICAL PERFORMANCE

Several comments were made to the effect that a dramatic performance was especially engaging because it involved real people; in these cases, people who had also been patients. Patients attending the performance shared that they heard thoughts and feelings expressed that mirrored their own, but which they were often afraid to utter to health care professionals. Physician faculty members remarked that the presentations were an experience in "enforced listening" to the voice of the patient, and that, despite their experience in their respective fields, they gleaned new insights into the patient perspective. Several faculty members even observed with some surprise that they were so involved that they identified with the patient rather than with the doctors represented in the shows. Students who had been involved in a literature and medicine elective noted that in many ways theatre impressed them as being more involving than reading a story or poem, yet at the same time it was not as overwhelming as actual patient care. "It's the patient [one] step removed," said [one] student. Another student commented that she was especially intrigued by the idea of performance, because as a beginning third[-]year student, she often felt as though she were play-acting. Seeing a performance by a patient helped her understand that we all assume roles, and that some are more comfortable than others. She concluded by recognising that some of the skills used in acting could be useful in medicine as well.

[...]

Conclusions

Mounting theatrical performances as an adjunct method of enhancing empathy towards patients in a self-selected subset of medical students proved highly successful. While this approach might not be effective for all medical students, those who participated were moved and felt they had gained important insights into the nature of the patient experience. The "live" nature of the performances reminded them of the humanity of people who become patients. The group aspect of the experience brought them closer not only to patients, but also to other members of the medical community and to each other. Sharing this event provided students with a greater sense of belonging to a community dedicated to healing in its largest sense.

6.3 Child abuse and family violence

from *Making the everyday extraordinary: A theatre in education project to prevent child abuse, neglect and family violence*
Peter O'Connor , Briar O'Connor and Marlane Welsh-Morris. (2006). *RIDE: Research in Drama Education, 11*(2), 235–245.

In September 2003 the New Zealand Department of Child, Youth and Family approached Applied Theatre Consultants Ltd (ATCo) to develop a proposal for a theatre in education programme to fit inside its *Everyday Communities* programme. Child, Youth and Family manage a wide range of services to carry out statutory and preventative social work practice. ATCo is a private company with a history of using applied theatre in public education programmes.

Everyday Communities is a social change and community engagement programme to prevent child abuse, neglect and family violence. . . . The primary message of *Everyday Communities* is that communities have a part to play in preventing abuse and in caring for all children within that community.
　　[…]

Negotiating the outcomes and their limits
　　In proposal documents drawn up by ATCo, the purpose and limitations of the programme and its underlying philosophy were clearly stated[:]

> *The purpose of the theatre in education programme is not to provide or teach simple solutions to the issues but to provide safe and structured environments for teachers and students to discuss these issues and find the answers relevant and suitable in their own contexts. The programme will allow students to think about, reflect on and talk about their own stories by investigating the story of someone else. This distancing process provides the necessary protection for students to both think and feel deeply about the issues but to do so in a protected manner.*
> […]

Everyday Theatre . . . was not expected to deliver the entire outcomes of the programme, but to provide one layer of it.

Everyday Theatre's structure in 2004

Particular attention was paid to developing *Everyday Theatre's* overarching structure to provide safety for all participants. This involved a four-stage engagement with each school. First, schools had to sign a contract to join the programme and agree to a range of preconditions. These included all parents being informed of the visit, and the principal and teachers signalling their commitment to the programme by agreeing to attend a meeting prior to the visit. The meeting was designed to ensure all teachers involved in the programme were aware and supportive of the work undertaken by the team . . . . As part of the safety structures, teachers at the meeting were informed they must remain with their students throughout the day. They were also encouraged to participate as fully as possible in all the process drama activities.

Dramatic structures for safety

On each day of *Everyday Theatre's* visit to a school, four classes, totalling on average 120 students, gather in the school hall to view a 25-minute performance. The performance tells a fictional story of a family in the local area. It is a complex family and the students meet its various members through the eyes of teenager Ramesh Patel, a video gamesmaster who sees life as a video game. He enrol[l]s the students as trainee gamesmasters, whose first job is to help fix the broken family game. At different times, the game requires the students to consider the perspectives of witnesses to abuse or confidantes, the victims of abuse and the perpetrators of abuse.

The teacher/actor focuses on helping the trainee gamesmasters through each level so they can gain the password to gain entry to the next level. Students work with the teacher/actors through four levels of the game, each level lasting an hour and with a different teacher/actor from the performance. Each workshop uses different dramatic conventions to explore the story and to work out answers to what might help the family. Conventions are presented as part of a video game structure. For example, at level one, students explore the narratives of the video game through two different game devices: circle story retelling and by hotseating different characters. In the circle story retelling, presented as the story wheel game, the trainee gamesmasters retell the story from a range of perspectives including family members, gossiping neighbours and visiting Martians. Hotseated characters (played by the teacher/actor initially and then by the students) are presented within the game with on-screen buttons that can be activated by the trainee gamesmasters. Button choices include a truth button, which requires the questioned character to tell the truth. The truth button can only be played once per character and all trainee gamesmasters must agree on when they want to play it. This encourages deeper questioning and careful reframing of questions—and usually results in the truth button not being used. Another button provides pieces of writing in role from each character that had previously been prepared about life in the family. This ensures significant "facts" about each character remain consistent throughout the workshops. A third button freezes the character on screen so questions can be asked, out of role, of the teacher. This allows the teacher/actor to slip in and out of role easily.

At level two, students create still images from the family's life to explore various issues which may sit underneath the violence. Students are asked to create frozen images to entice people further into the game by selecting dramatic moments from the family's life. Thought bubble buttons on the screen allow game players to hear the family's thoughts and feelings. Other buttons allow the frozen image to be "zoomed up" so detail can be questioned more intensively.

In level three, students play a decision game in small groups, where they decide what will happen to the children in the family. The video game allows only a limited number of decisions and a very short time press. The decisions are fed back into the video game and given to separate characters. The students determine which character is selected, that character being the one who will most dislike the decision. This difficulty recognises that trainee gamesmasters are working at a high level within the game. Having given the decision, the trainee gamesmasters are asked to create ten seconds of video showing the different family members waiting for the decision to be given, under the pretext that the video is to be uploaded as part of the game about the family. Gamesmasters often work for irony, providing dialogue and action for the waiting family.

In the final and most difficult level, students recreate what they have learnt in the previous levels and present it back in video game format. Finally, each student creates the game's opening screen by choosing the line from a character they think was the most important or interesting line of the day.

At the end of the day they have the full password: "Every child has hopes and dreams" which entitles them to become gamesmasters themselves.

At the conclusion of the day participating classroom teachers and the *Everyday Theatre* teacher/actors meet and reflect on the day. A list of suggested follow[-]up activities closely related to curriculum outcomes is left with the school. A written evaluation form is completed at this point. A follow[-]up cluster meeting six weeks later allows teachers to reflect and discuss issues that have arisen in their schools as a result of the work.

Double framing for safety

[...]

The double frame used in *Everyday Theatre* sees students engrossed in completing the tasks of assisting the family but as part of a tightly run video game. The fun and excitement of playing a "live" video game provides the distancing and protection for the students to engage with the serious and difficult issues that sit underneath the game structure. Students become so engrossed in making it to the end of the level to get the next words of the password, they actively engage in challenging and difficult work inside the game structure to help the family.

The double framing allows, as Gavin Bolton suggests, "for students to be protected into emotion" (1979), not from it. It provides a double protection but, paradoxically, a double opening for young people to feel the issues of the video game family. Students are motivated to engage with the drama by their desire to join Ramesh in fixing the game, and/or by wanting to help the video family.

Bolton, Gavin (1979). *Towards a Theory of Drama in Education.* London: Longman.

[…]

Students as active theatre makers were active makers, if only for a moment, in their own lives too. In *Everyday Theatre* we were intent on making theatre part of everyday life, of democratising theatre, where everyone is entitled to be theatre makers. Via *Everyday Theatre* we consciously made the everyday extraordinary, and the extraordinary power of drama was revealed as something that can be used as part of everyday life.

6.4 Drug abuse
from *Scratchin' the surface with Vita Nova*
Sharon Muiruri. (2000). *Drama Magazine, 28,* 24–30.

[…]

Scratchin' the Surface was devised as part of Bournemouth Borough Council's drugs education initiative. The community strand that began in February '99 with Sharon Muiruri and a group of recovering addicts led to the formation of a community theatre group [called] Vita Nova (meaning new life)….

A magical journey

There are in life special encounters, challenges and meetings that have a lasting impact. The making of *Scratchin' the Surface* was one of those times. The creation of the play had a profound effect on the group and myself as the key working practitioner on the project. I was not prepared for the intense emotions its making would provoke. This may have been naive of me because of course the nature of engaging in drama with a group of people who have been through drugs addiction was bound to bring up painful situations…. What we created together as a group was a play *Scratchin' the Surface* that we have shown to over 6000 young people and that has communicated a powerful and emotional story. It is of the journey of a young man, Jay, into the world of dance and drug culture. We discovered in rehearsal, through looking in detail at various situations— firstly alien experience taken from documentary material and then later from personal experiences—that the drama work was giving the group opportunities to gain different meanings, insights and perspectives with which to review their own stories.

- "I thought because my parents were a long way away that they were in some way shielded from the pain . . . but I realize now some of what they felt."
- "Every night I see the hospital scene it affects me."

These insights have continued as we have developed our play for over a year now. Part of the group's ongoing recovery program is to face up to the truth and counter the natural desire we all have to deny that which is too painful in our lives. In our memories we tend to see ourselves in the centre of situations. Drama moves those around. Seeing the whole picture had a profound effect on the group and this led to a mixture of emotions mainly focused on the distress they had caused their families. Geoff, who originally improvised Jay's dad in a "break-in" scene, later became the DJ Ginger, thus having the opportunity to watch what he had created. After watching the scene, Geoff said:

"I feel gutted[;] it brings it all back." (May 1999)

In April 2000, I interviewed Geoff on how he felt about the same scene after hearing and seeing it hundreds of times over the year:

Geoff: It's like a memory being acted out. It's helped me to see things from another angle. Like from my dad's point of view. A big part of my using was stealing from my family and stuff and that actual scene was created from some of my experiences.

Sharon: Putting yourself through it one of you said—I think it was Tim—was something you needed to do.

Geoff: For me part of the recovery process is to try and make amends for certain stuff we done . . . where I am at in my recovery at the moment. So happens Friday was the first time I saw it in months I could see it . . . it was painful. Most of the play I can relate to the recovery process. Actually you have to juggle it about a bit. A lot of what is there is what recovery people need to look at.

Sharon: Making amends, is that it?

Geoff: Yea, without a doubt. At the moment I am going through the painful task of writing down a list of people I have harmed in the past—making an effort to make amends to people. I am writing it down in three sections.

1   who I harmed
2   how I harmed them
3   how they must have felt

Dad's point of view may have taken me years from now if I had not had this experience. I think for myself constantly going over and over something. You can't deny it anymore. Seeing it there in my face. It is real. It is happening. It has made me aware of my behaviour in the past and through it helped me accept it. The discussions helped me too.

The epiphany Geoff has had over his father's pain has hastened his personal recovery. The play has made clear his past situation and embraces a similar development process to one the group were following as part of an ongoing and lifetime recovery plan. It appears that the drama process can enhance and complement the recovery process. We discovered that recovery demands disciplines similar to drama such as commitment, listening, sharing, not blocking ideas, and empathy. So that even though the group had done very little in the way of drama or performance, they had these fundamental skills.

Whenever we perform *Scratchin' the Surface* it reminds us of a ritual when the Raven almost inhabits Tim as he takes over the acting space. The Raven has fascinated all of our audiences and he is always a focus in the schools' discussions.

Who was the man with the tribal markings? Aboriginal markings . . . The weird one? . . . Was he the conscience? The drugs? . . . The spirit? Drug fairy?

Of course as Tim always points out in the discussion, if avoiding addiction were as easy as avoiding a six-foot-three geezer with make-up, none of us would be here.

The community audiences—who have included many people in recovery—have also responded to Raven:

- "The concept of the addiction was brilliant through the character of Raven who was seductive, empowering, dominating and totally convincing . . .["]
- "It blew me away! I'm a recovering addict and it was my story. Really authentic. The character of the addiction was brilliant."
- "I wake up with the Raven on my pillow every morning."

[...]

Scratchin' the Surface has brought up many issues apart from drugs. The group [is] pre-dominantly male. Seeing men involved in both a physical and emotional piece of theatre opened up the issue of sexuality. Men and women expressed their emotions in the play and discussion. . . .

There was for some observers an almost immediate recognition and identification. They felt this was speaking their language. Vice versa, the group could often see in the audience's faces themselves years before. These young people often had the beginnings of the tribal markings that we portray in the play through Raven: the dyed hair, the piercing, in some case the cuts and scratches on their arms of self-abuse. This is not in any way meant to stereotype these young people who wish to dress or portray an individual image of themselves.

The End and the Beginning

Jay, lying in [the] hospital sharing his pillow with Raven, with a monitor bleeping throughout, agrees to take just one more. There is a flat line on the monitor as Raven leads Jay through the arch. They exit leaving a mystery: [W]hat is that one more? Is Jay dead or living a living death or what? The end is where the real business of talk and discussion about the issue of drugs use begins. The young people are invited to write secret questions to be addressed by the group. . . .

- "My Uncle took a heroine [sic] overdose and after three days on a life support machine (last Christmas) he passed away. Do you think my family should feel guilty for not stopping his heroine [sic] addiction before he overdosed?"
- "My Dad took drugs for five years and was addicted to speed. He has not taken any for six months and now I'm afraid he might start again. The thing is, he has diabetes and if he takes it he will die."
- "My granddad takes pot and I know he won't listen to me. What would I be able to do? He says it helps but I can't see it does."
- "I want to take drugs as some of my friends do but I'm scared because I don't know what will happen to me. And my friend smokes pot all the time and I tell her not to but she doesn't listen to me and she spends all her money on it."

We have performed to a real variety of audiences including a Rehabilitation Centre. . . . A year on from the Rehab Centre we found ourselves on the wing of a new prison built on a Victorian design. We gave a raw version of our play with the background sounds of slamming doors, footsteps and keys and no stage lighting. As a group we thought hard before we took our work into a prison partly because some of our group had been inside for quite some time themselves. I started as usual by saying that we were Vita Nova, which means new life. A voice from behind one of the cells blurted out "What new life?" This comment broke the ice. . . . The most telling time was the coffee break. We found ourselves in the front of the queue receiving a great deal of respect from the prisoners. I spoke to someone who told me this was his fifth time inside but his first time in a drug-free environment. He said the Raven had f...king freaked him out. He thought the play was good and that young people need to know the realities. When we were leaving he came over to me again and said[,] "Thank you, Miss." I was shocked at how young some of them looked, not much older than the kids in school. Larry said afterwards[:]

"I was anxious but glad I did it. I know these men will think about this tonight when they are back in their cells." […]

From a personal point of view, I can only say that this work has been a life changing experience. . . . The group allowed me as a director/facilitator a freedom. They were willing to try out new ideas, have pieces of work swapped around and then put back again so we could look at how they worked. I never thought I would feel so proud of being dubbed an honorary addict but it's a strange old world. Because I had heard their stories, felt I had to ensure that they had the skills they needed to tell those stories clearly and confidently. We were constantly checking our material and what we were saying. Were we romanticizing drugs anyway? Because we were preparing for a young audience, and because of the near paranoia that is attached to the word drugs, the project was at times like walking on a tight rope. Thankfully we made it to the other side. Certainly the play, coupled with the discussion, made a profound impact on the young people who saw it. I strongly believe this was because the actors had real credibility. They have been there. Vita Nova was able to de-mystify the mystique around drug taking. The group was honest....

I have real hopes, although there are few certainties in life, that Vita Nova members have stopped some young people taking the wrong route or at least made them think about the consequences of where a journey into drug use can take them.

Further Reading

Ball, S. (1994). Theatre and health education: Meeting of the minds or marriage of convenience? *Health Education Journal*, 53, 222–225. See Introduction. Canadian Creative Arts in Health Training and Education. Retrieved on June 8, 2007 from www.cmclean.com. A Canadian online journal that presents research reports on health education and the arts and features articles involving drama and theatre.

Community University Research Alliance. Are we there yet? www.ualberta.ca/AWTY/index.html. This play about teen sexuality is part of a major study looking at effective interventions and educational strategies around healthy sexual choices in adolescence.

Gray, R. & Sinding, C. (2002). *Standing ovation: Performing social science research about cancer.* (With accompanying video). Walnut Creek, CA: AltaMira. Gray is an oncology researcher who has been using applied theatre in his work and documenting its effect on performers and audiences.

Gray, R. (2003). *Prostate tales: Men's experiences with prostate cancer*. Harriman, TN: Men's Studies Press. The next project on Gray's research agenda.

Lev-Aladgen, S. (2000). Carnivalesque enactment at the Children's Medical Centre of Rabin Hospital. *RIDE: Research in Drama Education*, 5(2), 166–174. This paper discusses the use of the particular performance genre of carnival and its therapeutic potential in performances for young patients. Includes an excellent description of the work "to mitigate frightening hospital stereotypes" (p. 173).

Mienczakowski, J. & Morgan, S. (1998). Finding closure and moving on: An examination of challenges presented to the constructors of research performances. *Drama*, 5(2), 22–29. A description of a project that examines schizophrenia and the events that occur within and around the performance in a psychiatric hospital.

Noble, S. (2007). Meeting myself for the first time while on stage: Learning that emerged from a community popular theatre project. *Applied Theatre Researcher*, 7, article 6. www.griffith.edu.au./centre/cpci/atr/content_journal_2005.html#6. Although the title suggests popular theatre, this description of a project designed to give voice to a group of psychiatric patients in Duncan, British Columbia, fits more appropriately under THE. Issues of power and identity as they affect all the participants emerge as they construct and perform *Shaken: Not Disturbed...with a Twist*.

O'Sullivan, J. (1996). Disorderly eating: *Anorexia nervosa* as a site of resistance in educational theatre. *NJ: Drama Australia Journal, 20*(1), 33–40. A look at the question of whether it is possible to perform the plight of an anorectic in theatre form. That is to say, how do we avoid representing a body image that may counteract the intentions of the project itself?

The Ryerson RBC Foundation Institute for Disability Studies Research and Education. www.ryerson.ca/ds/RBCindex.htm. This website includes links to Culture and Research on disability with many resources.

Saxton, J. & Miller, C. (2006). The relationship of context to content in the medical model: Exploring possible paradigms. In Balfour, M. & J. Somers (Eds.), *Drama as Social Intervention*, 129–141. Concord, ON: Captus Press. An overview of the continuum of THE practices from the private work to the public performance.

Strickling, C. A. (2002). Actual lives: Cripples in the house. *Theatre Topics, 12*(20), 143–162. A description of a project that critiques cultural and medical attitudes towards disability and engages the audience in re-envisioning what it means to live with disability.

Questions for Discussion and Reflection

1. Based on your understanding of good theatre, take each (or some) of the case studies in this chapter and identify what you would consider to be effective as theatrical moments.

2. How do these case studies reflect the definition of health given in the text box (from the World Health Organization) in the introduction to this chapter?

3. In the introduction to this chapter, Steve Ball writes about the shared philosophy of theatre and health education. What other common threads can you identify that connect theatre processes with healthy living?

4. There will be a number of ethnicities and cultural backgrounds within your group. What possibilities can you explore in drawing on a cultural practice, other than your own, to represent some aspect of health or illness in a metaphoric theatrical way?

Suggested Activities

1. How might you frame a response to an imagined (or role-played) encounter with a government official who has been responsible for funding your THE project? What could you say in response to questions about the value of applied theatre as a way to address issues in health education?

2. Look at some current local newspapers with a view to identifying a pressing health-related issue. Write a one-page applied theatre project proposal that outlines the topic you have chosen, the possibilities for education/change, the community group(s) that could be involved as participants and the potential audiences for the performance phase. Also consider what possibilities there are for follow-up work with both participants and audiences.

3. Visual artists through the ages have recorded experiences of illness (such as plagues, famines and so on). Create a small portfolio of those that engage you and describe how these artworks could be used as potential pre-texts for dramatic exploration in the context of a THE project.

Chapter Seven
Theatre for Development (TfD)

Introduction

Theatre for Development (TfD) involves the making and performing of plays in developing communities worldwide, although the bulk of research on this topic is predominantly focused in various African countries. The readings offered in this chapter take us into communities in Bangladesh, Laos, Uganda and Zimbabwe, where topical issues of relevance to community members are tackled through theatre. TfD is a potent educational tool for audiences struggling with illiteracy, as the method of delivery is both verbal and interactive and is most often reliant on indigenous cultural forms such as storytelling and dance.

> Theatre for development aims to interrogate the structures of fixed reality in order to "un-fix" them. It attempts to subvert the dominant ideology, to re-order the received unities of time, space and character through fictional reconstruction of those unities.
>
> Kennedy Chinyowa, 2007, p. 37

The TfD movement has gone through dramatic changes itself over time, moving away from its beginnings as a somewhat colonizing process of First World theatre artists/educators, university students and/or development agencies imposing their messages of "good" health and "good" democracy using Western theatrical forms in Third World settings. In a post-colonial world, this process has been inverted so that today TfD is, ideally, locally-driven with training and support offered by outside specialists and agencies, but control of the process is held by the community involved. Odhiambo (2001) says that the agenda for TfD is, "to alter and transform attitudes, habits and behaviours that are oppressive in nature and that come between a community and its imaginations towards development" (p. 86). Within this general definition we can begin to see

> As the need for a more thorough understanding of a community emerged[,] the concept of listening to what grassroots members had to say for and about themselves became key.
>
> Tim Prentki, 1996, p. 35

the ties between TfD and other more politically-oriented applied theatre genres, such as Popular Theatre and Theatre of the Oppressed (see chapters four and five of this book). Also, in the wake of the HIV/AIDS crises in many developing nations, TfD has served as a form of THE in presenting plays that educate audiences about the prevention, contracting and treatment of the virus.

Effective facilitation of TfD is dependent upon the ability to listen without a fixed agenda. This means that facilitators must understand the need to spend the necessary time within a community to build the trusting space where stories can be told and opinions shared without threat or fear of reprisals.

Odhiambo (2001) highlights the theatrical elements particular to TfD:

- *Subverting and democratizing the theatre space*; that is to say "both audience and actors have equal access to the space during and after the performance."
- *Privileging performance over the written script (text)*; the audience is offered "ample opportunities to intervene and interrogate the performance at the most critical moments."
- *Participation as a conscious act*; as well as the negotiation of the meaning in creating the performance, participation within a performance is regarded, as mentioned above, as another part of the process and not an interruption of a "final product."
- *Activating the audience: from spectator to spect-actor*; here "members of the audience, by interrupting the drama and becoming actors themselves, are made aware that they can change the direction of the drama. . ."
- *Choosing a viewpoint: the power of transformation*; "the transforming power" of TfD lies in its "ability to provide society with a lens through which it [can come to realize] . . . that reality and conditions can be changed" (pp. 89–92).

From these elements, we can see the central importance of community involvement that is key to all applied theatre practices is even more central to effective TfD practice.

TfD practitioners must also consider the thorny problem of follow-up, recognizing its importance but also its difficulties in practicality. Munier and Etherton (2006) return to the site of a Bangladeshi TfD project on children's rights (sponsored by Save the Children) to find that the promised follow-up had never happened because the children with whom they had worked no longer fit the age criteria. While they feel anger and guilt about this lack, at the same time they hear from the former child participants about how much they remember of their drama/theatre

As Theatre for Development evolves from being a channel of one-way communication of a propaganda message into a dialogical forum for the articulation and activation of community needs, so the assessment of its efficacy becomes increasingly problematic and its relationship to the existing power structures which control that community becomes complex and, at times contradictory.
Tim Prentki, 1996,
p. 40

work and how much it means to them. These "stories and discussions illustrate that it is extremely important for the initiators of the TfD process in a community to be aware and committed to long-term engagement, to see where it leads, and record what changes or impact it eventually brings" (p. 182).

Assessment of TfD projects is another area that presents challenges to facilitators. The context of any TfD project is unique, therefore how assessments are made around the perceived successes or failures of a theatrical intervention into a community must also be unique. While there are no easy answers to this challenge, close and careful attention must be paid to assessing the impact of a project on participants and audiences in a transparent and non-predetermined fashion. The concepts of open dialogue and democratic forums around community needs are key while, at the same time, facilitators must be aware of the power relationships within the community.

We all would hope to change the world, but the difficulties faced by TfD facilitators in many international communities remind us that change can happen in small and subtle ways. Sometimes, the experience of theatre-making and theatre-viewing is pleasure enough to have an impact in the lives of those who struggle daily with poverty, ignorance and disease.

> *The first case study looks at how an indigenous theatre form is applied to a production that explores the issue of human trafficking. Of interest is the use of a* bibek *(akin to the Joker in Theatre of the Oppressed) who narrates and comments on the action of the play, and engages the audience in dialogue. Second, we see a Ugandan TfD project intended to educate citizens of their voting rights in the development of a new constitution. Note how the government oversees the project and its eventual translation into a nationally broadcast television production. Finally, a Pakistani TfD theatre company addresses the difficult topic of honor killings in a culture where these practices are often kept hidden. The research carried out in this project involved gathering the stories of surviving men, women and children who had been victimized in these ways.*

7.1 A Bangladesh TfD project
from *Social theatre in Bangladesh*
Nazmul Ahsan. (2004). *TDR: The Drama Review, 48*(3), 50–58.

[...]

LOSAUK (*Loke Nattya O Sanskritik Unnayan Kendro*) bases its performances on the Bengali popular theatre forms *jatra* and *khaner gan*. Traditionally, *jatra* often told mythological stories that reflect the aspirations of the people. It relies on the audience's emotional identification with the mythological hero. *Jatra* is a living form, still very popular and always changing. For many, *jatra* goes beyond theatre. It is a concept of life, a way of life. Because *jatra* is so popular, it is an excellent tool for LOSAUK.

[...]

Jatra, in the hands of LOSAUK, becomes an instrument for creating awareness, social change, and transformation in Bangladesh. The extreme poverty of so many and the greed of others are the common causes of the trafficking in human lives that takes place over Bangladesh's unpatrolled border with India. Women are sold to brothels and children are taken to the Middle East to become camel jockeys. Sometimes people are murdered and their blood, kidneys, and limbs are sold. Combating these kinds of trafficking is a main goal of LOSAUK. The group begins by raising consciousness about trafficking. LOSAUK uses their short "sample" *jatras* to make people aware of the magnitude of the trafficking in Bangladesh. To develop sample *jatras*, LOSAUK conducts training workshops.

[...]

A sample *jatra* developed during the five-day workshop is shown in a courtyard for a limited audience. Later, the *jatra* is brought into various communities. People assemble at first to worship, then to listen to music. Finally, the actors appear in the acting area. There is little in the way of costumes or makeup, and any minimal props that are absolutely necessary, such as chairs or tables, are procured locally. They enact a *jatra* about the trafficking of women and children. This is a real story, a true story, not something mythological.

Sometimes at the beginning of the show, photographs of trafficking victims are shown to the audience—with no explanation given. The *jatra* performers display the photographs and start a discussion with the spectators. "Do you know what these pictures are about?" "Can you guess?" After a short discussion with the spectators, the main performance begins. As the *jatra* is performed, the *bibek*—an actor-teacher—sings a song about trafficking. The *bibek* is both an actor and a spectator to what is being performed. The word *bibek* means "conscience" and the *bibek* is the conscience of the performance. His songs express the ethical values of the performance. . . . He rouses the conscience of both the characters and the spectators. But the *bibek* is not like Boal's Joker. The *bibek* does not solve the problem as Boal's Joker does but rather gives characters and spectators the chance to choose right or wrong. The *bibek* describes the situation but does not offer a solution. The Joker stands apart from other characters but the *bibek* is very close to the characters. He sings directly to the spectators, explaining the various possibilities and dilemmas of the good and bad characters.

Because of the combination of wit and commentary, the *bibek* is similar to the fools of Shakespeare. The *bibek* also functions in somewhat the same way as the Greek tragic chorus. In Greek tragedy, the chorus often acts as a moderator and analyzes the behavior of the protagonists. The *bibek* similarly acts as a moderator and analyst—but always without solving the characters' problems. The *bibek* opens the eyes of the spectators to what is going on.

The *bibek* is a facilitator. He introduces the themes of the performance, interacts with the audience, and converses with them throughout the performance. At the end, the *bibek* draws the attention of the audience to what the play means. The protagonist conveys the key message of combating child trafficking. He puts the message before the audience in plain language. He says that everyone should carry a passport when they immigrate, that legal immigration with a valid passport can reduce trafficking.

Rural people are fond of *jatra* because it is a very emotional form. LOSAUK chose *jatra* because it is a perfect tool with which to raise consciousness. It is also fairly easy to perform. The actors do not have to memorize dialogue; a prompter coaches them as they improvise the main story line. Musicians sitting on both sides of the performing area create an atmosphere that carries the story along smoothly. The characters enter the stage one by one, and leave the stage accompanied by specific music that signals the coming of the next action.

In the film *The Constant Gardener* (Meirelles, 2005), you can see an applied theatre piece being performed. Note that each character is represented by three people, all dressed identically, as a means of projecting to a large crowd in the open air.

On 28 December 2002[,] a sample *jatra* dealing with child trafficking was performed in an open-air courtyard of Sachibunia school, a place under the jurisdiction of the Batiaghata police station of Khulna district. There were 200 men, 150 women, and 50 children present at the performance of *Haraye Khuji* (Search for the Missing) by Probir Biswas. The dialogue that created a strong emotional response in the spectators [relates the story] about a mother lost to trafficking:

- I don't know where your mother is now, Lipi!
- Your mother went to Dhaka for the job with that trafficker Ramjan.
- Perhaps we have lost your mother!

Another strong section of dialogue that shocked spectators was when Ramjan thunders:

- Ha ha ha—job!
- I shall give you such a job that you won't be able to return from there. Your job will be either at the brothel or I shall sell you to a rich man from an Arab country and I will get a very good price for you.
- Ha ha ha (*laughter*).

When the performance was over, a few spectators came to the microphone and spoke before the audience: "Everybody has to be united to combat against child trafficking, otherwise no good will prevail."

[...]

The impact of the sample *jatras* on the community is strong and positive. Spectators respond spontaneously. Sometimes audiences mingle with the performers and when they see a trafficker capturing children they take action to stop him. Once someone threw a brick at an actor-trafficker as he was luring three children. The acting was so natural that the spectator just had to intervene.

Generally LOSAUK plays in communities inhabited by farmers, grocers, and illiterate and under-educated men and women of the villages and slums. These people are not only the spectators of a *jatra* but also the victims of the very abuses the *jatra* enacts.

In such places the plays are very popular. Anywhere from 500 to 2,000 individuals gather without any prior publicity. If there is some publicity, another thousand can be expected. Sometimes there are microphones to aid the actors, sometimes they have to shout. Once people in a village or neighborhood hear the music associated with *jatra*, a crowd spontaneously materializes. The very high rate of unemployment guarantees that a sympathetic audience is always ready to attend.

[...]

If the idea of the performance is properly communicated, ordinary people are moved. It is important to follow up every performance with a discussion between the actors and the spectators. The immediate response and suggestions of the spectators increases the chance that the message of the performance will get through and lead to positive action. Nothing can happen unless there is active participation. And for there to be participation, the quality of the performance must be high, its message clear and transparent.

In the sample *jatras*, opinions are invited from the spectators on how to go forward in the next scene; spectators should not feel that the performance has been imposed. Participation becomes intense and everybody shares in developing the performance. The language of the performance is colloquial.

It is a general practice of LOSAUK that different themes are communicated in different styles. Discussions and idea[-]sharing procedures are not the same at all performances. It depends on the theme and presentation. The common feature is that there is an essential issue that is put forward and performed. In some cases, audience intervention happens at the beginning, in other cases in the middle, and in still others after the show is over. Everything is adjusted to the needs of specific circumstances.

Social theatre should be judged from a social point of view. Its aim is to enable the people of the community to establish their rights in society. Indigenous forms speak to the people who have for generations made and used these forms. Adapting indigenous forms to contemporary issues is an effective way of raising consciousness and advancing particular social programs.

7.2 Education for political process in Uganda

from *A theatrical approach to the making of a national constitution: The case of Uganda*
Mangeni Patrick wa'Ndeda. (2000). *NJ: Drama Australia Journal, 24*(1), 77–92.

[...]

The performances
Publicity and The Final Push

Prior to the performances, we had to adopt publicity strategies that targeted populated areas. Local Council and District and church leaders were approached to mobilise the people. The Commission prepared press releases for radio, television and newspapers inviting the audience. In the morning of the day of performance, the final publicity drive was done using a public address system mounted on a city council van. The publicity signature tune was the song ["]It Is Your Responsibility To Vote,["] then a "popular hit" on airwaves. Two hours to the production, the performers drove around playing drums announcing that the final hour had come.

The venue, the audience

A big audience was a factor in meeting nearly all considerations regarding our pre-performance strategies. The consideration for venues was their centrality; being public places and meeting points of all types and classes of people....

Except for University Hall (Makerere University), where the preview performance was staged, and the National Theatre, the open air venues were ideal for the construction of a temporary stage around which an unlimited audience would sit, allowing for a theatre in the round arrangement. This was viewed as a more democratic setting, enhancing audience-actor interaction.

The stage

The stage was an extended rostrum elevated to facilitate visibility. Papyrus mats marked the backstage. A second row of mats created a corridor which also doubled as dressing and back-room. The basement stored costumes, props, instruments, refreshments and personal effects of the performers.

There was no attempt to limit the audience from these areas of the stage except to leave a path for performers entering or going off stage. Seats were not provided for the audience[,] not even for the Commissioners. Everybody was "equal and level on the ground." To cater for acoustic limitations of the open air stage and the big audience, the CCA (Commission for the Constituent Assembly) provided a public address system.

The Commissioner intervenes

The Commissioners always kept in touch with the production and made it known to us that the showing of a scene detailing the nomination process was essential. Although we had promised to consider this, we, as directors/writers, didn't find it worthy of a separate scene. We therefore simply mentioned it in the dialogue. But during the inaugural show, the Consultant noticed this and told the actors not to proceed.

We were still considering how to handle the situation with the audience waiting when we noticed the Consultant talking to one of the actors. Other auxiliary characters had been mobilised "in a second" and, next, the Consultant was on stage "understudying" the Presiding Officer in a "make-it-up-as-you-go-along" improvisation, directly lecturing to the audience on the nomination procedure. Both the actors and directors were seeing this scene for the first time. And so, another character, another actor had been introduced and, although this scene had never been part of the original script, in this way it became an integral part of *The Shield*.

AUDIENCE ON ACTORS

During the inaugural performance, and for reasons the actor playing ECOK explained as "a spur of excitement" in the scene of vote counting, ECOK began tearing spoilt ballot papers. The audience chorused in protest. Rule 35 of the CA (Constituent Assembly) Statute classified such action as offence. "Arrest him," some demanded. The Presiding Officer chose to warn instead of arresting him because the play still needed the character.

COMING TO REGISTER AND VOTE

While playing to a capacity audience at Bugolobi with many watching from balconies, rooftops and tree tops, the actors moved to demonstrate the process of voting. Two men from the audience joined them. One explained that he had come to act while the other said he had realised that he had a civic responsibility. So he had come to register.

Yet in Rukungiri, while acting a translation of *The Shield*, members of the audience participated in the voting. It was not SUUBI (as per the script) but HOPE KISAKYE who won. The audience had exercised their "civic right and responsibility." There were hardly any spoilt ballot papers except those of the actors who spoilt them for aesthetic and didactic purposes. The audience changed the ending of this particular production and the directors had to accept the "results of their civic education."

Learning from the audience
VARYING THE LANGUAGE STRATEGY

After the inaugural performance at the constitutional square, we learned from audience members that some [had] difficulty following the play. We had to mix English, Luganda and Kiswahili in the subsequent performances. While in Mityana, a predominantly Luganda speaking area, much of the play was done in Luganda, courtesy of the linguistic proficiency of the predominately Bantu cast.

THE MITYANA EXPERIENCE

Playing to an audience of about 1,000 people, this production provided the most in-depth audience/actor interaction. During question time, ECOK stimulated participation by picking on actors deliberately "scattered" among the audience. Before three of the five actors had asked the designated questions, countless hands shot up. To respond, he had to rely on his knowledge of the CA Statute, as a character and performer. He also encouraged members of the audience to participate in answering some of the questions as need arose. When he [had] difficulty, he would call on the directors. For instance, people saw no sense in the use of *either* the tick or the cross to indicate preference. The lady who raised the complaint maintained that a tick was appropriate and enough. A cross was traditionally known to signify cancellation or a fail. This was a complaint we had received everywhere the play was performed. We, as writers, had expressed reservation about juxtaposing these two symbols as alternative indicators of choice. Even the actors had resisted it in rehearsal. ECOK's explanation of these symbols as a matter of the statute met with open disapproval. Finding himself in a fix, ECOK signalled the directors to come to his rescue. We in turn pointed to the Commissioners. ECOK then said: "Let me invite someone who knows more about the CA than myself. Those good people you see over there", he pointed to the right, "those are the Commissioners responsible for elections. I call upon one of them to come and explain that matter to us." The Consultant for Civic Education promised that the Commission would look into the people's view. And, by election time, that part of the statute had been corrected, with the cross being dropped.

This was a phase when the audience, the Commission and the actors put the play "behind" and dealt with issues that impacted on the electoral process. The production had to rely on the ingenuity of the actors to bring this session to a close without curtailing discussion. This session, normally lasting about ten minutes, ran close to an hour in Mityana. Darkness was descending and the last scene yet to be performed. ECOK exploited the flexibility of the scene and put the question to the audience.

By consensus, the audience agreed to only three more questions.

[...]

[These were] the last question[s] and the last of the production of *The Shield* in English. And as to whether [the] returns of this educational drive were positively reflected through high voter turnout, low ballot spoilage and voting for the right candidate, is as difficult to clinically quantify as to say they were not affected by the civic education through drama.

But, in view of the rationale behind the theatre strategy, there are certain things that stood out as conspicuously as an only tooth in an old gum. These were the mammoth audiences which kept growing in subsequent performances; the changes in voting rules that arose as a result of the alternative views of the audience; the play stimulating dialogue;

the significant level of attentiveness and participation; the audience and performers identifying with the characters; its diversity in class, sex and age. These were shouting indicators on the ground.

Yet another indication of its effectiveness was that the audience never made remarks against the play but sought corrections and clarifications without accusing the production or the Commission of being manipulative.

And, finally, the Commission saw fit to adapt *The Shield* for television and translate it for performance into the major languages of the country.

It may not be too much to say that *The Shield*, as a theatrical approach to the making of a national constitution[,] was a worthwhile case for Uganda.

7.3 Women's rights in Pakistan

from *Fitting the bill: Commissioned theatre projects on human rights in Pakistan: The work of Karachi-based theatre group Tehrik e Niswan*
Asma Mundrawala. (2007). *RIDE: Research in Drama Education*, *12*(2), 149–161.

[...]

Honour killings

. . . On behalf of the British Foreign and Commonwealth Office, the British Council Pakistan initiated in 2004 a multi-pronged project on honour killing to raise awareness. A number of initiatives were taken in the form of sensitization (workshops for the police and press), dissemination through electronic media (television plays and music video) and performance arts (mobile theatre) to diversify the outreach. *Akhir Kyun?* was therefore the theatre performance component of this multi-layered programme.

Honour killing is a term used to signify the murder of women (and men) under the pretext of restoring or reviving the "lost honour" of the family. Mostly victims of honour killings are accused of inappropriate sexual behaviour that, as claimed by the perpetrators of the murders, led to the loss of "family honour." This "inappropriate behaviour" for which hundreds of women have lost their lives can include exercising the right to marry or divorce or challenging oppressive traditions such as supporting the right of a daughter to marry through her own choice. In Pakistan[,] 1194 women and men were reported to have been victims of honour killing in 2004 alone, a figure that does not necessarily present the full picture as hundreds of cases go unreported. Honour killing is also signified by the term *Karo Kari* in Pakistan's southern province Sindh. *Karo* translated from Sindhi means "black," and in this context is used as a term of abuse for men. The term *Kari* signifies the same for women. Each province has a term for it in its own regional language, and essentially each one means the same: men and women condemned by their family and community for acts of misconduct.

Tehrik's [the theatre company] resource material for *Akhir Kyun?* was derived from manuscripts and real-life case studies collected from reports by various women's organisations and from consultations with women lawyers, activists and actors from rural Sindh. All contributors shared cases known to them or their own personal experiences. These actors had been part of *Tehrik's* theatre training workshops . . . and had maintained links with the group since. Their induction into the play not only enriched the performance but also added authenticity and cultural specificity in terms of local songs, language and dialect. The play is constructed around four stories and apart from the first, which is derived from one of the tales of *A Thousand and One Nights*, all of them are dramatised interpretations of case studies. In putting the stories together, *Tehrik* drew attention to the fact that men, women and children were all victims of this heinous crime, at the hands of individuals as well as various institutions such as the police, or the local village judiciary, known as the *Jirga.... Akhir Kyun?* is constructed around the stories of a girl, Marium...and Zainab, a 40-year-old mother who is killed by her husband because she supports her daughter to marry through choice. Zainab's case . . . reveals she was shot by her husband after a 22-year marriage for supporting her daughter's marriage. . . . She received a *Kari's* burial, which meant there was no ritual bathing or funeral prayer and her grave remained unmarked. The heinous nature of the crime is most evident in the Story of Marium, who was killed by her brothers. Her murder led to Marium being declared a *Kari*, together with the son of a poor farmer. Consequently the farmer had to pay blood money to save his son from being killed by either the brothers or through a decision of the *Jirga* [the local village judiciary]. The money extorted was just enough for the brothers to purchase a new tractor, the main motivation behind the crime.

The 60 performances, spread over a period of one year, provoked a mixed reaction amongst the audiences, ranging from vociferous approval to dismissal and verbal exchanges amongst the audience in the postproduction discussions. . . . Given the diversity of the responses, it also allowed the project initiators to identify sections of the society where support of honour killings was most prevalent. For example, the audience in Jamshoro Sindh consisted largely of intellectuals and educated people who agreed with the message behind the play. In this context, it was suggested that postproduction discussions were detrimental to the effectiveness of the play as it was probably more meaningful to allow the audience to go away with the dramatic impact of the play. On the other hand, other performances received silent responses, possibly reflecting the inhibition of people to speak up in front of their village elders or their inability to articulate their own opinions. One extreme response apparently denied the seriousness of the crime, when an audience member accused the sponsors of deliberately maligning the regions of rural Sindh and Southern Punjab and giving them a bad name internationally, in order to distract the world from more pending issues of the region.

Further Reading

Afzal-Khan, F. (2005). *A critical stage: The role of secular alternative theatre in Pakistan.* Calcutta: Seagull Books.

Gaskell, I. & Taylor, R. (2002). Getting the message: Measuring audience response to theatre for development. *Applied Theatre Researcher, 3,* unpaginated. Available at: www.griffith.edu.au/centre/cpci/atr/journal/volume5_article2.htm. Addresses assessment of the effects of TfD with awareness of the traditions and cultures of the local community and is focused on the theatre piece itself as a communicative art.

Kumar, S. (2004). ACTing: The Pandies' Theatre of Delhi. *TDR: The Drama Review, 48*(3), 79–95. Study of a Delhi theatre company with a twenty-year history that has moved from more traditional proscenium-style (often Western) productions to community-based projects addressing issues such as gender, children's rights and communal violence.

Munier, A. & Etherton, M. (2006). Child rights Theatre for Development in rural Bangladesh: A case study. *RIDE: Research in Drama Education, 11*(2), 175–183. A return by facilitators to assess the impact of a project that took place several years before. It addresses the issues of follow-up, one of which is that when children reach the age of 18 they are no longer considered children, and therefore schemes developed out of the project could no longer be supported.

Odhiambo, C. (2001). What has TfD got to do with it? Fixing, un-fixing and re-fixing of positions and conditions. *Drama Research: The Research Journal of National Drama, 2,* 85–94. Provides a useful examination of TfD principles in an African context.

Prentki, T. (1999). Big Mac – small change. *NJ: Drama Australia Journal, 23*(1), 97–108. Examines the potential for TfD to address the challenges and problems of globalization.

van Poppel, E. (1999). "El Güegüense Teatral": A possible synthesis of traditional and contemporary popular theatre. *NJ: Drama Australia Journal, 23*(1), 37–43. Gives a description of a popular three-hundred-year-old Nicaraguan play that includes contemporary socially critical satire.

Questions for Discussion and Reflection

1. Reread Odhiambo's theatrical elements of TfD (in chapter introduction). How do the case studies in this chapter follow these elements? Where do you see divergences from his model, and to what effect?

2. Many African countries, such as Uganda, depend on Western governments' funding. The conditions set for this funding demand observable processes of democratization, often in countries with long records of dictatorships. Given this context, what tensions you can identify in the case study by Mangeni around presenting government-funded theatre that teaches citizens about voting?

3. TfD has historically been created in developing nations. Where do you see the potential for applying TfD models in a First World context, as, for example, with immigrant groups?

4. Based on your reading of these TfD case studies, what can you identify as the key aesthetic qualities of a successful production? In other words, when performing to largely under-educated populations, what (beyond words) helps theatre artists to communicate their stories and messages?

Suggested Activities

1. Choose a developing nation and, in a small group, determine what novels, stories, films, plays, music and visual art (both traditional and contemporary) you can gather together that might create a cultural "toolbox" in preparation for entering into an imagined TfD project in that location. Who might you go to, to advise you on your choices?

2. If you have access to computers and the Internet, go to YouTube (or another video site) and search on the term "theatre for development." Select two or three examples of TfD projects. Develop viewing guides for each video and present these videos to other interested participants in your class or community.

3. Design and present a short theatre piece with the aim of educating your local audience about an issue or program created to support developing nations (for example, HIV/AIDS prevention, malaria prevention, safe/clean water, safe

agricultural methods, and conflict resolution). Consider the socio-political and/or cultural concerns arising from these issues. How are you going to deal with these sensitive areas in your process and presentation?

CHAPTER EIGHT
PRISON THEATRE

Introduction

The variety of forms of theatre in prisons explores the rich diversity of theatre and drama work in prison-related contexts. There are role-plays with street gangs in the US, comedic cabaret with drug users in Manchester, human rights performances staged in Brazilian penitentiaries, and psychodrama with violent and sexually abusive offenders in therapeutic communities (Balfour, 2004; Saldaña, 2005). From performances of *Don Quixote* in Mexican prisons (Morell, 2006) to *Shakespeare Comes to Broadmoor* (Cox, 1992), we can see and read about the work that is being done in prisons through theatre and drama. Yet other examples reflect the healing power of theatre in the most despairing of circumstances: the productions staged in the prisoner of war camps and concentration camps of World Wars I and II. Here, through theatre, "individual identity could be reclaimed and fear transformed into freedom...the act of making art suspended the collective nightmare...helping to sustain hope, a sense of self, and the will to live" (Dutlinger, 2001, p. 5).

> Prisoner: When you picked up the skull [in *Hamlet*] it really got to me; hit me right in the stomach. I've killed a person and I've done a lot of work on how the relatives must feel. I've played the role of the relatives; but it never crossed my mind until now that there is a corpse somewhere of the person I've killed. I have never thought about the corpse before.
>
> Murray Cox, 1992, p. 149

In order to understand the context of prison life, Balfour (2004) offers a number of institutional viewpoints that have developed historically:

- The prisoner is a rational person who offends of his/her own free will, choosing to commit a crime.

- The prisoner is at the whim of internal or external factors (as in "criminal types") or social problems of poverty, lack of education, family breakdown and so on.

119

Prisoner: I have just taken part in a workshop where I have cried, hugged, laughed, played in ways that I have never done in the past. I have changed totally. Perhaps next week I will have unsafe sex. I don't know why are you so obsessed with the future? What has happened now is most important.

Michael Balfour, 2004, p. 16

- The prisoner is an individual with an opportunity for rehabilitation who recognizes and can change certain self-images, attitudes, beliefs and behaviors (pp. 4–9).

With those suggestions in mind, consider Thompson's (2003) framework for understanding how applied theatre is viewed in prisons:

1. Some prison administrators consider rehabilitation as *futuritive*, in that the work is not valued in the present but for the promise of what it can achieve on the prisoner's release. However, while repeated activity can leave deep imprints, there is no simple extension to say that it can form the script for new actions.

2. Other prison officials feel work done by inmates is *constative*, done to fill time or as busy work. Theatre activities may not be taken seriously or with any commitment when framed in this way.

3. Ideally, theatre work done in prisons should be *performative*; that is, it should be done to have an immediate effect at the time it is being done (on self-identity, self-respect, self-efficacy) and focus on the inherent worth of participation, fun, debate, physical action and creativity (79–101).

Certain kinds of criminal activity involve skills and experiences which parallel those of artists. In a way, criminals live in a kind of parallel universe, a fictional world of their own making. To live outside the law means you're engaged in a very questioning relationship with conventional morality. To invent your own codes you need imagination, wit, bravado and courage.

John Somers, in Thompson, 1998, p. 132

Paul Heritage (2004) warns about placing too much emphasis on results-based work and instrumental benefits to the detriment of what the art itself can do for the people who engage with it. We have to understand that while such promotion may be a way into the institution, it can also become something that can and perhaps will constrain the potential of theatre and performance work.

Augusto Boal (2006), from his experiences working in prisons, makes a very clear distinction between working in communities and working in prisons:

When we work with social groups whose ethical values we share...we do not question their values because they are our own. In the adult prisons, or the reformatories for young people, the contrary is the case—we have partners who have committed acts we do not approve of. With these partners, we cannot identify, though we may be able to understand them... (p. 114).

Boal puts his finger on probably one of the greatest challenges of working in prisons. We may wish to assist others in this environment, but the human quality of empathy and identification with others must be held with care. Applied theatre actors and facilitators need to prepare themselves to work in these types of settings.

A young man, asked about what theme he would like the play we were about to create to have, answered: "How to kill a judge." When met with our refusal, he continued: "Who can I kill?"

> Augusto Boal, 2006, p. 128

The prison theatre case studies presented in this chapter take us from Israel to America to Brazil. The first study examines a long-term process and public performance on questions of justice as a social concern. The second project uses Theatre of the Oppressed strategies to work with inmates on issues around fatherhood and family violence. Finally, we read about a hugely ambitious project in Brazil that brought prison guards and prisoners together, through theatre, to present an original Declaration of Human Rights for everyone who lives and works in prisons.

8.1 Critical citizenship in prison

from *Prose and cons: Theatrical encounters with students and prisoners in Ma'asiyahu, Israel*
Sonja Kuftinec and Chen Alon. (2007). *RIDE: Research in Drama Education, 12*(3), 275–291.

[...]
A unique educational project conducted through Tel Aviv University's Community Theater program over a nine-month academic year in 2005–2006 (co-facilitated by one of this article's authors, Chen Alon) tackled the complex dynamics of the prison political system. The program focused on theatrical facilitations between mainly female students and male prisoners—two more or less homogenous groups that represent polarized social sub-cultures .... [T]he Tel Aviv program initiated by the head of the Community Theater Program . . . focuses on both long-term process and public performance.
[...]

Meeting once a week as an integrated group, and once separately with the theater facilitators (students' group) or a social worker and education officer (prisoners), the group engaged in theatrical activities designed to produce and transform conflict and sharing sessions that reflected on these activities. Theater workshops with prison staff ensure a context of support and a space for staff to reflect on their own attitudes towards prisoners. The final performance provided a reflective site for audiences of prisoners, prison staff, family members, university students and faculty, and those who might provide future jobs for prisoners.

[...]

Who is a hero?

SHAPING THE PLAY

Following seven months of group work that included the development of theatrical scenarios, the prisoners and students met together for a day-long workshop. The facilitators summed up the various conflicts they had explored so that the group could decide together upon their central premise. Exercises exposing what individuals most wanted to express to themselves, to their group, and to their society helped to formulate this premise. Several members of the group then volunteered to shape the scenarios within this structure. As the group decided that their central concerns were ethical—focused on individual choice and responsibility for one's actions in relation to their impact on others—they elected to work with the structure of a "morality play." They agreed that the journey of the piece needed to begin with an anonymous human being unrecognizable as either a prisoner or a "normative" individual. Dramaturgically, the play would commence with a peak moment in the individual's life, a celebration or emancipation from unknown constraints. The play's opening as well as its scenarios thus reflected the group's experience.

In the play, the Hero arrives at a party from an encounter with his mistress, immediately establishing the presence of an ethical crime while animating for the group the character of the mistress as figurative of the theater. The speech that the Hero makes at his party also maintained a triple meaning for the prisoners and students, as well as for the audience members who came to witness their work reflecting the thoughts of the character, the experience of the group developing the performance, and of the prisoners and students in their journey towards more ethical relationships.

> Hero: First of all I would like to thank each and every one of you who came to celebrate this important day with me . . . . Who knows better than you that it wasn't a simple path . . . but eventually, I made it, and a lot of it, if not most of it, is because of you.

The play unfolds its scenarios by adopting elements of the medieval play *Everyman* to the prisoners' experience and the group's work. In a scene reflecting a typical criminal arrest as well as the archetypal journey of Everyman, a winged Messenger takes the Hero away. Not knowing what crime he has been accused of committing, the Hero receives a 24-hour reprieve to try to find someone to take his place on the journey with the Messenger. Like Everyman, the Hero makes the request of significant individuals in his life, including his mistress, wife and daughters, the friend with whom he stole a bicycle at age seven, and his parents. Through these encounters, the group reflected on the notions of criminality and responsibility exhumed in their facilitation process.

The Messenger allows the Hero to return to the scenario in which he stole a bike at age seven, with the scenario working to illuminate the limitations of choice available in the situation. In a scene reminiscent of that explored in the significant object exercise, the Hero later encounters his daughters as young girls and as adults, one of whom accepts him while the other does not. Neither the young nor adult daughters offer to replace the Hero on his journey with the Messenger. Like Everyman's encounter with aspects of his sinful character, the Hero also encounters parts of himself that he must address in order to complete his journey, including Guilt, Memory, Education, and Self-rationalization[:] elements that the prisoners and the students had expressed they need to work through in their own transformations.

As an embodiment of their democratic process, the group also added a Chorus, designed to highlight questions emergent from their process (as well as to provide a stage opportunity for all 34 participants). Along with the Messenger, the Chorus addressed all of the crimes that were exposed within the group by both prisoners and students. "We all stole bicycles at the age of twelve, we all beat the shit out of someone until he lost consciousness, we all cheated on our girlfriends, murdered our wives, we all faked documents, sold drugs, drove without a license, hit and killed a girl on the road and ran away." The iteration of the crimes additionally signalled the act of taking responsibility for them.

In the final scene, after the Chorus sums up the ethical discussions of the group, the Messenger takes the Hero through passages of his life as possible sites of judgment for the audience as well as the prisoners.

> Hero: You want to say that no one ever stole a . . .
> Messenger: . . . a pack of gum? Downloaded a song or movie from the internet? Smoked something forbidden in India or in Israel? . . .
> Hero: So, what did I do?
> Messenger: Like always you looked for someone to replace you, who will go instead of you, so now you have a choice, now you can choose again. (*The Messenger hands him a knife.*) So, what do you choose?

The scene foregrounds the various shades of criminality within the group (and potentially within the audience) while highlighting an ethic of individual responsibility. It leaves the audience with a question unanswered by the production about their own responsibility: "What do you choose?" Will the prisoner choose to take someone else's life or take responsibility for his own being in relation with others?

[...]

ENCOUNTER WITH OTHER AUDIENCES

After relinquishing their IDs and passports at the prison checkpoint, and adjusting clothing to comply with the codes of modesty required, the audience entered the grounds of Ma'asiyahu's minimum security site. This journey upended assumptions about the prison disciplinary space. Laid out on a horizontal rather than vertical plane, the landscape featured sculptural gardens and exhibits of prisoners' photography. The gathered audience of friends and family of the prisoners and students waited by this exhibit outside the cellblock, not knowing for certain to which category each audience member belonged.

[...]

The hour-long performance concluded with an equally long interactive discussion with the audience. Response to the performance by various audience members implied a grappling with their own prejudices about both groups. A prison audience found it difficult that the performance had no clear, singular message. "I didn't understand," they asked the students, "Do you forgive us or not?" Without awaiting the students' answer another prisoner spoke up, indicating that he had collapsed the choral voices into a singular truth. "Why do you ask them? You didn't see in the show? They don't forgive and they will not accept us when we'll be released." A mixed audience produced more heterogeneous discussion allowing for anger, forgiveness, and compassion. These audiences also called for more responsive action. What should be done to transform both social polarities towards a less oppressive relationship? Still betraying their prejudice towards which group is educatable, several audience members asked only the students what they had learned from the project, expressing some astonishment that the education might flow in both directions between prisoners and students.

Responses and reflections on the process continued with both groups. In meetings with their social worker following the performance, prisoners were able to better verbalize and analyze the past choices they had made while also feeling that they had accumulated practical skills to speak with rhetorical force in front of a probationary panel. The students also used the process to re-socialize themselves in surprising and subversive manners.

[...]

What does it mean to become a critical citizen? It means to have the ability to recognize and transform not only individual actions, but also fields of social power. [It means t]o understand society not as a given structure but as a potentially transformable site that can ultimately be re-animated within a theatrical laboratory.

8.2 Fatherhood and family
from *Notes from inside: Forum Theatre in maximum security*
Tim Mitchell. (2001). *Theater, 31*(1), 55–61.

When you step into a prison you immediately notice the obvious constraints—the walls, the gates, the cells, and the regimentation of the lines and of the inmate count. There are also the less visible: the inmates' loss of privacy and control, isolation from friends and family, and the increasingly long sentences. Prisons differ from one another: high-tech centralized surveillance controls harsh new facilities while keys jangling on big rings lock up the cells of old plantation-style prisons; thick concrete and frosted windows demarcate the boundaries of a supermax while the walls of tent cities wobble in the wind. But dehumanization pervades them all. This affects the inmates the most, but it also spreads to guards and their families, administrators, and the communities that host the facilities.

For eight years I have worked in such environments through education programs in theater sponsored by two universities, Georgetown and Cornell. From 1992 to 1997 I worked in the maximum security blocks of Lorton (the Washington, D.C., prison in Virginia, now slated to close); recently, I have been working in the Louis Gossett Jr. Youth Residential Center in upstate New York. I have learned from the men I met, and I hope they have learned from me, as we have together engaged in a process of discovery that has led to some key theoretical and practical insights into theater and social change. Yet for the men inside, for me, and for the undergraduate volunteers who joined me, a tough question always looms over our endeavors: as Patricia O'Connor, the director and founder of the Friends of Lorton program at Georgetown asked the men in one of my for-credit drama courses there, "What kind of change can you know about in a place like this?"

I'd like to chronicle one change—which seems both modest and monumental—effected through Augusto Boal's Forum Theater techniques at Lorton in the summer of 1997, and through it to point to some tentative conclusions about the promise of such theater practice.

Working with community liaison Elvin Johnson, a former Lorton inmate who helped found the higher education program with Georgetown in the maximum security cellblock there, we planned to explore themes of fatherhood and family that summer by arranging to have family members bussed in from D.C. for a final interactive Forum Theater performance. Unfortunately, a change in city government and a new warden forced us to cancel these plans. Instead, each participant was allowed to bring guests from the block for the final performance, and several administrators attended as well. Here is one of the scenarios, based on actual life experiences, performed in the forum:

A man returns to his wife and his teenage son with a strong desire to reconnect with his family and to be a good husband and father. One way to get off to a good start, he thinks, would be to hold a special family dinner on his first weekend home. He imagines what it will be like—taking his long-empty place at the table and seeing his family around him again. When he returns home he tells his wife about the plan and she agrees to cook something special. But just before dinner, as he sits on the couch watching TV, his son comes into the room and announces that he is going out. "Where?" asks the man. "To be with my friends," replies the son. The father explains that he cannot go out because they have planned a special family meal. The boy begins to argue: "You've been in prison my whole life and now you want to tell me what to do? You can't tell me what to do. I'm going!" He stomps out of the house to meet his friends. The man yells after him to no avail. It is clear that no one knows who those friends are, where the boy is going, or when he will return home. As originally conceived, the father is the one with the problem here. How can he have a relationship with his son under these conditions? How could this scene end differently?

During our preparation of this forum (not the final performance), one of the men decided to replace the father right away. His intervention dismayed me but received great applause and approbation from the inmates. As soon as the son started to complain, he hit the boy hard with a slap to the face. Many of the men thought that this was a viable solution. As one of them explained, the son was making a move on the other man's power and authority. He saw the young man as the instigator, threatening his father with disrespect. Since nobody wanted to say anything against this position, we tried several other interventions, always replacing the father. One man who did so invited the son's friends in from the street and tried to include them in the family meal, but after begging off with lame excuses, the friends left with the son, laughing at the father on the way out. Another man tried to bring in the mother to contend with the boy, but after saying "I can't deal with him any more" and "This is what it's like all the time," she made only a feeble attempt to stop him, then let him go. Several others intervened, but the discussion kept returning to the first, violent solution as the best approach.

One of the criticisms commonly made about Theater of the Oppressed (T.O.) is that it often relies upon a sensitive or well-trained moderator, especially since one of the pitfalls and limitations of a forum is the danger of merely reifying the opinions held by the group. Sometimes the Joker (a moderator who can also act as a wild card) has to complicate the thinking of the group in order to touch on the soul of the matter. Perhaps this is why Boal now often refers to the Joker as the "difficultator" (Boal, 1995, p. xix). I was acting as the Joker on this occasion and finally felt that I had to "difficultate." I protested that the father's aggression immediately put the son in the position of the oppressed protagonist. I thought that his anger at his father and his reasons for wanting to go out had some basis and that it was natural for him to question his father's authority at this age. (I had the further, unstated concern that the proposed solution came close to child abuse.)

We agreed to play the scene again, this time replacing the young man. At first the interventions that followed made the son obedient and respectful. But this was "magic"—a T.O. term that refers to the solution of a problem by unlikely or unrealistic means. For example, if the problem is poverty and the solution is finding a winning lottery ticket, that's magic. Magic is a solution that fails to engage the problem at hand, in this case, the anger and expectations of the young man. So we continued to play the scene, and some remarkable results occurred.

As the boy reacted to his father's slap, the men playing him gave real dimension to his pain and anger. The discussion took a new turn. A few in the group started to talk about their own experiences as sons and about the consequences of creating a permanent split between fathers and sons. In the end, all the men agreed that the solution and the whole situation would be entirely different if the scene were about a daughter. Though they didn't explore the sexism or other assumptions underlying this unanimous opinion, inhabiting the character of the son enabled them to investigate how someone could be both oppressed and oppressor simultaneously.

Recognizing this dual role is a serious necessity in a prison. Though a majority of prisoners are in for nonviolent crimes, almost no crimes have neither consequences nor victims. In the theater classes we generally avoid working on anything as personal as victim reconciliation or reparation because we are not in the business of therapy (and in the juvenile facility, it's flatly prohibited). However, the ability to see "the other" within any scene and to develop skills of empathy is a crucial tool for change. Echoing Malcolm X, one participant in a Gossett workshop told me, "I learned that sometimes you have to accuse yourself before you can change."

What followed from the forum scene was a lengthy discussion about how prisons can follow a person out of prison and into the family, a discussion that eventually included two other key forums from the final performance. In "The Visitation[,]" a man receives a visit from his wife, and she tells him that she has a new man and his son a new father; the two men then negotiate these roles. In "Parents' Night," a man is denied access to his son's school on the orders of his own mother; he confronts her and the school principal, seeking a new way to get back into his son's life.

Following the final performance of the Fatherhood and Family Forum, one of the participants, a leader of the Lorton fathers' support group, took me aside. He told me that he and a couple of the Lorton fathers had joined our theater class when they heard about the theme. He enjoyed the discussions about the films and texts we had looked at, but he was really moved by our use of Image and Forum Theater to show fathers facing problems reconnecting with their families before, during, and after release from prison. He told me that he was excited to return to the fathers' support group and to change what they were doing there. He explained that the men had spoken in the group about becoming anti-role models to their children. As men inside, they were examples of what could happen to their children, and they wanted to warn them not to be like them and land up in a place like Lorton. But this man had had an epiphany: [h]e now wanted his group to focus on strategies that would put the men back in touch with their children before being released, and, more important, to focus on strategies that would help inmates recognize and grapple with larger societal and structural obstacles in the way of their family relationships. He wanted this support group of fathers to reinvent themselves and to do some of the thinking we had begun in our theater class.

This was a significant moment. It is always difficult to assess the effectiveness and usefulness of these projects for men in a prison, and after a program ends I typically lose touch with the participants. Lorton is closing now, and most of the men have been scattered and shipped out. I'm not even sure who has been released. I like to think that the men take with them something of use from the theater course, and I'm heartened by studies that have shown that adults who participate in higher education programs in prisons have startlingly low recidivism rates—though these studies do not look specifically at theater programs.

Certainly, I've seen forum scenes that were unworkable—because they presented a situation in which no change was imaginable (a trial about a criminal charge with a mandatory sentence, for example) or because they couldn't generate discussion (when, for example, the presence of a prison counselor acts as a silent censor). Overall, though, I have seen theater bring humanity into a heartless atmosphere, as it enables a sense of collaboration and shared stakes among the participants. It allows individuals to stand apart from their situation and consider alternatives and, as a physical activity, allows men who are often portrayed in mainstream culture as threatening and irredeemably criminal to represent themselves in their own bodies. Through the shared experiences of people in a theatrical space, it is possible to deconstruct the self, to look at the self within a problem situation from multiple points of view, and then to put it all back together into an ability to take action.

8.3 Human rights in a Brazilian prison
from *Taking hostages: Staging human rights*
Paul Heritage. (2004). *TDR: The Drama Review, 48*(3), 96–106.

[...]
Project Proposal Staging Human Rights

> "We committed a crime and we are paying our debt to society. But no one deserves to be treated like this—like animals" (a Brazilian prisoner cited in *No one here sleeps safely*, the report on the Brazilian prison system published by Amnesty International in 1999).

STAGING HUMAN RIGHTS is a programme being developed by People's Palace Projects with a range of partners in Brazil and the UK. It aims to work at ground level with the very people who must live and work together in prison on a daily basis. While it is acknowledged that there are very real concrete conditions that need to be improved in terms of accommodation, sanitation, and security, all reports on the prison system point to the dehumanising attitudes and environment that fosters the conditions in which abuse takes place. The discrimination against the prison population that is openly expressed in the Brazilian media ensures that public policy initiatives in prison reform are given a low priority against other pressing social needs. This in turn means that the families of those incarcerated suffer an equivalent sentence during the imprisonment of family members. By generating positive activities with the prisoners that seek to re-establish their roles as subjects and not objects within the system, the programme aims to begin a process of resocialisation within the prison that will also have an impact on their family lives. This in turn will produce different images of prisoners that can be reproduced in appropriate public media: theatrical representations, press reports on television and in newspapers.

"When prisoners forfeit their liberty[,] they do not forfeit their fundamental human rights. The Brazilian authorities have an obligation to ensure their rights are fully respected" (Brazilian prison reformer, cited in the Amnesty report). This programme aims to enable the prison population of Sao Paulo to begin to explore for themselves how these rights can be realised, so that the prison can begin to become the secure place that it is intended to be, and that ultimately society can be a safer place for all.

[...]

I announce that the program is also to be implemented as a pilot project for guards with the cooperation of the College of Prison Administration where they train. There is genuine disbelief. I represent for them the epitome of the sort of people that the prison directors have so often seen come from international NGOs [non-governmental organizations] to denounce abuse in their prisons. My assurances that our attention is not denunciation of abuse but declaration of rights is met with evident suspicion, but my promise that the guards will also have their space to talk about their rights has obviously had an impact.

[...]

12 December 2001

In the center of the choking metropolitan mess of Sao Paulo, there is the modernist vision of order and progress that the prize-winning Brazilian architect Oscar Niemeyer designed for the Latin American Parliament. There the project *Staging Human Rights* produces its final act.

During the eight months since the beginning of the project, over 2,000 prisoners have taken part in workshops organized by the FUNAP [the State Agency for Education and Work in Prisons] education monitors. The project has been staged in 34 prisons across the state of Sao Paulo.... In 21 of these prisons the monitors successfully staged Dialogues that allowed participants in different workshops to share their ideas and perform to an internal prison audience. On 10 occasions the prisons opened their gates to invited members of the public who came to debate human rights through the interactive theatre forums that were staged. More than 2,000 people saw these presentations, which included prisoners performing in the town square in Presidente Prudente and at the annual conference of prison psychiatrists in Bauru.

The final State Forum is an opportunity to bring together all of the monitors for one final act that will both demonstrate what has passed and perform what might be brought about through the urgent presence of the performers and their audience. . . . Here again was an instance when performance brought together impossible encounters: lawyers, lawmakers, guards, prisoners, their families, representatives from human rights agencies, students, and a battery of the press. And the hope behind the act lay in both its vivid present and its imagined future.

[...]

The format of the project's final day of performance was simple. The 400-seat auditorium is normally home to the members of the parliament of Latin America, but for this one day its ceremonial stage has been bordered with the banners for *Staging Human Rights*. Three forum theatre plays are presented: one by the guards, one by female prisoners, and one by male prisoners. Each tells of incidences of conflict from within the prison system where the participants believe their rights have been abused. After each of the 20-minute plays has been presented, the audience is given the opportunity to enter the stage and substitute for the protagonist in an attempt to bring about change when the play is rerun. Each of the sessions is facilitated by someone from the Center of the Theatre of the Oppressed team, who had helped to prepare the casts for these presentations.

[...]

The guards selected to present their play came from the prison in Sorocaba, some distance from the capital. They were not therefore the same guards [who] were escorting the two casts of prisoners. Backstage before the performance there is at first little sign of fraternization, as the prisoners arrive handcuffed and are shown to separate sides of the auditorium, away from the main body of the public. At all times they are watched over by armed guards in civilian uniform, lining the aisles. The actor-guards are to perform first and begin to take their positions onstage. Their play tells of the frustrations they experience when human rights agencies come into the prisons looking for instances of abuse. They feel invisible, both inside the prison and outside in the street. Nobody sees what they suffer and nobody listens. The play is funny and moving, and the interventions from the audience bring a blaze of anger from members of NGOs who feel that the picture presented is not an accurate portrayal of their behavior in prison. The debate is forthright, fulsome, and fierce. Quietly from the sides the prisoners are watching, fascinated to see guards dressed in prison uniforms and submitted to the humiliations of life in a make-believe prison. Horrified beside them are the real guards of the day, sensing that their own position is threatened by the subversion of order that is taking place.

Two other plays by the prisoners follow, with their desperate tales of the separation of mothers from babies and the inadequacies of the health care system in prisons. At lunch the actors all meet for the first time, sitting at tables together in the backstage area. Guards and prisoners share their fears and the pleasures of theatre, constantly monitored by the bemused guards of the day who stand dutifully at the side as the actors enjoy the familiar post-performance release in shared rites of food and drink. Perhaps in these minutes alone the promise of the project is most consummately performed.

[...]

To close the event, the education monitors of FUNAP [the State Agency for Education and Work in Prisons] enter the stage to read out the 36 declarations that have been produced by the project throughout the year. At the end of each workshop and performance, the participants were asked to write a declaration of a human right that was particular and precious to them. These were edited and collated for the final State Forum and presented to the Secretaries of Justice and Prison Administration who arrived for the final ritual. The education monitors are joined at this moment by two prisoners and two guards, who read out the declarations that have been written during that day as a response to the plays presented in the parliament.

[...]

The project *Staging Human Rights* set out to fight for the inalienable validity of prisoners as human beings. However, it was only through the process of the project that we realized the significance of the need to articulate that inalienability with reference to those who are perceived as the Other who denies them that right: the guards. Implicit in all declarations of rights is the relationship with another, who is recognized at that moment in which the rights are uttered. The respect for the rights of the Other, which is the basis for all such declarations, fundamentally frames the human subject in an interdependency of rights and obligations. And this is not an obligation to universal Man, but to a particular and unique other person with all her/his own demands and desires arising from the same enunciation. It is the declaration of our rights that binds us in a fight to protect the Other before we protect ourselves.

Further Reading

Balfour, M. (Ed.). (2004). *Theatre in prison: Theory and practice.* Bristol, UK: Intellect. A wide-ranging collection of practical and theoretical contributions, including creative pieces such as scripts and poems.

Boal, A. (2006). *The aesthetics of the oppressed.* A. Jackson, Trans. London, UK and New York, NY: Routledge. Boal's book features a chapter on his work in prisons and raises valuable questions around the ethics of doing theatre with the incarcerated.

Cox, M. (Ed.). (1992). *Shakespeare comes to Broadmoor: The performance of tragedy in a secure psychiatric hospital.* London, UK: Jessica Kingsley. A fascinating look at the relationship between theatre professionals, the Broadmoor inmates and professional staff who witness plays such as *Hamlet, King Lear* and *Romeo and Juliet.* Includes interviews with both actors and prisoners.

Fraden, R. (2001). *Imagining Medea: Rhodessa Jones and theater for incarcerated women.* Chapel Hill, NC: University of North Carolina. African-American theatre director Jones uses the Medea myth in working with female prisoners in San Francisco. Jones incorporates traditional myth, hip-hop, dance and autobiography that allows for connection between performers and audience.

Idoko, E.F. (2002). Doing theatre with young people in a reformation centre. *NJ: Drama Australia Journal, 26*(1), 27–34. Idoko worked with youth prisoners in Nigeria and searched for a way to overcome the problem of multiple languages spoken by his participants.

McAvinchey, C. (2006). Unexpected acts: Women, prison and performance. In M. Balfour & J. Somers (Eds.), *Drama as Social Intervention* (216–227). Concord, ON: Captus. The author explores three elements in a prison theatre program for women and highlights how difficult it is to make change in these institutional settings.

Taylor, P. (in press). *Theatre behind bars: Can the arts rehabilitate?* Stoke-on-Trent, UK: Trentham. This new contribution to the literature on prison theatre documents the author's projects carried out in New York state prisons and looks at the issues of rehabilitation, ethics and evaluation.

Thompson, J. (1998a). Theatre and offender rehabilitation: Observations from the USA. *RIDE: Research in Drama Education, 3*(2), 197–210.

Thompson, J. (1998b). *Prison theatre: Perspectives and practices.* London, UK: Jessica Kingsley.

Thompson, J. (2001). Making a break for it: Discourse and theatre in prisons. *Applied Theatre Researcher, 2,* unpaginated. www.griffith.edu.au/arts-languages-criminology/centre-public-culture-ideas/research/applied-theatre/publications/issues. Thompson is considered the foremost scholar in prison theatre and the three selections above are representative of his work, work that continually questions his own and others' practices.

Questions for Discussion and Reflection

1. Boal says, "When we work with social groups whose ethical values we share... we do not question their values because they are our own" (2006, p. 114). How is this relationship challenged when working in prisons?

2. What are the necessary stages involved in gaining permission and implementing a theatre program in a prison? What research can you do to find out how this process might go in your own community?

3. Prison theatre can include both accidental (public) and integral (imprisoned) audiences? What pre- and post-performance planning is necessary to ensure both types of audiences benefit from their experience?

4. In the Heritage case study, a prisoner is quoted: "When prisoners forfeit their liberty, they do not forfeit their fundamental human rights." In a group discussion, explore the range of opinions in response to this statement.

Suggested Activities

1. Five words or phrases are presented, each word on a large, individual piece of paper: FREEDOM; CONSTRAINTS; GUILT; REVENGE; HOPE. Each of five small groups chooses one paper. Brainstorm images, thoughts, phrases and so on generated by the word and write your responses on the paper. After 3 minutes, groups rotate to the next "station," read what is written and add their own thoughts. This continues until each group has visited each paper and returned to its own station. Read what has been added to your original thinking and discuss your responses. Each group creates a found poem using the text on their paper and shares it with the rest of the class/workshop (perhaps using images and movement).

2. Paul Heritage's (2004) Staging Human Rights project has the unique quality of including prison guards as part of the performance and dialogue. What other circumstantial partnerships might benefit from this approach (i.e., teachers/students, nurses/patients)? Generate a list of possible partnerships, select one pair and outline an applied theatre project proposal that includes both partners and present it.

3. Do an internet search on writing in prisons. Select some of this writing by prisoners—fiction, non-fiction and poetry—and create a dramatic anthology based around a theme (Invisibility, Surveillance, Witness, Privacy) that has emerged in your research and rehearsal using this material. What audiences would benefit most from seeing this work?

Introduction

Community-based theatre—of all the forms of applied theatre that we examine in this text—is rooted in a very particular setting within which contexts, participants and issues are all local. Like so much of the work here, community-based theatre has many names: "grassroots theatre;" "local theatre;" "ensemble theatre;" "people's theatre." Whatever the name, the emphasis is on creating and performing the stories of communities and community members in original productions that are specifically local. These stories may be celebratory or critical, or a combination of both. Community-based theatre is distinct from "community theatre" which is most often a theatre presenting previously scripted plays performed by amateurs for accidental audiences. While some applied theatre scholars/practitioners have used the term "community theatre," in a North American context the term "community-based" theatre clarifies the distinction between this form of applied theatre and what is generally regarded as amateur theatre.

> "Grassroots theatre is created in direct interaction with the community for whom it is intended. . . . The audience is not consumer of, but participant in the performance. Exemplary performance quickens the audience, the creation process challenges and vitalizes the community."
>
> Dudley Cocke, 1993, p. 9

Community-based theatre most often involves a group of community members coming together to explore and present a performance based on some shared issue or concern. However, Jonathan Neelands (1984) differentiates between *consensus* and *conspectus*; the former involves a homogeneity of perspectives, the latter a rainbow of differing opinions, all of which are to be recognized and included within a dramatic process (p. 40). In a community-based theatre project, an effective facilitator will aim for conspectus over consensus, ensuring that the voices and attitudes of each participant are represented in performance. These "artful collisions" (Leonard & Kilkelly, 2006, p. 31) and dissonances of identity and location allow for a theatre that challenges accepted beliefs and histories and works toward new visions of community action and social change. Within communities there are all sorts of perspectives on events that don't always agree with the public attitudes or the historic record. Theatre offers a method for presenting this broader range of "truths" that allow for open-ended reflection and dialogue with audiences.

Certainly, the challenges of listening to and working closely with a particular community demand a deep immersion, and many community-based theatre artists spend significant amounts of time living within the communities that are sites for projects. In this way, community-based theatre work is akin to the fieldwork of anthropologists who may live for months or years with a community in order to gain access to sometimes hidden or even secret stories, rituals, traditions and other cultural practices.

Community-based theatre projects can often be very large-scale events with dozens, if not hundreds, of participants. Various locations within a community may be used and the audience may move from site to site alongside performers. In order to manage and rehearse such projects, groups may work independently and come together only in or shortly before a performance. However, even when working with separate groupings of participants (such as school students and community members), it is important that there is some cross-collaboration so groups do not become isolated within the whole process. On performance days, community-based theatre projects may take on elements of a festival or celebration where food and drink, dances, parades and other kinds of shared activities may be incorporated into the experience.

> "[W]hen theatre is made in such intimate collaboration between artists and community, the histories, cultures, traditions, cares, concerns, questions, faiths, doubts, fears, perspectives and experiences of the community are more than present, they are essential to the plays made."
> Robert Leonard & Ann Kilkelly, 2006, p. 27

In reviewing a number of books and case studies on community-based theatre, it became clear to us that this theatre form can fall into one of two main areas. First, it is seen as a form of activist theatre, more closely connected to Theatre in Education and Theatre of the Oppressed with an intention to intervene within a community that is facing one or more challenges (such as racism, class divisions, loss of heritage). Second, it may take on a more celebratory form, more clearly rooted in Popular Theatre, that allows for communities to come together to share and reflect upon their own histories and present circumstances. In the end, all community-based theatre should address the implicit question, "What is community?" as it seeks to understand more deeply and come to terms with this complex and contested word.

The first case study is of a community-based theatre project in England involving students and community members working with a team of artists. Of interest is the focus on the experience of a group of teen participants. The second project takes us to a small Swedish community working against the loss of their culture in the face of corporate and government development. The play springs directly out of the community and is developed collectively by the participants with the aid of a local playwright and director/ producer. Finally, we present a community-university theatre project that focuses on a collaboration between a student group and a war veterans' group. The innovative aspect of this project is the interweaving of the Greek play Antigone with spoken monologues and videotaped interviews of the veterans' experiences of war. Throughout this unique project, great care was taken to provide safety for each member of the community in the interpretation of first-person narratives.

9.1 Large-scale community play
from *'B-O-U-R-N-E-M-O-U-T-H! Our Town!' Effects on male teenagers of participation in a community play*
Tony Horitz. (2001). *RIDE: Research in Drama Education*, 6(1), 69–84.

[...]

The Bournemouth Community Play 1997
Undercliff and over Heath was situated within this community play tradition. Participants collaborated in the creation of the play "text" and included 40 15[-]year-olds from an all boys' secondary school; 35 11[-]year-olds, 30 8[-]year-olds and 40 7[-]year-olds from three separate primary schools; and a voluntary group of 20 adults and older teenagers. Each group was responsible for creating one or two scenes for the play, with the assistance of a team of facilitators, including two members of the Bournemouth Theatre in Education Team, a musician, a dancer and an artist. As well as coordinating the project, I shared the direction of the play with my colleagues in the Theatre in Education team. During the [six]-week process, I also researched each constituent group's development whilst recording my own impressions of the play's progress. Participating pupils rehearsed during the school day while the adult group rehearsed in the evenings and at weekends. Starting in the sixth week, six evening performances were given to the public.

Content
After consultation with a research group and teachers of the four schools involved, we agreed to explore various episodes in the life of the town, from pre-history to the present day. Effectively, we then decided which group should tackle which historical era, based on teachers' preferences and curricular requirements. We designed a series of inputs for each group, aimed at stimulating active responses leading to improvised dialogue and movement. Through this process, the two infants' school groups explored Bournemouth's

natural environment before creating a legend about the birth of the town; the junior age group dramatized incidents from the lives of local children their age during the Second World War[;] and the General Certificate of Secondary Education Drama students devised two ensemble scenes making a statement about life in the town today, from their perspective. Finally, the community group explored the early years of Bournemouth during the Victorian era. As artistic directors, we took on the task of editing and shaping the resulting material, scripting it for later rehearsals and co-directing the end product, *Undercliff and over Heath.* By involving a wide range of young and older people in a mutual exploration of what it meant to be a member of their community, we hoped to create a strong sense of community, in which different perspectives found a voice. In terms of managing the different groups, we divided up the scenes and shared responsibility for devising and directing them amongst the three members of the Theatre in Education team, supported by a professional artist and musician. In view of my previous experience, I agreed to oversee the play as a whole and to provide a linking structure.

Form

The play was performed both inside and outside the town's principal art gallery and museum, with the audience travelling from one staged scene to another around the site, in the tradition of medieval mystery plays. There were three main reasons for this decision:

1. Our previous plays in similar open-air settings had brought positive responses from audience and casts; we now felt that this form was accessible and attractive to people unused to or deterred by the formalities of conventional theatre.

2. The local council's arts and museums officers were keen to collaborate and increase public access to the museum—which they offered us free of charge.

3. It provided a central, high profile venue that was an important historical building with a commanding view of the town centre, and the surrounding sea and landscape.

[...]

Ownership of the Content

The secondary students' contribution to the play involved two scenes portraying contemporary life for the young in the town and their hopes and fears for the new millennium. This focus was predetermined by the team to give the boys a thematic framework in which they could add their own ideas and so come to share ownership of the material. We had previously agreed with the school that they would work in their usual two class groups of 20, mainly during their normal school timetable for drama, so as not to disrupt other lessons. Each group would perform on alternate nights, keeping group sizes manageable and giving everyone an opportunity to participate. No selection of participants was made on grounds of artistic ability at any stage, hallmark of all our productions.

[...]

The creative process began with a discussion about what the boys liked and disliked about their town. The facilitators recorded all suggestions and then led the boys through a variety of drama activities. These included: games—to encourage relaxation and concentration; exercises—to develop trust and movement and speech skills; and improvisation and role-playing—to develop theme and context. By the end of the third week, they had two scenes roughly planned; these were edited and shaped collectively over the remaining 3 weeks, the sessions including regular phases of discussion.

In terms of favoured themes, both groups wanted to celebrate the natural beauty and modern resources of the town; negatives included teenagers being unfairly stereotyped by older members of the community, who confused youthful energy and humour with anti-social behaviour. Interestingly, this gelled with what was emerging in the other scenes of the community play: from its Victorian beginnings, the town had acquired a reputation for putting on "airs and graces" and turning its back on the needs of less affluent members of the community. In the Second World War, life for children was harsh, especially for those living in a home for orphaned children. So the creative team was able to link the students' concerns with a broader theme of looking beneath the surface to search for the true spirit of the town.

The boys' first scene was staged early in the play, just after the audience had heard two elderly women (from the community group) reminiscing about Bournemouth in "the good old days." To the accompaniment of drumming, the boys entered en masse from the adjacent cliff path, pushing open a large iron gate as if "invading" the grassy acting area in front of the Victorian museum, where the audience was waiting. The two women moved quickly away, strengthening the image of the boys as rival "gangs," chanting in unison, strange staccato chants they had invented, sounding ominously warlike. But at a given moment, the impending violence was diverted into an energetic display of gymnastics and tableaux illustrating the attractions of the town, such as the beach, the amusement arcades and the pier.

During the creation of the scene, some of the boys displayed anti-social and "macho" attitudes and behaviour that appeared to confirm the original image of the scene. Sensing that this was disturbing to the majority of the group, the creative team searched for ways of countering the tendency within the scene and inserted a female character, who became another link figure for the whole community play. "Seeker" was based on our research into the lives of homeless people living in the town—a theme in which many boys had expressed interest and concerns in the brainstorming session. Initially, the facilitator role-played this character, being hot-seated by the students about her reasons for coming to Bournemouth. These were mainly positive: she wanted to start a new life and find a job and had heard that Bournemouth was a friendly place. Including this character through process drama challenged some of the negative behaviour by the students and allowed for more sensitive and thoughtful attitudes to emerge, which were then woven into the fabric of the scene by the facilitator. After the all-male group first rebuffed Seeker, as she sang a song as a busker, a few approached tentatively and entered into her inner world—mirroring her song in freeze-frame images while speaking her feelings aloud. The scene finished with their rejoining the male gang and rushing off into the museum.

Their second scene came at the end of the play and was part theatre, part ritual. The audience was led out of the Victorian section of the museum, where they had been shown vignettes of the town's history, into the modern wing. The boys met them there and performed a movement piece around an open stairwell, simulating the passage of time. After illustrating their own hopes and fears for the future of the town, they invited the audience to write their wishes for the future onto cards. These were thrown into a net, hanging from the open stairwell. Finally, the students collected all the netted wishes and took them down to the beach where they were placed in a boat and rowed out to sea.

[...]

Reflecting at the end of the process, Amy, the drama facilitator, thought that she had tried her best to make the students feel "*their ideas had been listened to*," but that it had been a hard process, at times dominated by the "*strong members of the groups*." She had found it hard to find out what the quieter members were feeling and had felt frustrated at times by some of the latter just wanting her "*to tell them what to do*."

Attending the initial brainstorming session, I had also felt unsure as to the commitment of the majority of the boys and the value they placed on their contributions. But, reflecting in their coursework essays written several weeks later, many students valued the process highly, referring to a sense of satisfaction in being listened to and having their ideas respected. Not all agreed. Rick described it as "*the toughest moment of the entire process due to the lack of confidence in the group to speak up and voice their opinions*," though he thought things had improved when students were invited to write their ideas on paper. Most critical was Alan, who recorded that "*none of the others took the discussion very seriously as it was dominated by a few loudmouthed group members, the rest sounding rather shy*." But there was no doubting that Alan took the initial message of shared ownership very seriously. He criticized the ensuing sessions for being too controlled by the adult facilitators, even though based on the initial ideas from the brainstorming. Neil and Joe agreed, feeling that "*to start off we got told what to do*" and that this allowed some of the group to keep their distance without "*getting involved*." This suggests that they saw the consultative process as an important, practical way of sustaining group motivation, rather than merely a desirable ideological concept.

[...]

As the project developed, regular "run-throughs" of the scenes brought a different learning experience. While interviewees understood and valued the need for rigorous practising, they were frustrated when poor or careless behaviour by peers made extra practice essential. Interestingly, hardly any of the other students complained of feelings of boredom with this process in their essays or questionnaires. In fact, the data reveal a fairly positive picture of rehearsals, with negative expectations confounded. The same could be said for the challenging movement skills the students were asked to master. Early in the first scene, for example, they made a human pyramid and held it steady while they called out the letters of their town—"B-o-u-r-n-e-m-o-u-t-h!" This collapsed on several occasions during rehearsals, causing much frustration and some annoyance. But both groups persevered and finally succeeded.

[...]

. . . [T]he findings from the boy's group indicate substantial support for the claims by community practitioners. Many, though not all, boys were motivated by the prospect of a wider audience for their work; they gained valuable learning relevant to the school's curriculum objectives and in terms of their own discipline and self-confidence, and discovered a "voice" that was valued by the broader community. But in one respect in particular, the findings led me to question further our paradigm of community plays. The process revealed the weakness of the "jigsaw" approach (working with each group for several weeks and only putting them together at the dress rehearsal). The structure was practical to organise but prevented shared experience developing between the boys and other participants until the end of the process. In this case, the site did not help: there was limited space inside and outside the museum, making it impossible for all the cast to meet together in one location. As well as this, it was decided that the boys should not form part of the ensemble singing a song at the finale. They had found this extremely difficult in rehearsal and we feared they would lose concentration and distract other participants. This negative decision came from a lack of confidence in the extent to which the group was integrated within the whole cast. Though the secondary students appear to have made significant progress in bonding as a self-contained community in our production, they did not become part of the wider community of the whole cast. There was not a notable increase in "sympathy and understanding between young and old and, indeed, every section of the community"(Jellicoe, 1987, p. 5). I conclude that to develop a community play which breaks down social barriers, in the way claimed by Jellicoe and others, opportunities must be provided for all the cast to mix and feel part of a whole well in advance. The fragmented manner in which we have worked has prevented us from achieving this wider social end.

I have since modified my approach for a small-scale community play about Bournemouth with which I was very recently involved. The cast numbered 80, featuring 20 teenagers aged between 13 and 17, 50 children aged between 8 and 11, six adults with learning disabilities and three adult foreign students. Instead of devising the content and creating individual scenes in separate groups, the entire cast has worked together from the start. The play was divided into scenes[,] but constituent members of each scene ranged across ages and abilities. In this way, we hoped to break down barriers and shift stereotypical perspectives of what each age or ability group might achieve. I shall shortly be investigating participants' perceptions of this revised approach. Key questions will explore whether they have valued working together in a mixed-age, mixed-ability cast, or whether they would have preferred to have worked in separate phase groups. In this way, I hope to broaden my understanding of both the barriers and the bridges to building communities through theatre.

9.2 The "world of systems"/the "world of life"
from *Community theatre in a South Samic community: The challenges with working with theatre in small communities*
Tordis Landvik. (2005). *Applied Theatre Researcher, 6*, unpaginated.

[...]

A short description of the community of Björkevatn

Björkevatn is in a rural area. Back in 1951, it was composed of a cluster of 12 villages with a total of 174 people, which was eventually reduced to 10 villages with 39 people by 1991. Today the population of [the] Björkevatn area is about 50 people. After the Second World War, there was a strong urbanisation in Sweden. At the same time, a powerful and effective oppression of the language and culture of the Samic people occurred. Today, South Samic people don't even have a Swedish/South Samic dictionary anymore, so they have to resort to a Norwegian dictionary.

This project was born four years ago. Two women, Lena Östergren and Eva Helleberg, started the project in Björkevatnet. Lena wrote the play and was one of the actors. Eva directed, produced and performed in the show.

None of the actors in *Vattufall* spoke in South Samic; they all spoke Swedish. Many locals want to learn their old language. As a result, from 2005 all Samic theatre productions will be in South Samic. Everyone now has to begin to learn the local language if they want to perform in theatre productions organised by the Samic Theatre in Kiruna. This is a challenging goal.

The story of Vattufall/Waterfall and Björkevatn

The story of this performance is about how the world of systems penetrated the world of life during the 1950s and 1960s in Björkevatn. Locals made their living by farming, hunting and fishing. Their rights as Laps had been strengthened over generations. In this period, the Swedish government decided to develop this indigenous area for hydro-electric power production. They first sent anthropologists to document the local ways of life.

After the anthropologists had completed their research, engineers and workers were assigned to measure engineering requirements for the waterline (which is 13 metres higher than the tallest chimney). Then representatives were sent to convince the local population of the many financial benefits and improvements to their lives that they would experience from this hydro-electric project. The government's representatives visited every house, and counted every spoon, fork and knife, and every piece of furniture. Very carefully, all information was gathered and recorded.

The government invited the inhabitants to information meetings where the locals were promised a fantastic future filled with work and money and the newest modern appliances. Then the face-to-face negotiations began. The government's representatives employed money as power; for many of the inhabitants, the change from barter economy to money economy was substantial so they were only too easily persuaded. The locals used their pay-off money to buy the latest products available in both Sweden and Norway in the 1960s, including cars, typewriters and televisions—even though they had no idea of how to use many of these items. They bought television[s] without realising that there was no local electricity yet. The locals were promised free electricity for the rest of their lives—which they do now have. Unfortunately, however, the quantity of electricity they receive free is only enough to light a single lamp! Some people built new houses as close as they could to the lake, many people moved to the south of Sweden to work in factories. Others moved to the eastern coast. From the outside, it looked as if everyone was satisfied by this quick progress.

One of the consequences was fog. Another was that the local authorities appropriated local hunting and fishing rights from the South Samic people. Some even lost their status as Samic people because they farmed rather than worked with reindeer. The authorities claimed they needed to give these rights to some North Samic people who had to move their reindeer herds to the south. A barrier was placed to close the old road; it was locked and impossible to pass. At the information meetings, everyone had been promised a key to the gate, but that was only one among many promises that were broken. After about 30 years, the local people began to talk openly with each other about what they really felt about this "progress" and the negative impact it had had on their lives—particularly now that many of them have returned to the area to retire.

From a great idea to a final performance

Vattufall is an attempt to tell their story, and all scenes of the script are based on the history I have just reconstructed. The playwright, Lena Östergren, conducted detailed research. She attempted to study the official anthropological reports, but they were nowhere to be found. She read old local papers, held interviews and spoke at length with the local people. She took part in an academic course and received both response[s] and guidance from other playwrights. Then the scenes she wrote were workshopped, revised and developed in close collaboration with a local cast of 15 actors and musicians ranging in age from 12 to 72. Some of the adult and elderly participants remembered a lot of stories from the 1950s and 1960s.

The first performance was scheduled for July 2003, but during the spring one of the actors became ill and died. Two weeks after that, the playwright's father—an important contributor to the project—also died. Since this was such a small community, these events profoundly affected the group, so the production went into a temporary hiatus. It is difficult to replace personnel in a small local group like this. Eventually the grief passed, and replacements were found so that work on the production could resume.

[...]

To get people involved in a project like this is easy, but to keep them involved is very challenging for a community theatre facilitator. As Eva said:

> Every time we thought we had things under control, something happened. We were close to giving up, but the will and desire to tell this story were so strong, we simply couldn't. After each crisis always something positive took place—as if in the fairy-tale.

When I came into the production to work alongside Eva, my task was mostly to listen to the actors' storytelling and direct them into the script and scenes. There was a double purpose to this approach. The local actors contributed to the play with their own memories (what was said by whom) while the playwright, Lena, decided what of that material would be included in the script. There were more than enough memories for several more scripts.

Storytelling was also a therapy of sorts for the local participants. Their fictionalised role in the play gave them enough protection to tell it in public. For example, "the fog comes" scene opens with an old man, Arvid, sitting in his kitchen drinking his coffee looking out over the lake where the fog drifts in. He becomes frustrated as he has been many times before and calls the Vattufall/Electricity Board. But he hears only the mechanical voice of an operator offering him several choices and asking him to confirm his choice by pressing the "star" button. He gets mad at the voice, but gets no repl[y]. He hangs up and calls again. This time he tries to listen and eventually realises his old phone does not even have a star. He takes a cell phone from his pocket and tries one more time. Of course, it's the same telephone answering voice again, so this time he decides to write a letter. He goes to his typewriter and begins to spell out: "Till Vatufall," but he types it wrong and in frustration pulls the paper out of the typewriter. This is repeated several times.

[...]

In this way, during many of the rehearsals, we went deeper and deeper into what this story was really about. In many ways, it had been a taboo to confess their sense of lost identity, to confess some of the core feelings they felt about the local tradition and culture. Working in this project, the local actors began discussing these issues openly. The discussions continued during breaks. One of the greatest challenges for me was to let the actors talk—my method was to let it happen in its own time. Then I would use what was obviously important, focus and direct or lead the actors into what we were doing, and try to incorporate their perspectives into their roles or the situations.

Another challenge was dealing with the diminishing memory capacity of the old actors. I had to build their self-confidence in the scenes. There are always challenges in theatre direction which are not necessarily connected to old age, but when the actors are in the early stages of senility, things can become very difficult indeed. The more truthful an actor can be to himself in a role, the better the result will be.

The first performance

Finally the first performance came, and all went extremely well. The room where the performance took place only had seats for 40 persons, but about 55 were there from the village. Some had to sit on the stage behind the actors. During the performance, people commented out loud: "Yes, it was just like this." And they laughed. But the final scene ended with a blues that almost imperceptibly transformed into a *joik* [a Samic singing style that is deeply personal or spiritual]. It was very moving for everyone. Sitting there, my thoughts went to Augusto Boal and his experiences in the rural districts.

The audience was invited to join the cast and crew after the show, with food and drinks served. Someone from the audience thanked us because this performance had everything he could have hoped for: "Fun, serious drama, irony and sarcasm, love and poetry, power and humility. It was about life—our life and history." He was so grateful.

When all the important speeches were finished, it became dark. Believe it or not[,] we'd had a power blackout! Candles were placed on the table and now the real storytelling could begin. As mentioned earlier, storytelling is the truest form of theatre, both among Nordic people in general and Samic people in particular.

As it was told, one of the characters had his outboard boat engine sitting on the kitchen table. A lot of our scenes took place around this kitchen table while the man tried to fix the motor. This activity became the inspiration for 40 minutes of spontaneous outboard engine stories told by people in our audience. They were told in such a hilarious way that people were howling with laughter. I could not comprehend all the references, but I understood enough to follow the gist. The energy was incredible.

The power in Bjørkevatn did not return until 11.25 a.m. the next day, which was a Saturday. It was the end of April. During the night, the ground had become white with 20–25 centimetres of snow, which was unusual this late in the year, even for this part of the world. There was still no power in Mårbacka at noon, and I asked Eva if they were going to cancel the next show that was planned for that evening. "Nobody can stop us," she answered. "And least of all the Vattenfall [the Electric Power Company]! A lot of people are making coffee at home; someone else has arrived with a power generator so that we can use our theatre lights; a third person went home to get a large container holding 1000 litres of water so that we can have functioning toilets."

"See? Everything's under our control," said Eva. "They can do whatever they like to us and we don't care." They were an amazing group of people.

So this is community-based theatre the way we practise it up north. . . .

9.3 Working with war veterans
from *Devising community*
Crystal Brian. (2005). *Theatre Topics, 15*(1), 1–13.

[...]

The impetus for *The Antigone Project* was born [when a] group of theatre students . . . wanted to recreate, for a broader audience of students and community members as well, their experience as they listened to . . . veterans speak of the life-changing nature of combat. I suggested to this core group of five students that we devise a project which would allow them to further engage with the community of veterans in creating a work capable of communicating the thoughts and feelings stirred in them at the Veterans Day performance. The multiple goals the students wished to accomplish—forging links with veterans as well as with the campus community, deepening their own intellectual and emotional identification with the veterans' experience, and finding a theatrical structure flexible enough to allow for collaboration—could be most effectively accomplished, I felt, within the context of the applied theatre model.

[...]

Three primary goals were established: 1) to intellectually and emotionally engage performers with important social issues, seeking to transform students' understandings of their roles as citizens of the world; 2) to connect student performers with communities within and outside of the university; and 3) to create a theatre piece which would attract both campus and community-based audiences.

[...]

Although the students had no experience in adapting interviews into scripts, many of them were communications majors who had extensive experience with journalistic interviewing techniques. An adaptation with a documentary element offered the possibility of capitalizing on student training and expertise.

A Greek tragedy seemed the natural choice for our adaptation, since war is such a prevalent theme in so many of the plays. The students were also interested in exploring the issue of individual conscience as it comes into conflict with the dictates of the state, and they quickly settled upon *Antigone*.

[...]

As a first step, potential ensemble members were invited to write an essay in which they would describe their reasons for desiring to work on the project. Those actors invited to callbacks were asked to engage in a trial act of community-building by interviewing family members and friends who were combat veterans and then [writing] monologues drawn from the interviews. The students who designed the exercise hoped it would provide the actors with the opportunity to connect emotionally and intellectually with the thoughts and experiences of fathers, mothers, uncles, grandparents, and friends who had suffered the traumas of war. Additionally, the monologues could form a pool of original material upon which to draw for the adaptation.

Although in most cases students chose to interview family members whom they knew well, many of the veterans had never spoken of their experiences in combat. Bridges were created as memories were shared—as well as varied opinions about patriotism, war, and the role the United States has played in conflicts throughout the twentieth century. In retrospect[,] it is clear that the act of dialoguing with veterans who were not strangers also provided a valuable preparation for the conversations students would conduct with the veterans of the West Haven VA [Veterans Administration] Hospital, a community with which students had had little contact. Students performed their monologues at the callback auditions and the material was collected for future use. The monologues were compelling; the core group decided that each actor who had been called back would be invited to join the company.

[...]

Our next step was to set up a meeting with the veterans at which we would introduce ourselves and our project and determine which men and women wished to become collaborators.

[...]

Our next step was to structure the collaborative aspect of the work. Students who had attended the presentation in the fall felt that we should invite the eight members of the Homefront Theatre group to act in our project. But after meeting with the group at the VA Hospital, the ensemble felt that our production should be informed by the feelings and experiences of a larger group of veterans. Drama therapist Mary Lou Lauricella conducted a poll of the veterans who had attended the initial meeting; approximately seventeen expressed interest in working on the project, including all of the members of the Homefront Theatre. Lauricella, however, had reservations about the idea of the theatre group members actually appearing in the production. Some of the veterans had emotional and physical challenges that ruled out long rehearsals. Additionally, the troupe worked solely in an improvisational style; she felt the stress of memorizing dialogue would not be healthy for her patients, many of whom suffered from post-traumatic stress disorder (PTSD). The ensemble vetoed my suggestion that we include the veterans' perspectives as devised text that would be acted by student actors. Struck by the veterans' characterization of their experiences in the 1970s as resembling an "ambush," students were sensitive to the dangers of co-opting powerful material generated by the vets and using it to "glorify" ensemble members' performances. The students therefore felt it vital to the project that not only the veterans' words, but also their faces and voices, be presented to audiences. After exploring various options, the media production students, ensemble members, Lauricella, and the veterans ultimately decided that the veterans could effectively communicate their message through videotaped interviews. These warnings and insights would be presented as video montages interspersed throughout the production, with the veterans thus becoming a second chorus for our version of Sophocles' tragedy. The devised monologues and video chorus segments were included with the whole-hearted approval of those veterans who had given interviews for the project.

Notes made by the students during our initial session with the veterans, as well as input from Lauricella, were used to devise the list of questions for the videotaped interviews. Each veteran was given [these] in advance of the interview . . . .

[...]

Ensemble members, lacking therapeutic background, had no training in the techniques of interviewing in a clinical context, so Lauricella was present at each interview in order to create and enforce boundaries necessary to protect her clients' emotional well-being. Veterans were instructed at the beginning of the interview that they need not answer any question they chose not to address for whatever reason, and [they] could ask that the camera be turned off at any time. Each cast member conducted at least one video interview with a veteran; these conversations, conducted within the context of a two- to three-hour taping session, solidified relationships between veterans and students, enhancing the sense of community. Taping and editing the video interviews was a process that simultaneously accomplished all three of the goals we had established for the project. As students listened to the accounts of combat experience, their emotional identification with the veterans was strengthened; they found empathetic connection with the thoughts and feelings of the men and women whom they interviewed to a degree that had not occurred when researching historical accounts of war.

[...]

Developing monologues from the transcripts of the video interviews would create a dramatic device for incorporating more of the veterans' experiences within the live action of the play. In both the writing and the performing of these monologues, students were moved by the experience of playing characters whose thoughts and feelings were those of the real veterans the performers had interviewed. The monologues were delivered by students who were approximately the same ages as the veterans had been when they went to war; the performers were well aware that many of the vets felt their youth had been eradicated by the combat experience. For nineteen- and twenty-year-old actors who had no first-hand experience with war, the process of identifying with "characters" who had sacrificed their youth to war was especially poignant. The abstract nature of the student performers' understanding of war was challenged by the relationships they had forged with individual veterans. By expressing their emotional and intellectual responses to these human embodiments of the impact of war, some students experienced an awakening of their own social consciousness.

[...]

The monologues created from interview materials, as well as the video interviews edited by student dramaturges, provided aesthetically powerful material for the production, as our second chorus of veteran elders voiced their warnings, visions, and nightmares in ironic counterpoint to the elders of Thebes, caught up in Kreon's greed and blood lust. At talkbacks conducted after performances, audiences singled out the monologues—both those performed by actors and the video pieces—as the most powerful aspect of the production.

The visual aspects of the production were designed to emphasize the video pieces. Chorus members ringed the stage, seated on banks of risers of varying height and dressed—as were the principals—in black shirts, green camouflage pants, and army boots. White scrims, resembling Greek columns, were alternately flooded with color or used as projection screens for the speakers of the veterans['] chorus. Flute, drum, and electric guitar provided counterpoint for Brecht's choral odes. Three young women playing the messenger and handmaidens to Antigone also interspersed the action with broken fragments of war songs from the Civil War, WWI, and WWII eras. Kreon was frozen during key moments of his duplicitous oratory to the chorus by the sound of a young woman—seen in shadow through a scrim—singing fractured snatches of Bob Dylan's "Masters of War."

In addition to providing ironic counterpoint to Kreon's claims of glorious victory, the statements of the veterans' chorus were juxtaposed after certain scenes to create connections between the Greek story of ancient war and more contemporary perspectives. The scene in which Antigone describes to Ismene the burial of their dishonored brother was immediately followed by a poem written and spoken by one of the veterans who had served a year on grave registry in Vietnam:

Chu Lai Morgue
This building stands apart from all the others,
A wooden leper anchored in concrete
Poured by dead Marines
Behind its doors ride headless horsemen,
For death invades this place.
It layers up in corners like old wax,
And its drippings spot the floor in sad designs.
In this slaughterhouse are held
The world's most precious meats, delicacies
To be served up to mothers' nightmares—
The leftovers to mine.

—Alan Garry, Americal Division, US Army, Vietnam

Five of the monologues, delivered by actors behind scrims at the beginning of the production, provided a prologue for the Antigone story, framing it in the context of the American war experience. Each monologue identified the speaker by name, combat division, and war; later in the production each[,] of the identified speakers addressed the audience directly via video during the chorus pieces. In this manner[,] the audience, in a visceral fashion, was confronted with the toll war and time had taken on each veteran, as the ghosts of soldiers long gone, embodied by young students, were transformed into the aged faces of suffering.

[...]

The talkbacks after each performance of *The Antigone Project* became another forum for community[-]building. Any veteran sitting in the audience was invited to join the acting ensemble on stage for the conversation. News of the production had spread throughout the local veterans' community, and at each performance veterans would make their way to the stage. These dialogues—emotional and sometimes confrontational—were as effective as the production itself in giving voice to the many sentiments elicited by the topic of war. Dialogue took place between Vietnam veterans and audience members (a student's parent in one case) who had protested the war. During one exchange[,] a woman in the audience apologized to a veteran who had spoken movingly in his video interview about the shame he felt when college students spat on his uniform as he walked through the airport after returning from Vietnam. She admitted that she had been one of those students thirty years before who reviled the returning soldiers, citing a specific incident in which she had told a soldier entering a diner in which she worked that he wasn't welcome.

[...]

Family members of the veterans accompanied them to the production and spoke in the talkback sessions, thanking a father or husband for having the courage to share long-buried trauma. The veterans spoke of feeling empowered through their collaboration on the production. *The Antigone Project* had allowed their voices to be heard as they shared the realities of war with a new generation on the brink of conflict. The sight of grown men in tears—many of them speaking publicly for the first time about their combat experience and its aftermath—further intensified the identification ensemble members felt with their "characters," an identification stronger than they had experienced in previous acting endeavors in which more traditional research was conducted.

The bridge built between two isolated communities during the devising of *The Antigone Project* provided an avenue for healing for the veterans while engaging students with a political reality which holds increasing urgency for their generation. The community built between performers and audience created a forum for campus and community-wide discussion of the challenges that confront our nation at the beginning of the twenty-first century. For the student performers, the process of empathetically identifying with another individual—one integral to any acting experience—was deepened when the work of imagination and intellect conjoined with flesh-and-blood reality. In an era in which connections are so often void of immediate human contact, the touch and sound and sight of individual suffering is potent.

Further Reading

Cohen-Cruz, J. (2005). *Local acts: Community-based performance in the United States.* New Brunswick, NJ: Rutgers.

Haedicke, S.C. & Nellhaus, T. (Eds.) (2001). *Performing democracy: International perspectives on urban community-based performance.* Ann Arbor, MI: The University of Michigan Press.

Leonard, R. H. & Kilkelly, A. (2006). *Performing communities: Grassroots ensemble theaters deeply rooted in eight U.S. communities.* Oakland, CA: New Village Press.

van Erven, E. (2001). *Community theatre: Global perspectives.* London, UK & New York, NY: Routledge.

The four books listed above offer excellent introductions by the authors/editors and many case studies from America and around the world.

Cassidy, H. & Watts, V. (2004). To leave or not to leave: Rural youth gain a voice through theatre. *NJ: Drama Australia Journal, 28*(1), 35–45. This article discusses a "play about life for young people in rural communities" (p. 35) in Australia.

McConachie, B. (1998). Approaching the "structure of feeling" in grassroots theatre. *Theatre Topics, 8*(1), 33–53. McConachie is a well-known grassroots theatre practitioner who writes about a Virginia-based university-community partnership project investigating the recent racial histories experienced by participants.

Nogueira, M. P., Goncalves, R. M. & Scheibe, C. (1996). Community theatre in Florianópolis. *RIDE: Research in Drama Education, 1*(1), 121–128.

Nogueira, M. P. (2006). Reflections on the impact of a long term theatre for community development project in Southern Brazil. *RIDE: Research in Drama Education, 11*(2), 219–234. The two articles above offer reflections of a community-based project in Brazil over a ten-year period.

Sinclair, C. (2003). Collaboration, creativity and the purpose-built play. *NJ: Drama Australia Journal, 27*(1), 45–54. Sinclair writes about a project involving youth who researched and co-created a play about the history of their community.

Questions for Reflection and Discussion

1. How would you begin to go about researching a community in which you would like to work? What are the sources of information available to you, both in print (archival and contemporary) and in personal contacts?

2. What benefits for a community do you see arising from the creation of a community-based play? As a facilitator, what strategies would you employ to highlight and promote these benefits?

3. Jan Cohen-Cruz writes that community-based theatre "is about not just the play but the play in its community context" (Leonard & Kilkelly, 2006, p.5). How is this process different from mainstream theatre practices, and what are the implications for organization and facilitation?

Suggested Activities

1. Select a geographical area of a maximum ten-block radius with your own home location as the centre point. Determine and list how many different communities lie within this area (senior citizen's homes, schools, libraries, recreation centers and so on).

2. How might you discover what issues are central to each of these communities? Where can you see some potential performance sites in this area?

3. Propose a number of partnerships that emerge from your research as areas of joint concern and/or challenges. Create a promotional kit (leaflets, advertisements, posters, media) for a community meeting that will bring groups together to consider a community-based theatre project.

4. To prepare for this meeting, plan at least one activity-based game or exercise that will lead participants into a shared sense of community and purpose.

Introduction

A good definition for museum theatre is "the use of theatre and theatrical techniques as a means of mediating knowledge and understanding in the context of museum education" (Hughes, Jackson & Kidd, 2007, p. 680). Within that definition lie a number of performance possibilities:

> Theatre is a catalyst, a motivator, a means of encouraging audiences to want to encounter and wrestle with ideas. Theatre fosters an imaginative, creative and culturally diverse understanding of the objects we choose to display—and sometimes of those we don't choose to display. It achieves this by adding the personal—a sense of time, a sense of space, and a story.
>
> Tessa Bridal, 2004, p.6

> The use of "props" in the theatre sense, and the interpretation of "objects" in the museum sense are inherently different.... These categories are very important to the museum, which must distinguish antiques from teaching reproductions from "just plain props."
>
> Dorothy Napp-Schindel, 2002,
> pp. 11–12

- First-person interpretation is one form of museum theatre in which the interpreter takes on the role of a particular, usually historic, character and interacts with museum visitors in-role. At Fort Louisberg, Nova Scotia, for example, the site is populated with first-person interpreters engaged in activities of the settlement period.

- A theatre performance is presented to help people understand a particular time period or issue. For example, a transportation exhibit at the Smithsonian in Washington, DC demonstrates life in the US in the 1950s (see the initial examples in Chapter 1).

- Historical re-enactments can be theatrical recreations of historic events, often involving a large number of participants. In the United States, for example, re-enactments of Civil War battles is a popular pastime.

- Role-playing, also known as "second-person interpretation," is when the audience as well as the interpreters are working in-role together. For example, in the Victoria, BC, Craigflower Schoolhouse project, students take on the roles of turn-of-the-century schoolchildren over the course of a typical day.

Museum theatre, much like any applied theatre form, presents many challenges. One of the primary ones is that of moving a casual museum visitor into either an audience or participatory role. Museum theatre audiences may be the most accidental audiences found in all of applied theatre, as they are not usually coming to a museum for a theatre experience. However, research demonstrates that when a museum-based performance does gather the attention of an audience, it can be an effective learning tool that people tend to remember (Jackson & Rees-Leahy, 2005). Another challenge lies in how much perspective or multiple points of view can inform the historical storytelling enacted by performers. Actors working in museum settings need to be aware that museums, which are mainstream institutions, can be very traditional; therefore it takes a great deal of negotiation, research and tact on the part of theatre artists working in these settings to bring a more complex set of understandings to the process (www.imtal. org). It is also challenging to negotiate if and how actors may work with historic artifacts from a museum collection. A third challenge is the discipline required to repeat scenarios and monologues multiple times every day, plus the added challenge of being an effective improviser who can respond to visitor input while maintaining a role.

> Assumptions about the need for entertainment rather than education have led to historic sites being faced with a "double mandate": to act as both an entertaining tourist attraction and an educational resource and often end up caught between the two, satisfying neither objective.
>
> Jane Malcolm-Davies, 2004, p. 278

There are clear tensions in the heritage community that sometimes convey a suspicion of all things theatrical as "fake" and a belief that everything of heritage value must be "authentic." This brings into question how somebody enacting a historical figure, or a fictional character within a historic timeframe, is representing the "truth" while at the same time conforming to the mandate of a particular institution. Again, as in all applied theatre practices, the negotiation and preparation that happens beforehand is paramount in importance. Research has demonstrated that where a high investment is made in training, the visitor response has been extremely positive, both in appreciation of entertainment value and in perceived learning (Malcolm-Davies, 2004, p. 285).

The three case studies presented in this chapter offer three very different museum theatre projects. Margaret Burke and Juliana Saxton describe a Canadian TIE company working in collaboration with a museum's heritage conservation branch. Participants in this program took on the names of the original colonists who had been school children on the actual site they were visiting. The power of place to generate belief and commitment is key. That power can be seen again in Scott Magelssen's description of a one-time only historical reenactment of a slave auction at a historic site in Virginia and makes for powerful reading that raises many useful questions. Finally, Debra McLauchlan shares a museum-university partnership from the point of view of the facilitator. She encounters and negotiates a variety of institutional and student resistance to the project.

10.1 Golden school days

from *"Dear great grandchildren: when I was in school there was only one classroom and the school was as big as a house. . .": Craigflower Schoolhouse, 1860*
Juliana Saxton and Margaret Burke. (1986). *Drama Contact, 1*(10), 13–19.

A light skiffle of snow covers the ground. At the foot of the gentle slope, the water of the tidal inlet reflects the grey skies above. The air is full of the sound of children's laughter and the tinkle of a tiny bell. In the centre of a circle of excited children, a boy and girl wearing blindfolds attempt to catch a slight figure in a long gingham dress. Miss Dorothea McKenzie, a senior student of Craigflower School, is monitoring the outside play of her fellow students under the motherly eye of Mrs. Margaret McGregor.

Suddenly, the schoolhouse door opens and a formidable figure steps out onto the stoop, [shouting,] "What's going on here? Why hasn't the bell rung? It's one minute past the hour and school MUST begin on time. And Mrs. McGregor, I see you have allowed the girls and boys to play together again."

"But Mr. Clarke, in Scotland, where I come from, the boys and girls are accustomed to playing together in the schoolyard . . . ."

"In England, where I come from, they do not!" (Thirty pairs of eyes watch this adult altercation with delight.) "And, as I am in charge of this school, in future the boys will play on THIS side of the yard and the girls on THAT. Is that clear, Mrs. McGregor?"

"Line up in two straight lines; boys to my left, girls to my right. Who is the bell monitor? Henry Porter, be so good as to ring the bell if you please. Mrs. McGregor, march them in."

With a mixture of nervous giggles and attempted seriousness, the children file up the wooden steps. The outer door shuts firmly and the only sound lying in the air of the deserted yard is the echo of the school bell. Outside the school gate . . . the tanker trucks and four-by-fours roar by, but inside the schoolhouse, thirty Grade 5 children have stepped back 130 years to an ordinary day at Craigflower School, 1860.

Well, not quite an ordinary day, for "tomorrow" the Bishop of Victoria, the Reverend Mr. Cridge, will be conducting his annual inspection and public examinations and it is tomorrow that Dorothea McKenzie confidently expects to win the coveted Senior Scholarship for excellence from the hand of the Bishop himself.

The mandates:
[At the first meeting of the Museum and the theatre company], the interpretive goals . . . as presented to the team by the Museum, were that students leaving the Schoolhouse should know the following:

- Many materials manufactured at the site went into the buildings (sawn lumber, bricks, lime).
- Craigflower was largely a Scottish immigrant community.
- What subjects were taught in school.
- What school was like for children from 1855–1865.
- A child's role in the school and the community.
- The school's community role.

At the site students should have hands-on experience in such activities as:

- butter churning
- wood chopping
- sawing
- bell ringing
- writing on slates
- making quill pens
- writing with quills
- lighting and trimming candles
- participating in lessons appropriate to the period

Upon leaving the site the students should feel the following:

- satisfaction in their involvement with the site
- that old buildings are interesting and important
- encouraged to revisit the Schoolhouse and other historic sites in the future, on their own or with their parents

Although the team was not expected to fit every one of the above into the programme, the Museum people were [insistent] that whatever plot was developed, it must be historically accurate in terms of the motivations and dilemma of the characters in the story. . . . The devising problem was to develop a programme which was historically accurate and, at the same time, highly theatrical and which would meet the educational goals of both the Museum and the Grade 5 Social Studies curriculum.

Finding the framework:

. . . Many of the Museum's requirements could be encompassed but some were discarded on the grounds of safety (chopping and sawing wood), and no logical reason could be found for butter[-]churning at school! Trimming candles, writing on slates and making quill pens was not possible because of lack of money.

The choice of making the time "the day prior" to the annual inspection by the Bishop enabled the team to develop the dramatic dilemma, for not only did Dorothea McKenzie expect to receive the Bishop's prize but so also did Elizabeth Veitch. The competition between the two girls would have to be developed subtly during the school morning, culminating in some sort of face-to-face interaction which would call upon the children to intervene. [Each class would be visited in their own school in preparation for their visit to the Schoolhouse.] The first school visit became vitally important, for it would be in this visit that the children would:

   a. meet either Dorothea or Elizabeth[,]
   b. be invited to Craigflower School[,]
   c. find out the sort of things to expect (including the Headmaster's idiosyncrasies), and
   d. form some sort of sympathetic attachment to their visitor.

The teacher workshop:

[Teachers of the classes to be involved] were given a brief, concise history of the Craigflower Estate by [the museum officer] followed by an outline of the programme by [the director]. . . . The teachers were asked to:

   • teach one verse of the hymn "All creatures that on earth do dwell."
   • have the children memorize a short extract from the poem *Table Manners for Little folk* (Anonymous, circa 1858).
   • have the children do their "homework."

[. . .]

As there were often two or more family members attending the school, the teacher was asked to have each family group prepare a collage of pictures and sketches that depicted that family's life. [These would then become] the artwork displayed on the walls in preparation for the Bishop's visit. . . . Token costumes would be provided upon arrival: aprons for the girls, suspenders for the "big" boys and neckerchiefs for the "little" boys.

The plot:

In the Craigflower Project the team chose the familiar childhood issues of competition, fairness, and taking responsibility for one's own actions, glued together by the Victorian view of the sin of unpunctuality, a view which, without the rhetoric, remains much the same today! Thus the values used in the drama were right for the period and at the same time, valid for today's children.

The protagonists, Dorothea and Elizabeth, are not far distant in age from the children themselves. The dramatic plot concerns the "unfair" treatment of one girl over the other by the Headmaster, Mr. Clarke. It is supported by a sub-plot which reveals the historical reality of the two educational philosophies (English and Scottish) at work in the schoolroom. Dramatic tension is created through the slow but inexorable realization on the children's part that they, through their shared experiences with both girls, are unwittingly caught in a dilemma: the dilemma of knowing that although Dorothea's competition essay has proved, in Mr. Clarke's words, "most admirable," Elizabeth's is far superior in both content and sensitivity and more worthy of the Bishop's prize. [The] dilemma [is] compounded by the fact that Mr. Clarke's reasons for withholding the prize from Elizabeth are justified, for she *has* often been late; she *is* outspoken; she is *very* untidy and her penmanship leaves *much* to be desired! The plot, the sub-plot and the dramatic tension are woven into the fabric of the daily routine of Craigflower School circa 1860.

The value of the experience:

. . . [A]n experience of this nature in which information is absorbed in the context of a direct, personal encounter tends not only to last, but to fix itself in the memory. . . . [T]he Museum's curator has noted that a number of the children who were in the original Craigflower project have been returning to the Museum, bringing their friends with them and telling them "what it was like in the olden days."

- *I hope this show goes on forever and ever to let the children of tomorrow get to see how it was in 1860. Yours sincerely, "William Lidgate" aged 12.*
- *I think the past should be still going on. It[']s GREAT. "Ellen Little" aged 8.*

10.2 Re-examining history through museum theatre

from *Making history in the second person: Post-touristic considerations for living historical interpretations*
Scott Magelssen. (2006). *Theatre Journal, 58*(2), 291-312.

[...]

The 1994 Publick Times Estate Auction at Colonial Williamsburg [was] staged by what was then Williamsburg's African American Interpretations and Presentations Program (AAIP) . . . The auction reenactment, which included the dramatization of the sale of four slaves, drew substantial criticism from several groups, including the Southern Christian Leadership Conference and the NAACP. Protestors occupied the stage with the characters throughout the performance, condemning the auction as a demoralization of human dignity. This controversial reenactment was a moment of living history in which several performative and historiographic issues came to a head, specifically in the collision of the remembered pasts of the institution, the interpreter, and the museum visitor. In this space, a ritualized commemoration of a past identity (a site of potential) was forced into the structures of institutional history.

The auction conveyed and condensed several stories: Lucy and Daniel, married by common law, were sold to different bidders from counties fifty miles apart, their marriage and family broken up. Sukey, a laundress, was purchased by her husband, a "free Negro," who was able to outbid a wealthy white landowner. Another slave, a carpenter, was sold to a white bidder along with his tools. The staged auction lasted about thirty minutes, but by the end, a clear set of important themes and lessons had emerged to tie the stories together: (1) Whites bought and sold blacks like livestock; (2) Sometimes freed blacks could outbid whites to purchase and free enslaved individuals; (3) Sometimes white masters' desire for profit and/or frugality overpowered the bonds between two human beings. Several other narratives were possible, but unable to be contained in a dramatic presentation that sought to convey selected historical information and ideas in the most immediate and successful way possible. These other potential stories were left out of the narrative because they would not fit easily into the dramatic structure of singular plot, conflict, rising action, and denouement.

Audience members picked up on the missed opportunities in the talkback that followed, when AAIP Chair Christy Coleman (who also played Lucy in the performance) fielded questions from the audience. "Where do you show African Americans as fighters?" shouted one voice from a contingent of protesters holding banners demanding, "Say No to Racist Shows." Coleman responded that the AAIP shows resistance in all of its programming at Colonial Williamsburg, both active and passive (deciding not to work for the master one day, saying "I'm sick," or breaking a hoe). This answer did not, apparently, appease the dissatisfied spectators. Another question was hurled from the crowd: "Where was that today?"

The auction reenactment had negative effects on the costumed reenactors as well: in a May 2000 telephone conversation, Christy Coleman Matthews, now president of Charles H. Wright Museum of African American History in Detroit, spoke to me of how extremely difficult it was for the interpreters, who normally interact with visitors in the first or third person, to shift to a more traditional theatrical approach for the 1994 estate auction. According to Matthews, the interpreters experienced extreme emotional exhaustion, much of it caused by the need to internalize the characters' emotions in the performance, since, historically, the slaves on the auction block were not allowed to speak. When living history programming employs traditional theatre practices, the interpreters find the experience of immersing themselves in characters to be psychologically and emotionally more draining than their regular job of historical interaction. "They couldn't wear their interpreter hat [during the auction]. They were used to relying on both theatrical tricks for suspension of disbelief and the story told as an interpreter. . . . They had to dig into their personal psyche. That was a new experience for these people." Matthews cited this distress as the reason why the estate auction was only performed once. "The staff didn't want to do it," she said, "because it was too emotionally draining." The participants, both black and white, were taken aback by visitors' strong emotional responses to the reenactment and by their own emotions, which they had to repress in order to stay in character.

The estate auction failed to meet either interpreter or visitor/spectator expectations, and the museum's ethical, performative, and historiographic responsibilities were poorly defined. Acts of memory that would have been more personally empowering for contemporary performers and audiences, though not found in the Virginia Gazette records upon which the auction was based, could not be incorporated. The spectators, though, rather than passively accepting this institutional history, were instead allowed to unmask and voice the limiting conditions, because the liberating environment of protest enabled them to do so.

It is vital that the largely undocumented history of black oppression and experience continue to be voiced at such an educational institution and historical tourist [destination] as Williamsburg. But is there a way to do this that would allow more discussion and exploration than that which is available in a living history sound-bite like the estate auction?

[...]

"Second-person interpretation," a relatively recent term in the living history field, allows visitors to pretend to be part of the past and offers possibilities of co-creating the trajectory of the historiographic narrative with the staff, rather than merely passively consuming it. The vast bulk of this type of programming at living museums, though, does not involve any kind of impersonation or assuming of character on the part of the visitor.

[...]

Second-person interpretation is becoming one of living museums' most foregrounded programs. Social history, the wave of revisionist thinking that swept through the industry in the 1970s and 1980s, has much to do with its emergence. Museums have since changed the focus from displaying the lives of the Founding Fathers and have made significant steps toward showing the rest of the story, the mostly unrecorded histories of women, children, racial and ethnic minorities, and the very poor. Hence, second-person activities are geared toward hands-on learning about the kinds of crafts and chores these individuals would have done throughout their lives. Activities almost always include basket weaving and candle dipping. Musket drilling is conducted at Colonial Williamsburg using wooden sticks as dummy rifles. Other activities might include building a stone wall, throwing a pot, making ribbon, weaving on a loom, or working a plow. In summer 2001 at Living History Farms in Iowa, my fellow visitors and I were each given a pair of work gloves, stamped with the museum logo. The gloves served as a take-home souvenir, but we were encouraged to use them throughout our visit to the museum. For example, the interpreters at the 1850 Farm were using daub to patch holes in the walls of the log cabin homestead where the weather and hearth fires had dried and crumbled the earlier layers; they encouraged us to try our (gloved) hands at it.

[...]

Often, too, reenacted historical events (as opposed to the generalized common practices like ballgames and square dances) require the occasional crowd or cast of thousands in order to approximate an accurate picture of what originally transpired. Colonial Williamsburg makes heavy use of crowd participation, which often simply means that visitors chant lines on the cues given by the first-person reenactors. One June afternoon in 2000 (7 November 1769 in the Historic Area), I was one of the hundreds of visitors gathered for the "Convening of the General Assembly." After Williamsburg staff hand-picked a selection of middle-aged men from the audience to represent the burgesses marching through the gates of the Capitol building to begin that year's session, the crowd was led in a rousing chorus of "Rule Britannia!" in order to demonstrate that, at least in 1769, ties between Virginia and England were still strong. That was Sunday. By Tuesday morning of that week, we had skipped to April of 1775, and the crowd was enlisted in protesting the British Governor's middle-of-the-night removal of gunpowder from the Public Magazine; later that day, we jeered at the burning effigy of Alfred, Lord North, in protest of growing British sanctions.

With the exception of the 1994 estate auction at Colonial Williamsburg, there is no question about whether one will comply with the rules of these games, post-tourist or no. So effective is the tourist realism and family fun that to go against the grain and voice alternative histories, or to question the agenda of the institution (or to assume a character not assigned by the interpretive staff), would make one a spoilsport.

10.3 Museum-university partnership
from *Digging a ditch with undergraduates: A museum theatre experience*
Debra McLauchlan. (2008). *NJ: Drama Australia Journal, 31*(2), 83–94.

[I]n January 2003, the Museum Board of Directors formally approved my proposal to create an on-site theatre project using university drama students as playwrights and performers. The Board outlined three requirements: (1) that I would personally take charge of the project, (2) that the museum's education coordinator would select the topic of the play, and (3) that the production would increase museum publicity through media coverage and a preview performance for local politicians and museum supporters. The Board took responsibility for advertising, creating and distributing a program, financing and organizing an opening reception, and supplying a small production budget to cover extraneous costs.

[...]

In March, I met the museum's education coordinator to discuss potential topics for the play. A few weeks later, on the advice of teachers who regularly visit the museum with their classes, the coordinator decided on the topic of the Welland Canal for three reasons: (1) Lock 3 of the canal sits behind the museum, and artifacts about its history are located throughout the site; (2) the topic complements Ontario Ministry of Education guidelines for both social studies and science in Grades 4 to 6; and (3) the production would coincide with the canal's 175th anniversary. The coordinator requested a one-hour performance, with pre- and post-show discussion time, for seven Friday mornings in March and April. She assumed responsibility for advertising to schools, scheduling school visits, communicating with teachers before and after the performances, collecting feedback, and creating a study guide package to accompany the production.

[...]

In St. Catharines, the museum is accessed through an open foyer, overlooking the Welland Canal, with a permanent [three]-tiered riser close to the exhibit entrance. The exhibit area is a narrow, winding avenue of niches and display cases, some fixed and some moveable. Potential performance spaces included the façade of a shanty inhabited by canal workers, the helm of an old tugboat, a replica of a sea captain's office, stacks of barrels, and a large topographical model of the region. The curator took responsibility for providing costumes and print material about the Welland Canal.

. . . Ten months before the performance would be staged, preliminary arrangements with university and museum personnel were complete, and initial contact with potential audiences had been made. Groundwork of another sort now demanded attention. Meticulous planning would be necessary to enable the university students to learn about museum theatre concepts, research the Welland Canal, and devise and rehearse a one-hour performance in the short time available. Seven weeks of the 13-week course were already committed to performance, leaving six [three]-hour in-class sessions for the creation of the play! I made a few decisions to alleviate the scarcity of time issue.

First, I envisioned that the play would begin and end in modern-day scenes involving the entire class, the opening to occur on and around the foyer riser, and the closing to re-enact the annual Top Hat Ceremony that welcomes the first boat of the season through the canal each spring. The bulk of the play would be developed from topics selected by the students, working simultaneously in self-determined groups to build individual scenes of approximately seven minutes. The scenes would be linked by a narration strategy, also to be determined by the class, that would move the audience from one area of the museum to another. Next, after scripting their scenes, each group would schedule two [two]-hour rehearsals with me outside of class time. These focused sessions would provide uninterrupted opportunities to block and polish every section of the script. Finally, a local actor who frequently interprets the historical figure of William Hamilton Merritt, primary founder of the Welland Canal, agreed to visit the class, in character, during the first session. As Merritt, he would provide rich details about the canal's inception, while also modeling principles of first-person interpretation.

[...]

The first class consisted of introductions and warm-ups, a course overview, the in-role visit from "William Hamilton Merritt," and a structured exploration of possibilities for the opening scene. Of 18 students enrolled in the course, 14 were present. Although some displayed a knowledgeable approach to preliminary play-building tasks, others lacked the skill level in dramatic exploration that I had expected from a third-year group.

[...]

The final hour of class was devoted to the opening scene. I distributed factual information about the Welland Canal ("the ditch", as its creators labeled it) which groups translated into movement-with-narration vignettes. By fortunate coincidence, each vignette included depictions of a lock, water, and a boat. Merging the vignettes and staging them on the museum foyer riser would comprise the opening scene of the play.

[...]

We returned to the opening scene. After creating precise gestures for "lock," "water," and "boat" characters, we agreed on the order and transitional movements for vignettes devised during Week One. The role of Lockmaster Winston emerged as a character who would introduce the play and help narrate scene transitions. We choreographed an opening chant—"Inch by inch, meter by meter, we'll dig a ditch and dig it deeper"—that would bring performers into the performance space.

. . . For the second half of class, we traveled to the museum and met the site's educational coordinator, curator, and board chair. After touring the facility, students were free to decide what topic interested them about the canal, what classmates would work together on developing a scene about their selected topic, and where their scenes would be performed. The curator presented copious print material as research aids.

... Over the next two weeks, we hammered out tentative scenes for the play.
[...]

Meanwhile, as [Napp-]Schindel (2002) predicted, the museum denied access to authentic artifacts for use as theatrical props. In the end, actors performed certain actions in front of authentic objects, while either miming their use (especially in the case of shovels and other digging implements) or replacing them with replicas (especially in the case of documents).

Napp-Schindel, D. (2002). Museum theatre: Telling stories through objects. *Stage of the Art,* 14(4), 10–16.

... The play eventually developed into eight scenes that moved both chronologically and physically through the museum's exhibit space. Incorporating dance, song, mime, monologues, stylized movement and tableau work, it balanced episodes of despair with comic moments of light-heartedness, and included gender-blind depictions of both real and fictional characters. It ended as it began, in a full-cast scene set in present time.

... Aside from the initial visit, the class did not return to the museum until dress rehearsal, when we competed for space and time with both a work crew engaged in noisy repairs and a couple of bus tours. With the preview performance hours away—and an invited audience of media, city and tourism officials, university faculty, museum board members and supporters—no one had assumed responsibility for setting up seats in the foyer! Last-minute recruitment of labor went unnoticed by the audience, most of whom warmly applauded the show and praised its professionalism and entertainment value. Problems, however, demanded attention before the first performance for children.

... First, museum staff noted a couple of factual inaccuracies, one minor and a more significant one that prompted an additional rehearsal. Secondly, the curator wanted an actor to refrain from using a specific cart handle, requiring some restaging of a scene. Thirdly, docents worried that children's potential exuberance for the play might incite them not only to infringe on spaces, but also to touch objects restricted to the public. As a solution, the educational coordinator would make a welcoming speech before each performance, outlining rules of expected conduct in the museum. Children would also be supplied with small seating mats that would define their personal spatial boundaries.

Cast members complained that the preview had ended without a formal curtain call. A customary bow seemed inappropriate within the non-traditional setting of the final scene, which positioned the audience as crowd members in the Top Hat Ceremony. Yet, the ending of the play had seemed awkward without a mechanism to signal audience applause. We decided that I would speak a line at the end of each performance to thank everyone for attending. Afterward, the cast would bow and applaud the audience as a cue for the audience to return the applause.

... A potentially more serious concern emanated from a few museum supporters who complained that sections of the play were inappropriate for children. In particular, they wanted to eliminate the action of a husband slapping his wife, as well as any references to racial or religious hatred that sparked riots during the Welland Canal's construction. Although not in favor of sanitizing history, museum staff felt obliged to placate the supporters and asked my opinion about toning down these sections of the play. Fearing not only a revolt from the cast but also a severe wound to the play's integrity if I complied, I suggested a compromise that the museum supporters accepted. The script would be performed as written; however, during the post-show chat the actors would (a) demonstrate the stage slap technique and (b) denounce racial and religious intolerance in the play as unacceptable beliefs not shared by the performers in real life.

... Response from the seven school groups who attended the play was highly positive in terms of its entertainment value and professionalism. Obvious warmth developed between actors and audience in almost all performances. Most noticeable in post-show questioning was the children's interest in specific characters' reactions to dramatized events. The production achieved the museum's goal of increased school visits and publicity, with the result that the "Theatre for the Community" course has continued as a partnership between the museum and the university Dramatic Arts Department.

Further Reading

Bailey, C. H. (1987). "Soul clap its hands and sing": Living history theatre as a process of creation. *Activities, Adaptation & Aging, 9*(4), 1–43. A very detailed article looking at the aesthetics and assessment of performance in museum theatre and reminiscence theatre.

Bridal, T. (2004). *Exploring museum theatre.* Walnut Creek, CA: Altamira.

Hayes, J. & Napp-Schindel, D. (1994). *Pioneer journeys: Drama in museum education.* Charlottesville, VA: New Plays Incorporated. An award-winning text and informative overview of the then new and somewhat contested practice of theatre as a component of museum education.

Hughes, C. (1998). *Museum theatre: Communicating with visitors through drama.* Portsmouth, NH: Heinemann. These three books are worth looking at for their strong focus on this topic.

International Museum Theatre Alliance [IMTAL]. www.mos.org/learn_more/imtal. html. An informative website with links and projects.

Jackson, A. & Leahy, H. R. (2005). "Seeing it for real...?"—Authenticity, theatre and learning in museums. *RIDE: Research in Drama Education, 10*(3), 303–325. A look at the kinds of learning achieved in museum theatre education with children.

Malcolm-Davies, J. (2004). Borrowed robes: The educational value of costumed interpretation at historic sites. *International Journal of Heritage Studies, 10*(3), 277–293. This article looks at the value of costumed interpretation and the importance of sufficient training time for first-person interpreters.

Museum theatre: Many roles, many players, many places, many reasons [Special issue]. (1990). *Journal of Museum Education, 15*(2). Full of interesting and useful information.

Napp-Schindel, D. (2002). Museum theatre: Telling stories through objects. *Stage of the Art, 14*(4), 10–16. Addresses the significance of props in museum theatre practice.

Questions for Discussion and Reflection

1. In the three case studies you have just read, how does participation differ in each of these museum theatre activities? How do the different levels of participation potentially affect the learning intended in each project?

2. Re-read the concluding paragraph of Scott Magelssen's case study in which he describes how second-person interpretation usually offers little or no space for spectator-participants to resist the narrative they are re-creating. What are some possible strategies that might allow for more diverse opinions on historic events to be voiced in a museum setting?

3. Reflecting on one selected case study, identify what meanings could be drawn, what connections to the information could be made, what elements of surprise were evident (as in seeing something in a fresh way) and what possibilities exist for raising new questions.

Suggested Activities

1. Make a list of the museum and heritage sites in your area and find out, on the internet or by phoning the Education Director, if any museum theatre has been or is being done. (Note that science centres and art galleries may also offer first-person interpretation and/or theatre performances.) If possible,

make arrangements to attend a performance or interpretation and document it via notes and/or interviews with actors and institutional staff. Use these data as part of a post-performance analysis that examines the balance between entertainment and education.

2. Visit a local museum or heritage site with a view to determining possibilities for interpretation, presentation or interactive role-play in that setting. Write up your idea as a short proposal, keeping in mind the mandate of the institution and any potential challenges you can foresee.

3. Decide upon a museum or historic site as a setting for a first-person interpretation. Research the time period. You may want to identify a historic figure or create a composite fictional character. Write, rehearse and perform a monologue with a strong narrative that includes opportunities for audience interaction. In presenting this first-person interpretation, what educational opportunities are present for audience learning? If possible, present these monologues within your chosen museum site.

Introduction

Reminiscence drama uses the strategies and techniques of drama education to generate the recall of memories and experiences of the elderly. Often these experiences are simply shared and enjoyed by the group. Sometimes stories and experiences, stimulated by drama activities, are developed into performances that may be played either by the elderly themselves or by professional actors. This is reminiscence theatre: "dramatizing and making theatre from memories" (Schweitzer, 2006, p. 13).

The plays that are built from those shared reminiscences are generally performed in spaces that we would not recognize as theatre spaces but are ones in which the audiences feel comfortable. These plays have a double purpose: to generate memories and to use those memories to engender further memories and story-making from their audiences. The raw materials of the scripts are the tape-recorded or written recollections of older people, gleaned from group discussions, individual interviews, improvisations or pieces of writing. These stories are reflected back to an audience made up of the very people whose stories are being performed, as well as to their families, other seniors and their guests. Audiences are most often small groups so that seeing and hearing is easier for both players and watchers. After the performance, the serving of tea and cookies enables conversations that reflect the memories of the audience as they interact with the stories they have heard and the performers they meet.

> One of the things that we tend to forget is that people are living for much longer. It is estimated that by the year 2030, one in five people will be over age 65. Medical technology has helped to increase life expectancy and enhance the quality of living to such an extent that Americans over the age of 85 currently comprise the fastest-growing age bracket.
>
> Ann D. Basting, 1995, p. 113

A variation of this model is intergenerational and may happen in one of two ways. First, a group of young people elicit stories about life memories from seniors, dramatize these stories and then perform them for the seniors themselves. Second, a theatre group made up of senior players may choose to perform their reminiscences for young audiences who gain a deeper understanding of their grandparents' or great grandparents' generations.

Where there are improved diets, advances in medical technology, and understanding of the needs of the elderly in terms of safety, it is not surprising that more people live longer, and it is equally unsurprising that we do not yet know how to make those later years productive and engaging. Today, how we live our lives in our later years is an important area of research, and we are discovering that the needs of the elderly are the same things as humans of all ages: affirmation of their presence and value in the world.

Barbara Myerhoff (1992) notes that we have not created any meaning-making rituals for this period—what Myerhoff refers to as "definitional ceremonies" for this new longevity (Basting, 1995, p. 114). Such ceremonies could become, she suggests, "powerful tools" in the self-construction of elder identity; without them, it can be difficult to see one's later life as a fulfilling time (p. 113). Part of engendering that sense of fulfillment lies with the creation of time and space for memory prompting, storying and communicating.

> Storytellers . . . know that the problem of identity is always a problem, not just a problem of youth . . . [T]he nearest anyone can come to finding themselves at any given age is to find a story that somehow tells them about themselves.
>
> Norman Maclean, 1992, p. 145

The value of reminiscence theatre is that it uses theatre to reframe the stories of the elderly into performances that provide meaning and confirmation, not just to those whose stories are being told but also as prompts for the stories of its audiences who are most usually seniors and, often, their caregivers and family members. For these latter groups, reminiscence theatre pieces can become invigorating stimuli to promote reconnection and respect for the past through the conversations that ensue after the performance.

What we have described above reflects the approaches of a number of reminiscence theatre companies of which The Age Exchange in London, England has the strongest reputation. It is known for the variety of programs that it offers, the quality of the work itself by "in-house" or professional performers, and the international connections that it makes through its outreach activities, such as The Memory Box project (Schweitzer, 2006). There is, however, an equally strong body of work located in the United States and referred to as "senior theatre" (Basting, 1995). Senior theatre, not to be confused with reminiscence theatre, can be an extremely demanding vaudeville-style production that capitalizes on the talents of older adults (e.g., The

> In writing about children's theatre, Brecht said, " It is no different with grownups. Their education never finishes. Only the dead are beyond being altered by their fellow-men (sic). Think this over and you will realize how important the theatre is for forming characters."
>
> Bertolt Brecht in Willett, 1964, p. 152

Geritol Follies [Canada] or *The Geritol Frolics* [U.S.]). Senior theatre can also refer to the performances of scripted plays by senior actors. Western Gold Theatre, founded by Joy Coghill, produces "outstanding professional theatre that expands horizons and enriches the lives of mature artists and their audiences" (www.westerngoldtheatre.com).

In Victoria, BC, Target Theatre, which has the motto "empowering seniors by overcoming age stereotypes" (www.islandnet.com/target/), combines both kinds of theatre. In addition to working with scripts, the company has a repertoire of applied theatre pieces, often commissioned, addressing such issues as dementia, elder abuse, incontinence, death and dying. These plays are performed and facilitated at conferences for audiences of social workers, doctors, police and any who have a direct interest in the issues presented.

> *Our first case history offers an example of work from the Uhan Shii Theatre Group, a collective of non-professional elder women under an experienced theatre director. This excerpt describes only one part of a much larger work,* Echoes of Taiwan, *that focuses on cultural identity and traditions through reaffirmation and critique. The second study is an examination of an intergenerational project that focused more on the young interpreters than on the elders. What is useful is that it describes how the performances were moved from "authentic reproduction" to "dramatic representation"— from a simple retelling to a theatrical aesthetic. At a stage in life when they are dealing with medical issues, the third excerpt describes seniors creating plays that address these topics.* A Matter of Life *was first created to inform medical personnel and offers a model for post-performance interaction; later, restructuring the performance for older audiences shifted the focus. In the last example, an oral historian examines the purposes of storytelling in terms of its truth and its intentions. "How accurate," she asks, "are [these experiences] if the main narrative drive is to promote a sense of reconciliation and harmony in later life?" The answer to this question is one that any facilitator must consider when working with people's stories, whatever their age.*

11.1 Memory and transgression
from *The subversive practices of reminiscence theatre in Taiwan*
Wan-Jung Wang. (2006). *RIDE: Research in Drama Education, 11*(1), 77–87.

The background and context of the Uhan Shii Theatre Group

Taiwan has been ruled by different political regimes, undergoing colonisation by Japan and "re-colonisation" by the Kuomingtang nationalists (shortened to KMT) immediately after the Japanese occupation in the twentieth century. Culturally and historically, Taiwan has been influenced by Chinese and Japanese imperialism as well as "modernized" by Western neo-colonialism, and the hybrid culture of Taiwan indicates this post-coloniality. It was only after the lifting of Martial Law in 1987 that the Taiwanese began to reconstruct their own multiple histories and, as part of the process of decolonisation, started to renegotiate a more secure sense of their own identities. The Uhan Shii Theatre Group was founded in this emerging movement of cultural decolonisation in the 1990s.

[...]

The Uhan Shii Theatre Group is the first Taiwanese theatre company exclusively dedicated to the performance of the oral histories of community-based elders. By recovering and performing their buried memories, the company reconstructs Taiwanese historicised identity and, in the process, reaffirms it.

[...]

In *Echoes of Taiwan VI—We Are Here*, [which] premiered in 2000, a migration epic story of Hakka (the second largest ethnic group in Taiwan) was delivered for the first time on the Taiwanese stage in the Hakka language. The story spans the past to the present, from the countryside to the metropolis, and the experience of Hakka women is the main focus. These women use their Hakka dialect to tell their life stories and project themselves into a public space, thereby countering their previous absence in public and creating a new spatial reproduction. They employ the Hakka language and singing to reclaim a space for Hakka women whose experiences and voices had been previously marginalised by the double oppressions of [Kuomintang]'s nationalism and patriarchy. They share their personal stories of migration, showing how they make a living in the metropolis and how they have moved from the confines of the domestic place to the public space. Furthermore, their numerous tours (the production has toured to remote Hakka villages for more than 50 performances and has travelled as far as Wupertale, Germany in 2001) has meant that their stories have been seen on various public platforms both in and out of Taiwan.

Echoes of Taiwan VI—We Are Here reveals the hidden tradition of adopted daughters in Hakka history for the first time on a Taiwanese stage. Some of the female cast are "adopted daughters" themselves, some of their mothers and sisters were "adopted daughters" who were given to another family in exchange for their labour. Sharing collective memories of this exploitative system of adoption helps them to come to terms with their suffering. In turn, the performance enables them to show the inner feelings of these exploited daughters through dramatic narratives and singing. In the scene of "Wrapping the Wound for the Little Girl," enacted by an all-female cast, they pass a long white strip of cloth towards each other slowly. It occupies and involves the whole stage and symbolises a cleansing meandering river. It represents a healing ritual to comfort their traumas. The healing space sometimes extends beyond the stage and reaches the audience who may have endured similar afflictions.

The production also portrays how Hakka women break free from their domestic constraints and economic dependency. Women start to make a living to support their families by tailoring or selling merchandise, and this is shown theatrically in Jyu-Ing's and Yu-Ching's stories, both of whom are self-reliant Hakka mothers and career women in real life. They either walk out of their domestic space and create their own career in the public domain or transform their domestic space into their workplace. In contrast with the confinement, financial worries, suppression and anger that Jyu-Ing had to put up with at home, she dances with her customers, using her tape-measure and mannequin to celebrate the economic independence she has gained by transforming her home into a tailor's studio.

In the last scene, the circling parade "Opening up the Bundle of Memory," projects the Hakka women's memories into the auditorium. Each woman opens a blue bundle, which traditional Hakka people wrap up and carry around their shoulders when they embark upon a far[-]away journey, and she shares her most treasured memory with the audience. Xiou-Ching's memory is a family photograph in which her mother holds her tight and loves her dearly; Jyu-Ing's blue bundle contains her diary which accompanies her migration journey from village to city. One after another, they circle around the auditorium and pass on the blue bundles to children as passing on their Hakka heritage. The procession encompasses the space with their memories of migration and projects them into their prospective futures. This play has toured around the metropolis and remote Hakka towns twice in the past five years with the intention of re-inscribing Taiwanese history with Hakka women's oral histories and re-affirming their identities through theatre practice.

These examples illustrate how the Uhan Shii Theatre Group not only presents the traditions of Taiwanese culture, but also subverts them by new representations of contemporary female experience.... The presentation of the Taiwanese stories performed by the women themselves also subverts the "orientalist" imagination about Asian women and challenges passive stereotypes with which they are sometimes associated. Although the director Peng Ya-Ling never stresses their political aim as a "feminist group" (Wang, 2004), the process of women acting their own stories is part of a continual process of striving towards social justice and gender equality. Through these cultural and theatrical strategies the company intends to transcend binarism and open multiple choices and spaces for different voices in Taiwan.

Wang, W-J. (2004). [12 interviews with the director Peng Ya-Ling about Uhan Shii Theatre Group's methods and process in rehearsal, September 2003-January 2004, Taipei.].Unpublished raw data.

11.2 Intergenerational reminiscence theatre
from *The performance of memory: Drama, reminiscence and autobiography*
Helen Nicholson. (2003). *NJ: Drama Australia Journal, 27*(2), 79–92.

[...]

In educational terms, the dramatisation of oral narratives, particularly when students are involved in interviews and research, presents particular challenges. How are interviews conducted and interpreted? Whose stories are chosen for development in drama? Who controls the texts? Do the actors have the authority to fictionalise the stories? How are the narratives shaped into dramatic form? How is the work presented and received? These were some of the questions faced by a group of fifteen[-] and sixteen[-]year-old students who worked with me on a project in which oral histories were developed into a piece of devised theatre. From my point of view, I was interested in interrogating the social purposes of drama in relation to oral history and in developing the students' artistic skills in devised drama.

The starting point for the devised work involved students interviewing their grandparents and other members of the local community about events that had shaped their lives. In part, we were drawing on the work of a local community writing group— Bristol Broadsides—whose members had documented their memories of growing up. I saw this process as communitarian and social rather than therapeutic, although the psychological benefits of reminiscence work with the elderly are well[-]documented and were growing in popularity during the 1980s. My own grandmother was invited by social workers to attend a reminiscence group around that time when, in her 80s, she became depressed. By then she was blind but the touch of particular kinds of woollen cloth made in the Yorkshire mills where she had worked in the early 1920s prompted her to tell many stories. She enjoyed reminiscing, benefited from the companionship which came from sharing memories, but she had to stop going when her depression lifted and she felt better. But in my first drama education project of this type, the effects of the work on the elderly were not my immediate concern. Retrospectively, I think I was naïve about this. When I first started working on intergenerational work, I tended to use old people as a resource. They were "happy to help"— and enjoyed the contact with young people I am sure—but I think I took them for granted. My primary focus was on the young people who were largely responsible for re-presenting their stories, with elderly members of the community having small walk-on parts and sometimes seen at different ages on excerpts of ciné film (recorded before the days of video!).

Portelli, A. (1998). What makes oral history different. In R. Perks & A. Thomson (Eds.), *The oral history reader* (pp. 63-74). London, UK: Routledge.

. . .

From the interviews the students conducted, two distinct narratives emerged. One concerned the experiences of those who moved to England from previously colonised countries during the 1960s. The other story which captured the students' imagination was told by Lucy's grandmother, who had worked in the local cigarette factory during the second world war, where flirtatious "tobacco girls" used to put their names and addresses in cigarette packets destined to be sent to soldiers. Interestingly, both sets of stories included humour; there appeared, however, to be an element of self-censoring on the part of the people they interviewed which excluded more painful or difficult memories. As Portelli (1998) points out, it is often the silences and omissions in the stories which are most revealing[:]

> ... [T]he most precious information may lie in what the informants *hide*,
> and in the fact they *do* hide it, rather than in what they *tell*. (p. 69)

It is possible to speculate on why more painful memories were hidden. Many interviewees had family relationships with the students and they presumably selected aspects which they deemed appropriate to the context. Some stories were illustrated by treasured possessions; small, private mementos—an aeroplane ticket, a hat, immigration papers—which symbolised particular events. They also served to focus the students' attention on the content of the narratives as visible signs of lived experience.

In the process of devising, the students were concerned to tell the stories as "authentically" and "faithfully" as they could. I found this desire to **reproduce** events rather than **represent** them troubling. Some students expressed an understandable anxiety about misrepresenting the very personal stories they had been told, and responded to this by insisting on a dramatic form which was heavily dependent on naturalistic acting styles in a linear and episodic dramaturgical structure. Their reluctance to experiment meant that their drama was limited by the confines of a form which, whilst it suited a rather simplistic re-telling of events, did not really capture or fit the feelings. Conceptually, this suggested that the students had a partial understanding of the ways in which personal history is constructed in memory, accepting without question that everything that had been told was literally true. They were actively resistant to alternative readings, feeling with some justification that they should honour personal narratives they had heard. This central dilemma—how to both validate the testimony of the original speaker *and* open the narratives for critical interrogation—or, in this case, creative interpretation—has

Tait, P. (1994). *Converging realities.* Sydney, NSW: Curreny Press.

Personal Narratives Group (Eds.). (1989). Truths. In *Interpreting women's lives: Feminist theory and personal narratives.* Bloomington, IN: Indiana University Press.

been theorised by oral historians. The Personal Narratives Group (1989) sum up the debate:

> When people talk about their lives, people lie sometimes, forget a little, exaggerate, become confused, get things wrong. Yet they are revealing truths...the guiding principle could be that all autobiographical memory is true: it is up to the interpreter to discover in what sense, where, and for what purpose (p. 261).

The idea that there are multiple interpretations of truth in autobiographical memory suggests that a dramatic style which relies heavily on realist forms of representation is politically, as well as artistically, constricting. As Peta Tait (1994, p. 33) convincingly argues, to represent social experience as a "coherently ordered, stable pattern of reality" in theatre is implicitly to accept hegemonic values.

To encourage the students to question the boundaries between the fictive and the real, I suggested that they asked to hear the stories again, this time listening particularly for *how* the speakers commented on past events and to notice any differences in the details. The act of re-telling personal experience creates ... a dialectical relationship between the past and present in which the speaker does not "relive" events but "re-writes" them. The students discovered that description[s] of past events were interwoven with new insights and explanatory comment, sometimes contextualising the moment, at other times pointing out how the events had influenced the tellers in later life. By acknowledge the similarities and differences between the past and the present, the students recognised how the storytellers both situated themselves in the present and negotiated their relationship with the past. Observant students noticed how performative elements of the storytelling—use of voice, enactment and gesture, for example[—]suggested particular emotional connections with specific events; whilst the stories were not substantially different in content from the "original," on second hearing the interpretation and emphasis was. They became aware of the rehearsed elements of autobiographical stories where it was obvious from the "performance," they had been told and retold many times and when the elderly people were recalling details of life events which they had not spoken about for many years. Oral history invites this kind of self-reflexivity and, in so doing, enables participants to construct their own identities in relation to others.

The awareness that the tellers themselves moved between the past and the present and between multiple "realities" gave the students licence to break the pattern of linearity in their drama. Until that moment, the students had been searching, in Derridean terms, for the "myth of origin," for the single, unmediated presence of truth. The process of devising became more concerned with what Derrida describes as absence than presence; the artefacts, tape recordings and other ephemera used as props symbolising the missing originators of the stories. This sense of absence weighed the students down. Educationally it inhibited their development as theatre practitioners as they were reluctant to experiment with dramatic form. It also prevented them from trying out ideas spontaneously; they were not representing lived experience creatively but were engaged in a form of ventriloquising. The process felt, and was, second hand. Furthermore, their insistence on accurate presentation of the material culture of the times, particularly in the form of props and costumes, had prevented them from asking more abstract questions about memory and the interpretation of the past in dramatic form. From the moment when they began to interrogate the stories more closely, they recognised the dialectic between past and present and they wove this into their drama, using the comments they had heard to frame the dramatic action. This was used most interestingly by one group of students who spoke in Urdu when representing the story of the past and English for the contemporary commentary, thus fluctuating between the official and the domestic, indicating multiple identities and realities in powerful dramatic moments.

The shift in emphasis from "authentic" reproduction to dramatic representation moved the work from an unmediated and uncritical retelling to a popular theatrical aesthetic. By introducing Brechtian devices such as montage and popular songs of the period, they succeeded in creating a dramatic atmosphere which, to borrow John McGrath's phrase, made the shows a "good night out" with audience members joining in the songs.

[...]

Pedagogically, however, one of the strengths of the project lay in how students learnt explicitly about the genre of social realism. In the process of working they found that an understanding of genre was liberating and creative. Once the students had stopped trying to reproduce events "authentically" they were able to gain an embodied understanding of the opportunities and constraints presented by working in this dramatic form. In particular, it became clear that the popular aesthetic of social realism was appropriate for devised drama which was built on oral history; readings of oral history frequently challenge dominant accounts of the past by providing interpretations of events which differ from those of the governing classes. The research processes—conducting interviews, plundering local archives and family histories—necessarily involved dialogue between students and different members of the community which had obvious social benefits. By enacting other people's stories, students gained insights into the lives of others. This kind of social dialogue and cultural exchange invites self-reflexivity, a process which Charles Taylor (1992) describes as "dialogical action." He argues that dialogic action has a social purpose, in which other-understanding changes self-understanding:

Taylor, C. (1992). *Sources of the self.* Cambridge, UK: Cambridge University Press.

Much of our understanding of self, society and world is carried through dialogical action ... This means that our identity is never simply defined in terms of our individual properties. It also takes place in some social space (p. 173).

By encouraging young people to work with people of different ages and from diverse sectors of the community, I hoped to provide opportunities for them to extend the social space which they inhabited. Perhaps one of the most moving aspects of the work was the reaction of originators of the stories and the presentation of the students' devised work led to dialogue and exchange between the elderly members of different ethnic communities whose previous personal contact had been limited and sometimes strained. In this way, the combination of oral history and drama education had a social purpose insofar as it began to make hidden histories visible and public. But its weakness lay in the fact that the work did not really capture the aesthetic of memory, its instability and its contingency, with the effect that the past was presented as rational and ordered. As Paul Thompson (1978) points out, "oral history is not necessarily an instrument for change; it depends on the spirit in which it is used" (p. 22).

11.3 The evolution of a piece of reminiscence theatre
from *Older people act up: Making the ordinary extraordinary*
Howard Pflanzer. (1992). *TDR: The Drama Review, 36*(1), 115–123.

The JASA (Jewish Association for Services for the Aged) Theatre Ensemble, an older adult performing group . . . founded in 1984 by Dr. Susan Miller and myself with eight actors (four men, four women)[,] develops theatre pieces dealing with issues important to older people: doctors and health, rituals of daily life, childhood memories, and ageism. These pieces have been presented for diverse audiences ranging from medical students to school children and older adults.

[...]

The first public presentation of *A Matter of Life* (then titled *Cases: Doctors and Patients*) was a staged reading in November 1986 in a dimly lit student lounge area of the Health Sciences building of the Columbia College of Physicians and Surgeons. It was a dreary, rainy fall day but the atmosphere in the lounge was lively as 150 first-year medical students seated themselves on the floor ten rows deep, eagerly anticipating the start of the show.

[...]

The opening scene in the medical center waiting room began tentatively but as the students began to laugh uninhibitedly the actors forgot their fears and fully assumed their multiple roles as patients and doctors. Buoyed by the positive response, the performance was energetic. The issues had a real impact on the audience. During the discussion session afterwards a young woman asked: "Is there anything you can recommend to physicians whose patients are lonely and isolated and don't leave the house because of pain?" Minna answered without hesitation: "It's just showing caring." After the discussion the medical students broke up into 10 smaller groups (12–15 people each) led by the preceptors, with one of the actors as a resource person for each group. Each group focused on different topics and students engaged in open discussions with actors. As Dr. Constance Park, director of Columbia's Patient/Physician Relations course, said in her follow-up letter to us: "The course instructors as well as the students felt it was the high point of the semester." Everyone was "most engaged by this substantive production, by a skillful mixture of humor and matter-of-fact revelation which alerted them to the ways that physicians can either facilitate or hinder competent and caring health care delivery to the elderly." As evidence of the strong impact the theatre piece had on the students, she told us that a dozen students wrote "insightful, moving accounts of their grandparents' lives," which were "stunning in the openness, insight, and humanity the students revealed." She felt "the JASA Theatre Ensemble had played a significant role in encouraging these students to speak in their own voices, connecting deeply felt personal experiences with important issues in care of the elderly" and called the group "a significant educational force" (personal communication, 1987).

We were all excited by the success of the reading at Columbia. With extensive discussion and feedback from group members, we decided to expand the piece. . . . While reworking the piece we became less interested in it as an educational tool for medical personnel and more involved in it as a consciousness-raising piece for older audiences. The new version, now called *A Matter of Life,* was more negative. We forthrightly presented problems relating to health care but did not offer solutions. We attempted to empower both the members of the Ensemble and the audience to deal with these issues. As Augusto Boal (1985) says: "It is not the place of the theatre to show the correct path but only to offer the means by which all paths must be examined" (p. 141).

[...]

When Dr. Park spoke after the last performance we realized how far our political agendas diverged. She looked at our theatre piece as an "educational tool" for developing good medical practices for her students, while we saw it as a vehicle for criticism of the medical establishment and consciousness[-]raising for our audiences. She attacked the piece, calling it "polarizing" and dismissed *A Matter of Life* as exaggerated. Some of us felt she was blaming the victims for the problems of the system. Though we were all looking to improve medical care for older adults, our means were totally different. But after Dr. Park privately discussed the issues with us, we agreed to examine *A Matter of Life* with the members of the ensemble to see if we were treating the issues fairly. Eli suggested we end the piece with a clear presentation of both the older person's point of view and the doctors' point of view, emphasizing the need for cooperation between doctors and older patients.

To our surprise, in November 1987 we were invited by Dr. Park to perform at Columbia again. We had finished a third version of the script, which we later had misgivings about because its razor-sharp attacks had been somewhat blunted. The medical students were much more subdued during this performance than at our first appearance. The discussion that followed was a dialog mostly between the students and their professors.

Boal, A. (1985). *Theatre of the oppressed.* (C. & M. McBride, Trans.). New York, NY: Theatre Communications Group.

The actors were relegated to the margin.

Responding to the piece, one student asked: "What can we do to relate to the needs of older patients?" Dr. Park and the other professors answered with a litany: listening carefully, having the proper attitude, saving time by taking detailed histories, seeing patients more often for shorter periods of time. Dr. Park was caught in a dilemma. She wanted doctors to be sensitive to patients' needs, yet she had to defend the concerns of the medical profession.

A different audience in a different setting was encountered at Hunter College's Little Theatre. This performance was sponsored by the Brookdale/Mt. Sinai Geriatric Education Center for fourth-year medical students, nursing students, social workers, Touro College undergraduates, and older adults. The show was warmly received and there were some lively exchanges afterward. Talking of illness, a medical student said: "You have to learn to live with it." One of the older people replied: "You're in your residency and I'm much older[;] find another way to say it." Ida added: "Don't treat the age, treat the ailment." One woman did not like being called by her first name: "It was a lack of respect." Another felt doctors scoffed at complaints like dizziness. Several older people felt doctors were not interested in them medically or personally.

Fields, S. (1989). Miscellany: A matter of life. *The Gerontologist, 29*(2), 287-288.

Under the barrage of attacks[,] the medical students seemed defensive. But Dr. Suzanne Fields of Mt. Sinai Medical School seemed supportive of open dialog leading to changed attitudes and procedures. When she reviewed our video of *A Matter of Life* in *The Gerontologist* (1989) she wrote:

> Fourth-year medical students who viewed the play found it overwhelmingly negative in tone. They could not believe that health professionals could be so callous towards elderly patients and therefore could not relate to the characters (p. 288).

She felt our work "does succeed in raising one's consciousness about ageist biases that younger health professionals have towards elderly patients" (p. 289).

11.4 Interrogating reminiscence

from *Reminiscence and oral history: parallel universes or shared endeavour?* Joanna Bornat. (2001). *Ageing and Society, 21*, 219–241.

[...]

The Good Companions are a London-based group of older people, nine women and one man, who devised a play *Our Century and Us* with Pam Schweitzer, a well-known producer of reminiscence projects in the theatre, community and institutional settings.

The play dramatizes their memories through their words and, in so doing, presents a history of the 20th century which is both personal and public. Some memories are collective, others are quite individual. With songs and stories the play begins at the time of the performers' births in the 1920s and early 1930s, tracks through their growing-up years, their World War II experiences, their working lives and the changing pattern of family life, up to the present day. It is designed for audiences of older people, deliberately making links with audiences through shared experience and reinforcing messages with the help of contemporary songs and music. I was co-organiser of an international conference on "Biographical Methods and Professional Practice" held in London in October 2000. We invited *The Good Companions* to present this play as part of the programme.

As a member of the audience, I have a first-hand impression of the dynamics of the event. My understanding of the process has been further built up from reports and interviews with those involved. The experience was both moving and enlightening. Although we were confident about the skills of the performers and the relevance of the play to the content of our conference, we were worried that a group of amateur players, older people at that, might not be well received by the delegates. We should have addressed our own prejudices instead. The performance was wildly received by a group of academics, whose emotional responses belied the objectivity and detachment of their own highly professionalised presentations. Clearly something was at work here. The stories narrated by the performers had meanings which communicated across national and international boundaries with people whose backgrounds and ages implied quite different experiences of the 20th century. The performance ended with a standing ovation and lively discussions between the audience and the ten performers. . . .

During the play, one of the women takes the stage on her own to describe her experience of divorce in the 1950s. She describes the stigma, the exclusion and rejection which her erstwhile friends and neighbours visited on her. The other performers then joined in with brief exchanges to illustrate this cold and wounding behaviour.

The background to this scene was complex, as we discovered. In devising the play, the performers had discussed at some length how personal the play should be. In particular, in playing out her own real experience of divorce, was this actor in danger of "re-living" her humiliation and pain? In the end the scene was included and, in my view, the play was the better for it. Divorce in the middle years of the 20th century was difficult for many people, men and women. The performers recognised this and, for a while, the balance of the play shifted away from celebration and humour.

The process of arriving at this particular scene involved interrogation, on an individual and group basis. More than that, the scene inevitably interrogates audiences that include people who themselves are divorced or who have to come to terms with their own actions in relation to divorcing neighbours and relatives. The process of reminiscence is also interrogative and, while the individual account stands out as a performative act (whether in a play, a group or in a one-to-one exchange), the extent of that interrogation is set by the individuals taking part. Indeed, the background to the performance illustrates that people arrive at some kind of reconciliation with past life events by taking different paths. *The Good Companions* actor who played out her experience of divorce had not previously found a way to talk about this painful experience. The process of interrogation from her group members[,] and the shaping of the account for wider audiences, provided her with the means. Working in a reminiscence context enabled her to find a method, in this case a public performance.

In summary, this review of the methods of oral historians and reminiscence workers suggests that there are aspects which can usefully be shared. Awareness of the influence of age and life stage on how a story is narrated can help to broaden oral history, giving it relevance in policy and practice terms. Identifying the dialogic and interrogative nature of oral history helps to remind us that participation involves agency and decision-making, and that the interview is essentially an interactive process involving two parties, each with their own agendas and purposes.

Further Reading

Basting, A. D. (1995). The stages of age: The growth of senior theatre. *TDR: The Drama Review, 39*(3), 112–130. A good overview of the history of senior theatre and a case study from The Grandparent's Living Theatre.

Basting, A. D. (1998). *The stages of age: Performing age in contemporary American culture.* Ann Arbor, MI: University of Michigan Press. A collection of performance analyses of theatre projects with and by the elderly.

Basting, A. D. (2001). The time of our lives: International festival of reminiscence theatre [Review]. *Theatre Journal, 53*(1), 155–157. This festival was held at The Age Exchange and showcases performances by fourteen companies from eight different countries. Clear descriptions of shows reviewed.

O'Brien, B. C. (1985). *Encore!: Drama and theater with older players.* Eganville, ON: O'Brien Resource Center. This very rare book can be found through Worldcat Library Database. It is valuable as one of the first texts to document effective work with the elderly.

Kelin, D. A. (2005). *To feel as our ancestors did: Collecting and performing oral histories.* Toronto, ON: Pearson Education Canada. Useful information on the important and tactful ways of engendering memories and respecting the stories.

Schweitzer, P. (2007). *Reminiscence theatre: Making theatre from memories.* London: Jessica Kingsley. The text pretty well covers the waterfront. Pam Schweitzer, who began her career in Theatre in Education, has been working in reminiscence theatre for over twenty years, and this is a compendium of her experiences with many case studies.

Strimling, A. (2004). *Roots and branches: Creating multigenerational theatre.* Portsmouth, NH: Heinemann. A practical text that includes workshop and playbuilding activities with an appendix of monologues and scenes.

Questions for Discussion and Reflection

1. Who is the oldest person you know, what is your relationship with them, and how much do you know about them?

2. When is old, "old"?

3. What considerations we should have when a painful memory that has strong dramatic potential is shared?

4. What are some foundations for ethical practice when working with senior participants, some of whom may have impaired memory?

5. Within a culture so focused on celebrating youth, what responsibility does reminiscence theatre work have to counter the invisibility of the elderly? What positive examples of vital and engaged seniors can you contribute to the discussion?

Suggested Activities

1. Working collaboratively with others, identify two potential partner groups (e.g., an elementary school, high school, youth or university group and a neighborhood senior care facility) for an intergenerational reminiscence theatre project in your community. Write a letter of invitation to each, outlining the structure of the project and its benefits to those involved.

2. Working with a partner, generate a list of questions from which to conduct an interview focused on eliciting life memories. Using these, carry out an

interview—ideally, with a senior member of your family. You might like to practice with a classmate first.

3. Gather some examples from film, television, plays and other sources (novels, short stories, etc.) where senior characters are *central*, rather than peripheral. Present your research in a creative way—dramatically or visually (as in a poster)—in order to generate a discussion on how are these characters portrayed and what are the stereotypes and prejudices often embedded in these representations.

PART FOUR

Challenges for Practice

CHAPTER 12
PARTICIPATION, AESTHETICS, ETHICS AND ASSESSMENT

[D]rama is a politically incorrect and corrupting medium; it corrupts the certainties of received truths and identities with both dangers and possibilities.... It even-handedly shows the commonalities as well as the differences: our common humanness within the very otherness. But of course, like the contents of Pandora's box, drama is powerful and it is morally neutral so we have to be careful how we use it.

John O'Toole, 2004,
pp. 11–12

At the end of Chapter 2 of this text, we suggested that we would return to issues that were discussed briefly in that chapter and suggested some questions to think about as you moved through the various practices. You will have noticed, in every case study, that participation, aesthetics, ethics, and assessment are present in some form or other. These four motifs raise issues that are central to the practices of applied theatre. Much of what this chapter addresses falls with the designation of "contested" applications in the sense that while most agree that these four areas are significant, there is often disagreement about who or what they represent in applied theatre and how to go about structuring the work in ways that address these issues. Certainly, as a first motif, **participation** throughout all stages of a performance project is an ingredient that makes applied theatre work markedly different from mainstream theatre. Big Brum Theatre reminds us of that when in its mandate, it speaks of the "fluid boundary" that allows audiences to become active participants within the safety of the fictional action (www.bigbrum.org.uk).

The second motif is that of **aesthetics**. Lowell Swortzell in Jackson (1993) regretted the difficulties he had in "trying to like" Theatre in Education performances but he found it hard to accept the poor production values and the seeming lack of aesthetic sensibility. Why should schools not expect the very best production values, he wondered? In applied theatre performances today his objections still hold true in many cases. Denzin (1997) suggests that we "suspend normal aesthetic frameworks so that co-participatory performances can be produced" (p. 121). Whatever conclusions we come to, Jackson (1999), in discussing the educational experience of theatre, points out that the "aesthetic dimension must form an integral part of any serious evaluation" (p. 51). Feelings cannot be separated from thought or intellect but are, to put it crudely, the "glue" that makes things stick in the memory and accumulated remembered experiences comprise our learning (Damasio, 1999, pp. 54–56). That aesthetic learning enables us to see not only ourselves but also to reflect on the perspectives of others, helping us to wonder and imagine things "as if they could be otherwise" (Greene, 1988, p. 3). Does that mean we have to see aesthetic appreciation differently in applied theatre?

Applied theatre practices tend to be seen as always beneficial and certainly, it is unlikely that anyone would want to engage in a social practice that was not so. Yet, theatre is, as John O'Toole (2004) says, "morally neutral and so we have to be careful how we use it" (p. 12). Nicholson (1999) adds, "It has been claimed that the aesthetic enables individuals to reflect on the contrast between the conditions of everyday life and human potential and, as such, it acts as a powerful means of educating the political imagination" (p. 83) but the imagination, as we all know from our own experiences, can generate nasty as well as "nice" visions. As Eagleton (2008) reminds us, a lethal weapon is the result of an act of the imagination. The implications of that recognition demand that we pay more attention to the third motif of the **ethics** suffusing our work than perhaps we have heretofore. We need to be more careful, for example, in examining the way in which power is held and distributed, whose agendas are really being served by what we do, and how we leave the project sites.

> [Chantal] Mouffe argues that to accept that there are differing versions of the good life is to begin to recognise the plurality of cultures and multiplicity of voices in contemporary society.
> Helen Nicholson, 1999, p. 84

Lastly, how do we value what we do? By what criteria do we judge the effectiveness of the work? What are the implications of short-term results when laid against what traces remain years later? What claims can we make for "transformation" when the money has run out, the project is over and the facilitators have moved on? What is the language we are using to describe what we do and how is it helpful? What language is demanded by those to whom we are accountable? How can the languages of others assist us to make our case and how can we negotiate these languages so that everyone is clear about the results? Such questions lie at the heart of our fourth motif: **assessment.**

Assessment is an important element in the acquisition of funds and in justifying those expenditures. More significantly, how we assess, what we assess, and how we frame our assessments are central to effective research that will, in turn, promote advocacy that can stand on firm ground. At a purely personal level, we have a need to find satisfaction in what we do. With appropriate assessment, the field of applied theatre will grow and develop. Without it, the field will always remain vulnerable, subject to the economic bottom line and the whims of those who can help us to make this work happen: institutions; communities; donor organizations; and the prospective participants themselves.

Of course, these four motifs are always bound together, but this chapter attempts to separate them so that we can see them more clearly. We acknowledge that, in doing so, something may be lost.

12.1 Participation

In the traditional mainstream theatre (especially that of the Western world from the late 19th century on), audiences have been defined by their passivity, their submission to "theatre rules." We ask our audiences to come on time, sit still, refrain from talking (either to each other or to the actors), refrain from eating or drinking, to pay attention, and to suspend their disbelief. In order to help the audience to focus and to discourage any interaction, we place them in rows facing towards the stage, an arrangement that also makes it difficult for them to move around. They sit in darkness while the stage is lit in order to command their attention to the place and action that matters. While there is an understanding that a performance needs an audience in order to complete the act and that what is happening on stage is a reflection of the human condition of which the play and actors are representative, audiences in mainstream theatre are often viewed merely as "bums on seats" rather than as co-creators in the meaning-making (Butsch, 2000; Prendergast, 2008).

Paulus (2006) suggests that only when theatre is prepared to refocus its attention on the audience by waking them up and allowing them freedom of movement and choice; only when "the rules of audience etiquette" are rethought and the audience is regarded as co-collaborators can the "flow of energy that can only happen live in the presence of both parties" actually occur (p. 335). When it is clear to the audience that their presence is both appreciated and necessary, effective participation practices should allow audiences to decide the level of their involvement for themselves (p. 340).

In a productive postshow, audiences talk back, talk to each other and (with good facilitation) also listen to one another, making sense together of common experience... ."

Janna Goodwin, 2004, p. 317

For performer-participants in applied theatre, whose lives and words are the material of the performance, questions of ownership may arise. And while Jackson (2000) reminds us that this work is so localized that it does not generally "ou'live its historical moment" (p. 104), ownership can be a point of ethical contention if it is reproduced as script or as material for scholars; for example, in conference presentations and/or peer-reviewed publications.

When audiences become participants, we must honor the culture, rituals and characteristics of their context in order to enhance the flow of meaning. The audience is the source and the judge of the process and the performance. Their feedback needs to be constantly encouraged and not seen as something that only happens at "appropriate" or "safe" moments. For facilitators, this level of participation can be very difficult, as it requires an open mind, ability to put aside one's own agenda(s), and the grace to see value in critical responses.

Participation in applied theatre is not just confined to audiences, however. For many applied theatre companies, their partnerships within the local community are central to their practice, especially when members of that community become resources for the information upon which the work is based and may also be performers in the project. Time must be taken to ensure that each of the parties involved are clear about "what's up" and how everyone will be included within the communication loop. Maiter, Simich, Jacobson and Wise (2008), in their examination of the ethics of community-based participatory action research, point out the importance of this kind of contextual knowing for strengthening community partnerships that can only be productively built through taking time to build relationships and communicative networks (pp. 307-310). Central to this partnership must be the recognition that things may turn out differently from the original expectations. If people are included in the design and planning as experts in their own cultures, they will be aware of these shifts—when they occur and how the direction has changed—and why. To accept engagement with a creative process means that surprises are to be expected; how the partnerships are to be kept informed must be a part of the structuring of the project. One of the most important elements of feedback is that the stories and words that are drawn from the community must be "served back" to them before public performances as a way of checking the authenticity of the work and receiving permission for use. It is here that those whose stories are involved have the opportunity to withdraw them if they are not comfortable with having them played publicly. This is one of those matters that mesh participation, aesthetics and ethics and scenes that are aesthetically "right" may have to go because, ethically, it would not be right to use them.

Often, in addition to building a relationship with the community, there will be a partnership with a funding body, donor organization or institution. Again, the agendas need to be opened up for scrutiny and a continuing means of information exchange agreed upon. This does not mean that, having proposed and been accepted, the facilitator(s) are expected to be in touch with funders constantly and, indeed, such a thing may not be possible for many reasons. But the context that surrounds an applied theatre project must be a participatory one for all involved if the work is to be effective and seen to be effective. The most effective partnerships are those in which the conditions for participation are followed. Dudley Cocke (2004) writes eloquently about these issues in his discussion of how art interacts with democracy in applied theatre work.

...there is a growing appetite among citizens to do more than watch. This is cause for optimism, because the vitality of the arts in a democracy, like the vitality of democracy itself, rests on the participation of not just a few, but many.

Dudley Cocke, 2004, p. 173

The goal of the participatory component of applied theatre practice is one in which all those engaged with the performance (sources, players and audiences) are moved to become active and reflective through "wrestl[ing] with the consequences of their choices and actions" (Haedicke, 2003, p. 79). By participating in building and/or performing a fictional or parallel world, audiences (and players) gain the kind of distance that sets them free from their own bodies, specific situations and lives. It is this distance that allows participants to explore areas that, in real life, may have remained hidden or unexamined, perhaps through ignorance or fear (p. 78).

12.2 Artistry and Aesthetics

In traditional theatre, the focus is on the artistic making with a trust that if done "well," those attending the performance will have an aesthetic experience. Actors and directors meet together to interpret a scene artistically but, of course, the receptive aesthetic is at work in the process of creating a piece of theatre as much as it affects an audience's response. Maxine Greene (2001) defines this experience as new connections made, new patterns formed, new vistas opened; after an aesthetic experience, "persons see differently, resonate differently" (p. 6). The idea that "aesthetics" refers to the sensory, centering on the visceral and physical (Neelands & Goode, 1995, pp. 42, 44), places the practices of applied theatre as part of what Eric Booth (1999) calls "the everyday work of art," where the aesthetic lies not necessarily in an escape from reality but often in a return to it. When we find ways to talk about our hopes and dreams, our desires and wants and to share these through theatre as

> We should be clear about the fact that the Aesthetic Process is not the Work of Art. Its importance and its value reside in its stimulation and development of perceptive and creative capacities which may be atrophied in the subject—in developing the capacity, however small it may be, that every subject has for metaphorising reality. We are all artists, but few of us exercise our aesthetic capacities.
>
> Augusto Boal, 2006,
> p. 18

process and as product, we discover that we can make a difference to other's lives. In applied theatre, this can make it extremely difficult for any viewers who do not share the context—who come to the work as "outsiders," as accidental audiences.

In the early days of what, in Canada, was then called Popular Theatre, a group of women created a play from their experiences of domestic violence. The work was incredibly powerful for them, their small, mainly female, audiences, and for the facilitators. The women were persuaded to show their play as part of a conference of theatre scholars. The scholars responded in much the same way as Dr. Swortzell had in his attempts to enjoy TIE as an aesthetic experience. They had difficulty hearing the actors, the acting was unskilled and the production values completely absent. They saw the presentation as raw and unframed; they were confronted with a theatre experience they did not recognize and the subject matter was presented without the distancing devices of traditional production, leaving the audience with no idea of how to respond. For that accidental audience, there was no "aesthetic" present. And yet, for the integral audiences who first saw the work, there was an immediate recognition that promoted a powerful response both at a feeling and a thinking level. What creates this apparent dichotomy?

In mainstream theatre that is required to connect with an accidental audience— whoever it is that happens by—the work of transmitting the message can be extremely difficult. You will remember, of course, being told that the first 15 minutes of any play are the hardest—hardest for audiences "getting the picture" and hardest for actors helping them to do so. A traditional performance experience follows the Taxonomy of Engagement (Morgan & Saxton, 1987) by first attracting your interest, then engaging you (generally through its theatricality, force of argument or subtle manipulation of the elements of tension, contrast and/or symbolization). Once engaged, you have to be held long enough in the logic of what is happening for you to commit to the "idea" or world you are seeing and hearing; only then can you begin to internalize, unconsciously laying your own experience against that of the play to discover its truth by gathering its meanings—another way to say you begin to "get the message" (pp. 21–29).

In applied theatre, the first three parts of the taxonomy are almost always already in place; that is to say (unlike, for example, that audience of bewildered scholars), an integral audience is already interested and engaged (we recognize this, it is about us and concerns us). For the most part, they are committed to the content (if it's about us, we should listen) whether it is a celebration or a critique, and so the messages begin to arrive almost at once.

Christine Bailey (1987), writing about what we now call reminiscence theatre, says that, "Those who feel the art object...is a self-contained entity separate from its extrinsic contexts, will have difficulty seeing [applied] theatre as an artistic medium." "The seeming banality (at times), of [applied theatre] presentations," Bailey suggests, "is minimized because the audience is sympathetic to both the presentations and their sub-texts." As a result, she goes on, "an interaction takes place between performer and spectator that is an integral part of the process...[and] for those involved, it is an aesthetic experience. The intensity and degree of that experience varies from individual to individual and depends on the degree to which performers [and audiences] connect with the performance" (pp. 19–20). It is the full aesthetic impact of a performance that makes itself felt, as Jackson (2005) puts it, through the "'liveness' of the event, the emotional resonances it can offer, the dialogues that can be generated [either within or after the performance] and the complexity of texture that defies easy closure" (p. 117).

12.3 Ethics

"Ethics" refers to the principles or values by which a culture or group agrees to function, as in professional codes of conduct. "Ethical" refers to the ways in which someone functions in accordance with the cultural values or standards of the group. "Morals" and "morally" can be used interchangeably with ethics and ethically (see any dictionary definition), but for most people, morality suggests a set of values that has some sort of religious connotation (Hart, 2000, p. 96). We need to remember, however, that there are many people today who are extremely ethical and yet would not admit to a religious belief.

> ...[T]here is always the need to be vigilant about whether the practice is accepted as a generous exercise of care or whether, however well-intentioned, it is regarded as an unwelcome intrusion. It is easy for trust to become dependence, for generosity to be interpreted as patronage, for interest in others, to be experienced as the gaze of surveillance.
>
> Helen Nicholson, 2005, p. 160

All of us, whoever we are and wherever we live, conduct our lives by a set of standards. The standards under which we operate—often without even thinking about them—may be very different from those that govern the lives of the people with whom we are working. Applied theatre practitioners work with groups in their cultural contexts all the time and that "being inside" means that the ways in which facilitators conduct themselves are open to scrutiny. Facilitators generally are invited or appointed to work with a community, usually one with which they are not familiar; for instance, in a facilitating role, you may need to work in an institution such as a prison or a museum or with a group of disadvantaged people in a country different from your own. Even before you begin this work, you need to be clear about your own understanding of what is important to you, what it is that you value and see as fair, what it is that you are prepared to give up. You need to create a sense of safety for yourself and others that will free you and them to work at optimum.

Equally, the group and the individuals within that group may be governed by different views from you (and from each other) of what is important and valuable. You need always to be aware not only of those standards but what the implications of living within those standards mean. No group of people is wholly homogenous and it is helpful to discover how the community defines itself as a "community"—what does that mean to them and how is it manifested? For example, you may see the independence of women in a very different way from the societal group with whom you are working.

Always the work follows what it is that the group *together* with the facilitator develops and sometimes that work begins to move in directions that are different from what you had in mind. How prepared are you to follow the group's interest and, if it applies, to support that shift when reporting back to your funding agency? This is a particularly difficult question if the work you are doing is funded by an agency that has its own agenda, standards and educational history. In HIV/AIDS education in Africa, for example, there has been difficulty with the government funding from the United States. This funding is generous and well-intentioned; however, when the practices of abstinence over condom use is a condition of funding—contrary to the traditional practices of the societies for whom the funding is provided—the funding recipients find themselves between the proverbial "rock and a hard place" (Dalrymple, 2005).

Ethical practice depends upon *reflection* as a key means of intra- and inter-personal discovery, not only for the facilitator but also for the group. But many may not find reflection very easy or desirable in that it may pull up issues that have been deliberately hidden or cause participants to see things about themselves that they have heretofore self-censored. Safety in these instances is both imperative and an ethical requirement if insight is to be encouraged and supported. Maiter et al. (2008) suggest that reciprocity and trust are fundamental to effective ethical practice. Trust must be carefully built between facilitator and group and between the participants so that an atmosphere is built in which everyone feels comfortable in expressing their ideas, feelings and actions without censure. With trust established, the feedback loops then can become reciprocal—exchanges that are open and in which the power is equally shared. Power-sharing is possible because everyone is aware and informed about the process as it is taking place. While this is easy to describe in words, it is extremely difficult in practice.

Whether we are facilitators or facilitator-researchers, "the very last thing we might aim to do is 'dominate[,]' but the ethical dilemmas we invariably face demand that we choose to acknowledge and trouble the power inherent in our...roles," writes Gallagher (2006, p. 97), reminding us that facilitators must ever be aware of their status positions. Awareness through continuous reflection is one way to keep our work, ourselves and our fellow-participants in ethical balance. Gallagher also reminds us of Conquergood's (1985) four "ethical pitfalls"—the Custodian's Rip-off (using texts [often sacred] without permission); the Enthusiast's Infatuation (trivializing the lives of participants by allowing our enthusiasm to prevent us from becoming deeply involved in their cultural setting); the Curator's Exhibitionism (presenting the material as a kind of curiosity for others to wonder at); and the Skeptic's Cop-out (refusing to face up to the "ethical tensions and moral ambiguities of performing culturally sensitive materials") (p. 8).

In the end, ethical practice is about being aware that "every time a text is performed, a performance ethics is enacted" (Denzin, 1997, p. 120), reminding us to ask the question, "What are we doing here in someone else's cultural context?" and to take responsibility for what is interpreted, what points of view are espoused, and who it is that makes up our audience (p. 121). Denzin concludes by writing, "empowerment begins in that ethical moment when individuals are led into the troubling spaces once occupied by others. In the moment of co-performing, lives are joined and the struggle [begins] anew" (p. 122). How we co-perform is, Denzin suggests, a matter of seeing that what we perform is "dialogic." He means that we need to be aware at all times that we are not "speaking about," but rather, "to and with others, keeping [the work] open-ended; critiquing, interrupting and empowering" (p. 121). Through those facilitated dialogues emerge the questions that participants need to ask and the language with which to ask them. The ethical demands of applied theatre practice are energy, imagination, commitment and the ability, as Maxine Greene (1995, p. 31) puts it, to decenter ourselves in the interests of the greater good—a good that derives from the participants' communally agreed-upon agenda.

12.4 Assessment/Evaluation

How can we assess the impact of applied theatre work, not just in terms of what an applied theatre performance transmits (the learning) but also in terms of its aesthetic impact (the reception)? Elliot Eisner (2007) is perhaps the most helpful when he writes, "there is no hard and fact distinction between assessment and evaluation, but there is a tendency to think about assessment as pertaining to judgments about individuals and evaluation as pertaining to the appraisals of programs" (p. 423).

Whatever the kind of theatre we practice, one of the most persistent questions is, "Well, how did it work?" In applied theatre practice, there are many things that we could talk about in answer to this question and many areas of assessment and/or evaluation. Each of those areas can be fraught with difficulty because, as Nicholson (1999) points out, whatever we are assessing or evaluating is "bound" by the context, the conditions and, we would add, the capacities of the participants. Paul Newman, in an interview (2008) once remarked that "in films, the definition of 'good' is always murky" and "murky" is indeed an appropriate adjective when we are discussing how and what we value in the arts.

[A]ll evaluations, including aesthetic judgments, are contingent [dependent upon conditions] and contextually [the circumstances that surround events] bound.

Helen Nicholson, 1999, p. 84

In mainstream theatre, success is judged by the response of the critics (single voices also bound by their own context, conditions and capabilities) and, contingent upon that subjective judgment, by the financial returns that must both cover the costs of production and the investments of backers. In applied theatre, judging success is very different depending upon the type of project; it is the nature of the project that will dictate, to a greater or lesser degree, the sorts of evaluative procedures that can be undertaken. The three major project types are: those that are generated in response to a perceived need; those that are funded for a specific purpose; and those that are created for research purposes. In each case, there will be an assortment of guidelines, goals, aims, objectives and purposes—some will be set out specifically and others will be more general in their descriptions. For each type, facilitators will need to address the question: How will this (goal, objective, aim, purpose or outcome) be demonstrated?

The following supplementary questions apply both to any project as a whole and to each element of a project as it emerges. Assessment considers everything from the initial meetings and setting up, the research, development and rehearsal phases, the presentation itself and, of course, the organization and facilitation of the interactions with the audience at the presentation as well as those interactions that may take place before and/or after the presentation.

- What will be seen?
- What skills will be required in order for that to take place?
- What will be looked at specifically in order to consider (and value) the effect?

These questions refer only to the actual elements that make up the event. Beyond that, facilitators will need to consider such things as:

- The degree and quality of participation
- The rhythm, form, pace and structuring (aesthetic)
- The risks, trust, sharing and caring of participants (ethics)

These in turn, are balanced by:

- The conditions that surround the creation of the event (space, time, support and so on)
- The skills that are brought to the work by the facilitator(s)
- The response(s) of the audience
- The ways in which the participants and the project may be provided for after the facilitators leave

One of the least-addressed, but not the least important, planning points are the exit strategies; in exiting from an applied theatre process, practitioners are ethically bound to create—preferably in collaboration with participants—an action plan that aims to continue the process following their departure. A "good" project should contain "clear evidence of effective planning to sustain [the partnership] beyond the funding support" (Burnaford, Aprill & Weiss, 2001, p. 240). A significant aspect of applied theatre practice is a knowledge of teaching in order to be able to facilitate the transfer of skills from practitioners to participants. For the whole list of prompts, the evaluators must factor in their own biases and preferences and how these affect their assessment. This is where field notes, in the form of a log and/or reflective journal, become key.

Even after the grant is over, and the "passion" of the funding subsides, you gave birth to a child that needs nurturing.

Jorge Merced, Associate
Director of Pregones
Theater in Sato, 2005, p. 55

All this sounds a bit like counting the angels on the head of a pin and, for that reason, many practitioners do not pay much attention to assessment because, in the end, they know that whatever they may value and offer in proof, they can often be wrong. For example, Ross Prior (2005) points out that one of the difficulties of group playbuilding is that shared meanings may not be shared at the deepest level; that players can "own" the work but not necessarily the content (p. 62). His experience is paralleled by final year drama student collectives who created, over a number of years as their final assignment, excellent pieces of playbuilt work about drinking and driving, supported by MADD (Mothers Against Drunk Driving) and local police organizations in Lower Vancouver Island. All those who supported it deemed the project successful: teachers, including the facilitating teacher, and outside agents, present not only at the performances but also at the talkback and workshop sessions. They all agreed that the audiences learned a great deal (demonstrated by the questions they asked), were thoughtful and concerned (as shown through their improvised scenes in follow-up workshops), and were able to generate useful suggestions for further action (writing). But despite the participants' research, their commitment to the project and the demands of touring to local schools, they themselves, it was later discovered, did not follow their own advice. Anthony Jackson (personal communication, July 2008) has noted that same disconnect and suggests that this may be because "school" and the "real world" are seen as totally separate: what participants learn in school is not seen as being connected with their lives outside. Although it met all the criteria, can the drinking and driving project be truly judged a success?

This example does not, however, reduce the need and the importance of considering project assessment as a fundamental component of effective practice and, importantly, central to advocating for the field itself. Assessment is not something to be done only by facilitators. Participants need to be included in assessment/evaluation processes, not simply as resources for feedback but as designers of that feedback. In this way, participants feel a sense of true ownership of the project over its entire course; they are enabled to feel that they are people who are capable of doing and not simply of being done to. Journaling, interviews, focus groups, a series of follow-up sessions (see Jackson's elegant research on the effects of museum education projects, 2000, 2002, 2005) are all valuable means of recording,

> Heisenberg's theory of uncertainty... dictates that anything under observation will change its course as a direct result of being observed. If that is the case, can anything be observed with any accuracy, be it the movement of particles or the interplay of human motives?
>
> Richard Eyre & Nicholas Wright, 2001, pp. 331–332

> In 20 years of activist theatre I do not believe I have raised anyone's consciousness, or liberated them, or brought them new understanding. I have, however, been changed with and through others, and they I hope, with and through me....in theatre, as in life, we develop one another.
>
> Bertolt Brecht, in McDonnell, 2005, p. 73

discovering and validating raised awareness, changes in behavior and action taken or advanced. In the end, we are guided by the ethical principle that an "aesthetics of cultural democracy be considered in the light of its intentions and values and evaluated on its own terms; Rustom Bharucha's question—"Is it right?"—is primary" (Little, 2008, p. 3).

There are many who make claims for applied theatre's transformative powers. "Transformation" is a theatre term used to signify an "apparently miraculous change in a stage set" (Stein, 1966, p. 1505) and the verb "to transform" is a synonym for "to convert." Until there is a way to assess, quantitatively and/or qualitatively, such theatrical power, we are on stronger ground when we limit our claims to what we know applied theatre can do. It is a theatre that, in the words of Australian scholar Kate Donelan (2007), provides "space for social dreaming." It encourages participants to create dialogue through imagining and enacting possibilities. It is a theatre that does not tell what *must* be done but, rather, in offering a multiplicity of perspectives, invites questions that may, perhaps, initiate action in the search for answers (see Paterson, 2001, p. 65). As Kushner (2001) reminds us, "art is not merely contemplation, it is also action and all action changes the world, at least a little" (p. 62). It is possible that, as Heritage (2004) points out, too much emphasis on results and the instrumental benefits can submerge the very real power of what art itself can do for the people who engage with it. "Do no harm" applies equally to the art form itself.

Summary

Motifs are distinctive ideas that recur as forms or shapes in a work of art. The four motifs presented in this chapter—participation, aesthetics, ethics and assessment—are recursive constants in any applied theatre process. We acknowledge the contestation and murkiness of these areas and recognize that debate around these motifs will continue—the mark of a growing and vigorous field. The art that lies within applied theatre practices is reflective and dynamic, giving us the social spaces in which to dream. Applied theatre presents us with a mirror of our lives and is the imaginative tutor of our future possibilities and action.

Further Reading

Participation

Haedicke, S. (2003). The challenge of participation: Audiences at Living Stage Theatre Company. In S. Kattwinkel (Ed.), *Audience Participation: Essays on inclusion in performance* (pp. 71–87). Westport. CN: Praeger. This chapter uses the work of the Living Stage Theatre company that lies more firmly in the semi-private than semi-public. However, their use of professionals as facilitators provides valuable insight into those processes.

Paulus, D. (2006). It's all about the audience. *Contemporary Theatre Review, 16*(3), 334–347. Paulus describes two shows that, like the reading above, blur the line, this time between semi-public and public, but what the author has to say about how audiences can be engaged through contemporary methods is very useful information.

Aesthetics

Boal, A. (2006). *The Aesthetics of the Oppressed* (A. Jackson, Trans.). London, UK: Routledge. This text is a whirlwind ride in Boal's inimitable style, through his years of practice. Many useful examples of his practice and the philosophy that underlies it.

Samson, F. (2005). Drama in aesthetic education: An invitation to imagine the world as if it could be otherwise. *The Journal of Aesthetic Education, 39*(4), 70–81. A thorough description of the use of Ping Chong's documentary theatre to develop an understanding of aesthetic education in pre-service teachers and teachers in the field attending a Lincoln Centre Institute course.

Ethics

Maiter, S., Simich, L., Jacobson, N. and Wise, J. (2008). Reciprocity: An ethic for community-based research. *Action Research, 6*(3), 305–325. For practitioners and researchers, this is a rich discussion of procedures for setting up and maintaining a communicative network with a focus on power sharing.

Shaughnessy, N. (2005). Truth and lies: Exploring the ethics of performance applications. *RIDE: Research in Drama Education, 10*(2), 201–212. Apart from the interesting issues raised by the basics of theatre performance (it is all a "big lie"), there are two useful case studies that examine the "lies" in practice and the ethical questions that derive from them.

Assessment/Evaluation

Eisner, E. (2007). Assessment and evaluation in education and the arts. In L. Bresler (Ed.), *International Handbook of Research in Arts Education* (pp. 423–426). Dordrecht, NL: Springer. This synthesis of the problems of assessment/evaluation should be required reading for anyone involved in measuring outcomes in applied theatre.

Robinson, K. (1993). Evaluating TIE. In A. Jackson (Ed.), *Learning through Theatre* (pp. 251–266). London, UK: Routledge. Although the date is early, this discussion and examination of the "areas of evaluative action" is really indispensable, particularly as it uses a Theatre in Education program as its model and is therefore rooted in the realities of the practice.

Questions for Reflection and Discussion

1. In developing a new understanding of the function of the audience, what changes do you see that might need to be made in actor training? In learning to be a director?

2. If audiences are to be recognized and involved, what practical implications are there in constructing a presentation and its audience intervention strategies?

3. What other kinds of theatre have encouraged audience participation and what was the quality of that participation? What can we learn from these historical antecedents?

4. What kinds of questions do you need to ask yourself before you begin your work and where will you find those answers? What are you listening for as you introduce the work and what sorts of concerns should you have about what you hear?

5. Two useful questions from Shaughnessy (2005) to chew upon: 1) When is it right to make the private public? 2) The actor is a master of pretense, mimicry and artifice; what are the ethics of using these methodologies when we are working with real lives? (p. 202).

6. Some other questions worth thinking about: Who decides what stories are told? Who decides whose stories are told? When may a discussion about a presentation not be safe for the participants? What needs to be done to make it safe?

Suggested Activity

The situation: A funding agency has provided information and project guidelines for facilitators they have hired to work with homeless men in an effort to help them to build job-seeking skills. The facilitators have consulted widely with social agencies and drawn up a plan that will extend over ten weeks, with a possibility of some kind of presentation—to whom and what about will be decided by the participants. As the facilitators meet with the community and get to know them, it becomes clear that the need the agency sees as being important is not what the men have identified. Libraries and other public spaces do not tolerate people who have simply come in to get out of the weather; the men are constantly being moved on. They need a place to go to be warm in the winter, dry in the rain, and out of the weather. They need somewhere that is open daily where they can remain for as long as they need until it is time to seek the night shelter. Keeping warm and having a safe place are two most basic of Maslow's (1968) hierarchy of needs. Without these assurances, finding a job is, for the men, an exercise in futility, not to mention that they have a tendency to see the whole "exercise" as an opportunity for "do-gooders" to slum a little! It is clear to the facilitators that the funding agency is not up to date with—and perhaps not sympathetic to—the needs of this constituency.

1. What research do you need to do to familiarize yourself with the issue of homelessness? What areas of importance can you identify to bring forward to your group?

2. With your group, search out an agency that works with street people. What do they believe to be the needs of their clients?

3. Search out a potential group of participants, preferably with the cooperation of the agency. What do these homeless people identify as their needs?

4. With your group, create a proposal for an applied theatre project to work with this clientele. As you do so, consider the following:

    a) What information would be helpful to you in deciding what to do? What strategies might you use? What exit strategies are available?
    b) Identify any potential ethical dilemmas that facilitators may face.
    c) Outline a procedure for addressing these possible shifts in intentions.
    d) Consider how you will go about dealing with shifting intentions with your own group members, with the funding agency, with the clients, with the community at large, and with the local government.
    e) Look at the assessment instruments used by the agency and use it as a template for an assessment instrument. How will you include the participants in designing your assessment procedures?

5. Present your proposal and ask the funding agency to provide you with feedback as to how they see the project as appropriate to their mandate.

6. If the funding agency or participants suggest a shift in focus, what changes would need to be made to the proposal, keeping ethical issues in mind?

7. Continue to revise your proposal until the agency, participants and you, as facilitators, are all comfortable with the guidelines for the project.

8. If it is possible, implement your project.

Reflection

The quality of reflection usually reflects the quality of the experience but, strangely enough, even a rather flat or mundane experience can often be lifted into something much greater than itself through reflection. The act of simply thinking about something with other people can enable insights into things that were not apparent while inside the experience; when reflection happens together, shared insights deepen and extend that experience. When there is no time for reflection, the opportunity is lost and at the same time, we lose the ability to see ourselves and our actions in relation to our community and the environment. Shared reflections help to build, extend and enhance collective visions. To slight or forget reflection as an imperative element in the operation of applied theatre is to lose the opportunity to exercise what Antonio Damasio (1995) calls "our unique human properties"—the ability to anticipate what may happen, make plans, look after ourselves and other people responsibly and maintain our lives with thought and care (p. 10).

> [O]nly humans are capable of observing themselves in action. By observing myself in action, this dichotomization allows me to change my way. That's why culture is possible: because we humans are capable of looking at ourselves in action. . . . We observe ourselves and say, "If I am here I can go there. If I have done like this, I can do like that."
>
> Augusto Boal, in Delgado & Heritage, 1996, p. 35

The heart of the reflective process is the space it provides to bring into existence a personal relationship with the material. Reflection allows time to consider the moral attitudes, principles, and beliefs that lie beneath actions and to see these in relation to the views, actions and feelings of others. Reflection lets us see how ideas are mediated and how thought is changed when it becomes concretized through action. Eric Booth (1999) notes how hard it is for people to reflect. "Many," he writes, "have an ingrained bias" against such an activity, deeming their thoughts not 'worth noticing'" (p. 54). For facilitators, reflection can be one of the most difficult activities to initiate but, once begun, as Booth points out, participants "come to respect experience-awareness as a skill that directly taps into the feeling of being alive" (p. 54).

The arts allow those who practice them and those who consume them to imagine alternative states of mind and being. This is a political function of art. Imagined communities allow us to get critical distance and critical perspectives on our own political condition and potentially to transform it.

> Garth Allen, 2006,
> p. 291

Reflection is taking experience and looking at it critically, variously, publicly ... Reflection steps back and examines past experiences in the light of other connections and experiences. It is a reconstruction of actions taken; it is a re-look at meanings made.

> William Doll, Jr. 1993,
> p. 141.

... landings of past thought ..are also stations of departure for subsequent thought.

> John Dewey, 1933/1971,
> p. 75

Jerome Bruner in *Acts of Meaning* writes about our two "dazzling" intellectual capacities: first, the ability to "turn around on the past and alter the present in its light, or to alter the past in the light of the present" and, second, the capacity "to envision alternatives, to conceive of other ways of being, of acting, of striving."

> 1990, pp. 109–110

If, as Garth Allen (2006) says, the arts enable the kind of distance and viewpoints that help participants to understand where they have positioned ourselves, the potential for change and perhaps, transformation will only occur through reflecting on what has happened in the safety of a metaphoric world that the theatre experience has created. When groups reflect, they bring past experiences into relationship with the present and, in so doing, are better able to see where it is that they want to go. This sense of the future generates motivation and hope and is important for building a sense of identity within the group and for each member of that group. Reflection develops the skills of assessment, helping participants think about their work and to see how what they have been doing has substance and purpose, that their work has real value. Reflection helps participants to organize their thoughts and legitimizes the place of feelings within their own work.

Reflection:

- encourages participants to think about how and what they could have done differently;
- presses participants to consider that no action is without implications for themselves and others;
- enables them to be aware of the innovative ideas that can emerge when they work together;
- encourages participants, through a safe and trusting environment, to develop their critical and analytical skills that, in turn,
- builds participants' aesthetic and artistic standards.

Through reflection, participants have an opportunity to consider the ethical and moral

It is through experience that we make reasoned choices; not the experience of just doing but of reflecting on what we do; experience that is analyzed through the lenses of culture, language and personal bias.

> William Doll, Jr., 1993,
> p. 130

implications of their work and to set those considerations within the wider contexts of their culture. It is, writes Doll (1993), the "only reliable guide to further action" (p. 141).

The best reflection is recursive, functioning in the same way that the theatrical rehearsal process works; that is to say, by going back and back again over things experienced by the group, participants are enabled to see how their ideas, thoughts and feelings work together to build the group's sense of efficacy in the world. But such reflective activity is not something that works for the participants only. Reflection is an essential strategy for facilitators: it is something that, with more and more experience, can be used in the midst of what is happening—reflection-in-action (Schön, 1984). Reflection-on-action is more easily acquired; here the reflection is on what has happened in order to know how to move the work forward, on what worked or was not effective, on one's own ideas, thoughts and feelings, on what needs to be done again, what needs to be let go. As Freire (2000) argues, action without reflection is unproductive both for ourselves and for our participants (p. 87). And reflection is not something to be used only for closure; it must occur throughout the process, building new awareness upon which the work can capitalize.

In his discussion of genius, Malcolm Gladwell (1999) writes that the best candidates are those who have "the ability to rethink everything they have done and imagine how they might have done it differently" (p. 60). Such reflection is not limited to the genius; it also makes effective the work of applied theatre facilitators and their groups. And those groups include the audiences to which the act of theatre is applied. While it may not always be applicable or, indeed, politically safe to reflect with the audience, reflection—generally speaking—is an important extension of the performance for everyone concerned.

Theatre is not just a place, not simply a profession. It is a metaphor. It helps to make the process of life more clear.... [W]hen the population assembles in a special place under special conditions to partake in a mystery, the scattered limbs are drawn together and a momentary healing reunites the larger body, in which each member, re-membered, finds its place.

> Peter Brook, 1998,
> p. 196

In reflection, the first simple thoughts, as they bounce back and forth, become more complex ideas as they mix together. Within the richness created through reflection can always be found new ways of thinking about ourselves and the world; within those thoughts lie the unlimited opportunities for healing, as the community is re-membered through the act of theatre.

Further Reading

What are the books and journals that you would like on your bookshelves to help you build your understanding and strengthen your practice?

Questions for Discussion

What questions would you now want to pose to colleagues for discussion?

Suggested Activity

With your group, create a number of scenarios that mark your learning in applied theatre and share them with the class.

BIBLIOGRAPHY

Note: Texts, articles and media sources listed under Further Reading in each chapter are not repeated here.

Afzal-Khan, F. (2001). Exposed by Pakistani street theater: The unholy alliance of postmodern capitalism, patriarchy, and fundamentalism. *Social Text, 19*(4), 67–91.

Allen, G. (2006). The arts and the cult of performance. *Arts & Humanities in Higher Education, 5*(3), 291–304.

Anouilh, J. (1951). *Antigone* (L. Golantiere, Trans.). London, UK: Methuen. (Original work published in 1942).

Arnold, R. (1998). The drama in research and articulating dynamics—a unique theatre. In J. Saxton & C. Miller (Eds.), *Drama and theatre in education: The research of practice/the practice of research* (pp. 110–131). Victoria, BC: IDEA Publications.

Arnold, R. (2005). *Empathic intelligence: Teaching, learning, relating.* Sydney, NSW: UNSW Press.

Arrabal, F. (1973). *The panic.* Paris, France: Union générale d'Édition.

Bailey, C. (1987). "Soul clap its hands and sing": Living History Theatre as a process of creation. *Activities, Adaptation, Aging, 9*(4), 1–43.

Balfour, M. (Ed.). (2004). *Theatre in prisons: Theory and practice.* Bristol, UK: Intellect Books.

207

Ball, S. (1994). Theatre and health education: Meeting of minds or marriage of convenience? *Health Education Journal, 53,* 222–225.

Barnhart, C.L. (Ed.). (1965). *Thorndike-Barnhart comprehensive desk dictionary.* New York, NY: Doubleday and Company.

Basting, A. (1995). The stages of age: The growth of senior theatre. *TDR: The Drama Review, 39*(3), 112–130.

Baugh, C. (1994). Brecht and stage design. In P. Thomson & G. Sacks (Eds.), *The Cambridge companion to Brecht* (pp. 235–253). Cambridge, MA: Cambridge University Press.

Beckerman, B. (1990). *Theatrical presentation: Performer, audience and act.* New York, NY: Routledge.

Blau, H. (1965). *The impossible theatre: A manifesto.* New York, NY: Collier.

Boal, A. (1979). *Theatre of the oppressed.* London, UK: Pluto Press.

Boal, A. (1992). *Games for actors and non-actors* (A. Jackson, Trans.). London, UK: Routledge.

Boal, A. (1995). *The rainbow of desire: The Boal method of theatre and therapy* (A. Jackson, Trans.). London, UK: Routledge.

Boal, A. (1998). *Legislative theatre: Using performance to make politics* (A. Jackson, Trans.). London, UK: Routledge.

Boal, A. (2006). *The aesthetics of the oppressed* (A. Jackson, Trans.). London, UK: Routledge.

Bond, E. (1996). Notes on imagination. In *Coffee, xxxxiv.* London, UK: Methuen Drama.

Booth, E. (1999). *The everyday work of art: Awakening the extraordinary in your daily life.* Napierville, IL: Sourcebooks.

Bray, E. (1991). *Playbuilding: A guide for group creation of plays with young people.* Sydney, NSW: Currency Press.

Bridal, T. (2004). *Exploring museum theatre.* Walnut Creek, CA: Altamira.

Brook, P. (1968). *The empty space.* London, UK: Penguin.

Brook, P. (1998). *Threads of time.* Washington, DC: Counterpoint.

Bruner, J. (1990). *Acts of meaning.* Cambridge, MA: Harvard University Press.

Burnaford, G., Aprill, A. & Weiss, C. (Eds.). (2001). *Renaissance in the classroom: Arts integration and meaningful learning.* Mahwah, NJ: Lawrence Erlbaum Associates Inc.

Bury, A., Popple, K. & Barker, J. (1998). "You've got to think really hard": Children making sense of the aims and content of theatre in health education. *RIDE: Research in Drama Education, 3*(1), 13–27.

Butsch, R. (2000). *The making of American audiences: From stage to television, 1750–1990.* Cambridge, UK: Cambridge University Press.

Butterwick, S. & Selman, J. (2003). Deep listening in a popular feminist theatre project: Upsetting the position of audience in participatory education. *Adult Education Quarterly, 54*(1), 7–22.

Carlson, M. (1993). *Theories of the theatre: A historical and critical survey, from the Greeks to the present* (Expanded edition). London, UK: Cornell University Press.

Chinyowa, K. (2007). Frames of metacommunication: Examples from African theatre for development. *NJ: Drama Australia Journal, 31*(1), 33–43.

Cocke, D. (1993). The aesthetics of community-based artmaking. Unpublished essay.

Cocke, D. (2004). Art in a democracy. *TDR: The Drama Review, 48*(3), 165–178.

Coleridge, S. T. (1817). *Biographia literaria.* Retrieved February 28, 2007 from www. english.upenn.edu/~mgamer/Etexts/biographia.html.

Conquergood, D. (1985). Performing as a moral act: Ethical dimensions of the ethnography of performance. *Literature in Performance, 5*, 1–13.

Copfermann, E. (1972). *La mise en crise théâtrale*. Paris, France: François Maspéro.

Cox, M. (Ed.). (1992). *Shakespeare comes to Broadmoor: The performance of tragedy in a secure psychiatric hospital*. London, UK: Jessica Kingsley.

Croyden, M. (2003). *Conversations with Peter Brook, 1970–2000*. New York, NY: Faber & Faber.

Dalrymple, L. (2005). Dramaide: An evaluation of interactive drama and theatre for HIV/AIDS education in South Africa. Paper given at the 5th International Conference on Researching Drama and Theatre Education, University of Exeter, April.

Damasio, A. (1995). *Descartes error: Emotion, reason and the human brain*. New York, NY: Penguin.

Damasio, A. (1999). *The feeling of what happens: Body and emotion in the making of consciousness*. New York, NY: Harcourt.

Delgado, M. & Heritage, P. (Eds.). (1996). Augusto Boal. In M. Delgado & P. Heritage (Eds.), *Contact with the gods? Directors talk theatre* (pp. 15–35). Manchester, UK: Manchester University Press.

Denzin, N. (1997). *Interpretive ethnography*. London, UK: Sage.

Dewey, J. (1933/1971). *How we think*. Chicago, IL: Henry Regnery.

Doll, W. (1993). *A post-modern perspective on curriculum*. New York, NY: Teachers College Press.

Donelan, K. (2007). Drama in the 21st Century curriculum: An Australian perspective. Keynote paper presented at IDEA World Congress, Hong Kong, July 18.

Dutlinger, A. (2001). *Art, music and education as strategies for survival: Theresienstadt 1941–45*. New York, NY: Herodias.

Eagleton, T. (2008). "Coruscating on thin ice." Review of *Creation, artists, gods and origins* by Peter Conrad. *London Review of Books*. 24 January.

Edson, M. (1999). *Wit*. New York, NY: Broadway Play Publishing.

Eisner, E. (2007). Interlude 26: Assessment and evaluation in education and the arts. In L. Bresler (Ed.), *International handbook of research in arts education* (pp. 423–426). Dordrecht, The Netherlands: Springer.

Ellis, A. (2000). The art of community conversation. *Theatre Topics, 10*(2), 91–100.

Esslin, M. (1976). *Anatomy of drama.* New York, NY: Hill and Wang.

Eyre, R. & Wright, N. (2001). *Changing Stages: A view of British theatre in the twentieth century.* London, UK: Bloomsbury.

Filewod, A. (1987). *Collective encounters: Documentary theatre in English Canada.* Toronto, ON: University of Toronto Press.

Foreman, R. (1976). *Plays and manifestos.* New York, NY: New York University Press.

Freire, M. (2007). A different kind of community theatre: Performance projects with GLBT adolescents. *Teaching Artist Journal, 5*(4), 243–252.

Freire, P. (2000). *Pedagogy of the oppressed: 30ᵗʰ anniversary edition* (M.B. Ramos, Trans.). New York, NY: Continuum (Original work published in 1970).

Gallagher, K. (2006). Pondering ethics: Viewpoints. *RIDE: Research in Drama Education, 1*(1), 96–98.

Giannachi, G. & Luckurst, M. (1997). *On directing.* New York, NY: St. Martin's Griffin.

Giesekam, G. (2006). Applied theatre/Drama: An e-debate in 2004: Viewpoints. *RIDE: Research in Drama and Education, 1*(1), 96–98.

Gladwell, M. (1999). The physical genius. *New Yorker*, August 2, 57–65.

Goleman, D. (1995). *Emotional Intelligence.* New York, NY: Random House.

Goleman, D. (2006). *Social Intelligence.* New York, NY: Random House.

Goodwin, J. (2004). The productive postshow: Facilitating, understanding and optimizing personal narratives in audience talk following a personal narrative performance. *Theatre Topics, 14*(1), 317–338.

Gray, R. (2003). *Prostate tales: Men's experiences with prostate cancer.* Harriman, TN: Men's Studies Press.

Gray, R. (2004). Performing for whom? Spotlight on the audience. In A. Cole, L. Neilsen, J. G. Knowles, & T. Luciani (Eds.), *Provoked by art: Theorizing arts-informed research* (pp. 238–249). Halifax, NS: Backalong Books & Centre for Arts-informed Research.

Gray, R., Fitch, M. I., LaBrecque, M. & Greenberg, M. (2003). Reactions of health professionals to a research-based theatre production. *Journal of Cancer Education, 18*(4), 223–229.

Gray, R. & Sinding, C. (2002). *Standing ovation: Performing social science research about cancer.* Walnut Creek, CA: Alta Mira Press.

Greene, M. (1988). *The dialectic of freedom.* New York, NY: Teachers College Press.

Greene, M. (1995). *Releasing the imagination: Essays on education, the arts, and social change.* San Francisco, CA: Jossey-Bass.

Greene, M. (2001). *Variations on a blue guitar: The Lincoln Center Institute lectures on aesthetic education.* New York, NY: Teacher College Press.

Grotowski, J. (1968). *Towards a poor theatre.* New York, NY: Simon & Schuster.

Haedicke, S. (2003). The challenge of participation: Audiences at Living Stage Theatre Company. In S. Kattwinkel (Ed.), *Audience participation: Essays on inclusion in performance* (pp. 71–87). Westport, CN: Praeger.

Handke, P. (1971). *Offending the audience/Self-accusation.* London, UK: Methuen.

Hart, H. (2000). Religious conflicts, public policy, and moral authority. In J. Olthuis (Ed.), *Towards an ethics of community: Negotiations of difference in a pluralistic society* (pp. 91–126). Waterloo, ON: Wilfred Laurier University Press.

Hennessy, J. (1998). The theatre in education actor as researcher. *RIDE: Research in Drama Education, 3*(1), 85–92.

Heritage, P. (2004). Taking hostages: Staging human rights. *TDR: The Drama Review, 48*(3), 96–106.

Hughes, C., Jackson, A. & Kidd, J. (2007). The role of theatre in museums and historic sites: Visitors, audiences, and learners. In L. Bresler (Ed.), *International handbook of research in arts education* (pp. 679–696). Dordrecht, The Netherlands: Springer.

Jackson, Adrian. (1995). Translator's introduction. In A. Boal, *The rainbow of desire: The Boal method of theatre and therapy* (pp. xvii–xxvi). London, UK: Routledge.

Jackson, A. (1993). *Learning through theatre: New perspectives on theatre in education.* London, UK and New York, NY: Routledge.

Jackson, A. (1999). The centrality of the aesthetic in educational theatre, *Drama Australia, 23*(2), 51–63.

Jackson, A. (2000). Interacting with the past: The uses of participatory theatre at heritage sites. *RIDE: Research in Drama Education, 5*(2), 199–215.

Jackson, A. (2002). Between evaluation and research: Theatre as an educational tool in museum theatre. *Stage of the Art, 15*(1), 6–9.

Jackson, A. (2005). The dialogic and the aesthetic: Some reflections on theatre as a learning medium. *Journal of Aesthetic Education, 39*(4), 104–118.

Jackson, A. & Lev-Aladgem, S. (2004). Rethinking audience participation: Audiences in alternative and educational theatre. In V. A., Cremona, P. Eversmann, H. van Maanen, W. Sauter & J. Tulloch (Eds.), *Theatrical events: Borders, dynamics, frames* (pp. 207–238). Amsterdam, The Netherlands & New York, NY: Rodopi.

Jackson, A., Rees Leahy, H. (2005). "Seeing it for real...?" Authenticity, theatre and learning in museums. *RIDE: Research in Drama Education, 10*(3), 303–325.

Jellicoe, A. (1987). *Community plays: How to put them on.* London, UK: Methuen.

King, N. (1981). *A movement approach to acting.* Englewood Cliffs, NJ: Prentice-Hall.

Kirby, M. (1965). *Happenings. An illustrated anthology.* New York, NY: E. P. Dutton Inc.

Knowles, D. (1989). *Armand Gatti in the theatre: Wild duck against the wind.* London, UK: The Athlone Press.

Kostelanetz, R. (1968). *Theatre of mixed means.* New York, NY: Dial Press.

Kuppers, P. & Robertson, G. (Eds.). (2007). *The community performance reader.* London, UK & New York, NY: Routledge.

Kushner, T. (1993). *Angels in America: Parts one and two.* New York, NY: Theatre Communications Group.

Kushner, T. (2001). "In praise of contradiction and conundrum:" How do you make social change? *Theater, 31*(3), 61–64.

Lamden, G. (2000). *Devising: A handbook for drama and theatre students.* Abingdon, UK: Hodder & Stoughton.

Leonard, R. H. & Kilkelly, A. (2006). *Performing communities: Grassroots ensemble theaters deeply rooted in eight U.S. communities.* Oakland, CA: New Village Press.

Little, E. (2008). Editorial: Ethics and aesthetics. *alt. theatre, 4*(1), 3.

Maclean, N. (1992). *Young men and fire.* Chicago, IL: University of Chicago Press.

Maiter, S., Simich, L., Jacobson, N. &Wise, J. (2008). Reciprocity: An ethic for community-based participatory action research. *Action Research, 6*(3), 305–325.

Malcolm-Davies, J. (2004). Borrowed robes: The educational value of costumed interpretation at historic sites. *International Journal of Heritage Studies, 10*(3), 277–293.

Maslow, A. H. (1968). *Toward a psychology of being.* Ann Arbor, MI: University of Michigan Press.

McDonnell, B. (2005). Towards a theatre of "little changes:" A dialogue about dialogue. *RIDE: Research in Drama Education, 10*(1), 67–73.

McDonnell, B. (2006). Theatre, resistance and community—some reflections on "hard" interventionary theatre. In M. Balfour & J. Somers (Eds.), *Drama as Social Intervention* (2–11). Concord, ON: Captus Press.

McKenzie, J. (2001). *Perform or else: From discipline to performance.* London, UK & New York, NY: Routledge.

Meirelles, F. (Director) (2005). *The constant gardener* [motion picture]. London, UK: Potboiler Productions.

Morell, A. (2006). El teatro como herramienta para la contrucción. In L. McCammon & D. McLauchlan (Eds.), *Universal mosaic of drama and theatre: The IDEA dialogues* (pp. 213–220). City East, QLD: IDEA Publications.

Morgan, N. & Saxton, J. (1987). *Teaching drama: A mind of many wonders.* London, UK: Hutchinson Education.

Morgan, N. & Saxton, J. (1995/2006). *Asking better questions* (2nd ed.). Markham, ON: Pembroke.

Munier, A. & Etherton, M. (2006). Child rights theatre for development in rural Bangladesh: A case study. *RIDE: Research in Drama Education, 11*(2), 175–183.

Mutnick, D. (2006). Critical interventions: The meaning of praxis. In J. Cohen Cruz and M. Schutzman (Eds.), *A Boal companion: Dialogues on theatre and cultural politics* (pp. 33–45). London, UK: Routledge.

Myerhoff, B. (1992). *Remembered lives.* Ann Arbor, MI: University of Michigan Press.

Napp-Schindel, D. (2002). Museum theatre: Telling stories through objects. *Stage of the Art, 14*(4), 10–16.

National Health and Medical Research Council (Australia). (1996). Retrieved June 10, 2007 from www.who.int/bulletin/bulletin_board/83/ustun11051/en/print.html.

Neelands, J. (1984). *Making sense of drama: A guide to classroom practice.* Portsmouth, NH: Heinemann.

Neelands, J. & Goode, T. (1995). Playing in the margins of meaning: The ritual aesthetic in community performance. *NJ: Drama Australia Journal, 19*(1), 40–57.

Newman, P. (2008). Memorial retrospective. *Weekend Edition* with Lianne Hanson (September 28). *National Public Radio* (KPLU).

Nicholson, H. (1999). Aesthetic values, drama education and the politics of difference. *NJ: Drama Australia Journal, 23*(2), 81–90.

Nicholson, H. (2005). *Applied drama: The gift of theatre.* New York, NY: Palgrave Macmillan.

Oddey, A. (1996). *Devising Theatre: A practical and theoretical handbook.* London, UK: Routledge.

Odhiambo, C. (2001). What has TfD got to do with it? Fixing, un-fixing and refixing of positions and conditions. *Drama Research: The Research Journal of National Drama, 2,* 85–94.

Orenstein, C. (1998). *Festive revolutions: The politics of popular theater and the San Francisco Mime Troupe.* Jackson, MS: University of Mississippi.

O'Toole, J. (1976). *Theatre in education: New objectives for theatre—new techniques for education.* London, UK: Hodder & Stoughton.

O'Toole, J. (2004). Illuminated texts: From Homer to the home-page. *NJ: Drama Australia Journal, 28*(2), 5–13.

Paterson, D. (2001). The TASC is: Theatre and social change: How do you make social change? *Theater, 31*(3), 65–67.

Paulus, D. (2006). It's all about the audience. *Contemporary Theatre Review, 16* (3), 334–347.

Pavis, P. (1998). *Dictionary of the theatre: Terms, concepts, and analysis* (C. Shantz, Trans.). Toronto, ON: University of Toronto Press.

Pflanzer, H. (1992). Older people act up: Making the ordinary extraordinary. *TDR: The Drama Review, 36*(1), 115–123.

Prendergast, M. (2008). *Teaching spectatorship: Essays and poems on audience in performance.* Amherst, NY: Cambria Press.

Prentki, T. (1996). Big Mac—small change. *NJ: Drama Australia Journal, 23*(1), 97–108.

Prentki, T. & Preston, S. (Eds.). (2008). *The applied theatre reader.* London, UK: Routledge.

Prentki, T. & Selman, J. (Eds.). (2000). *Popular theatre in political culture: Britain and Canada in focus.* Bristol, UK: Intellect Books.

Prior, R. (2005). Looking around in awareness: Playbuilding on HIV/AIDS. *RIDE: Research in Drama Education, 10*(1), 54–64.

Saldaña, J. (2005). *Ethnodrama: An anthology of reality theatre.* Walnut Creek, CA: AltaMira Press.

Salverson, J. (1999). Anxiety and contact in attending to a play about land mines. In R. Simon, S. Rosenberg & C. Eppert (Eds.), *Between hope & despair: Pedagogy and the remembrance of historical trauma* (pp. 59–74). New York, NY: Rowman & Littlefield.

Salverson, J. (2000). Risking friendship in a play about landmines. In Prentki, T. & Selman, J. (Eds.), *Popular theatre in political culture: Britain and Canada in focus* (pp. 23–29). Bristol, UK: Intellect Books.

Sato, S.M. (2005, January). The audience as art. *American Theatre,* 50–58.

Saxton, J. (2006). [Personal notes on Smithsonian Institute visit]. Unpublished raw data.

Saxton, J. & Miller, C. (2006). The relationship of context to content in the medical model: Exploring possible paradigms. In M. Balfour & J. Somers (Eds.), *Drama as social intervention* (pp. 118–128). Concord, ON: Captus Press.

Schechner, R. (1997). Believed-in theatre. *Performance Research, 2*(2), 76–91.

Schechner, R. (1998/2003). *Performance theory* (2nd Ed.). New York, NY: Routledge.

Schechner, R. (2002/2006). *Performance studies: An introduction* (2nd Ed.). New York, NY: Routledge.

Schechter, J. (Ed.) (2003). *Popular theatre: A sourcebook.* London, UK: Routledge.

Schön, D. (1984). *The reflective practitioner: How professionals think in action.* New York, NY: Basic Books.

Schweitzer, P. (2006). *Reminiscence theatre: Making theatre from memories.* London, UK: Jessica Kingsley.

Shaughnessy, N. (2005). Truth and lies: Exploring the ethics of performance applications. *RIDE: Research in Drama Education, 10*(2), 201–212.

Shaw, G.B. (1906/2004). *The doctor's dilemma.* Fairfield, IA: 1ˢᵗ World.

Shepherd, S. & Wallis, M. (2004). *Drama/Theatre/Performance.* London, UK: Routledge.

Sills, P. (1971). *Story theatre.* New York, NY: Samuel French.

Sills, P. (2000). *Paul Sills' Story theatre: Four shows.* New York, NY: Applause Books.

Somers, J. (1998). Interview in "Trusting paradoxes" by Chris Johnston. In J. Thompson (Ed.), *Prison theatre: Perspectives and practices* (pp. 127–148). London, UK: Jessica Kingsley.

Somers, J. & Roberts, G. (2006). "On the edge:" Reflection on an interventionist theatre programme. In M. Balfour & J. Somers (Eds.), *Drama as social intervention* (pp. 26–39). Concord, ON: Captus.

Stein, J. (Ed.). (1966). *Random House dictionary of the English language: Unabridged edition.* New York, NY: Random House.

Sullivan, J. (2004). Community environmental forum theatre: A dramatic model for dialogue and participatory research among citizens and scientists. *Stage of the Art, 16*(1), 17–23.

Swartz, L. (1995/2002). *The new dramathemes* (3ʳᵈ Ed.). Markham, ON: Pembroke.

Swortzell, L. (1993). Trying to like TIE: An American critic hopes TIE can be saved. In A. Jackson (Ed.), *Learning through theatre* (pp. 239–250). London, UK: Routledge.

Tarlington, C. & Michaels, W. (1995). *Building Plays: Simple playbuilding techniques at work.* Markham, ON: Pembroke.

Taylor, P. (2003). *Applied theatre: Creating transformative encounters in the community.* Portsmouth, NH: Heinemann.

Taylor, P. (2006). Applied Theatre/Drama: An e-debate in 2004: Viewpoints. *RIDE: Research in Drama and Education, 11*(1), 90–95.

Thompson, J. (1998). *Prison theatre: Perspectives and practices.* London, UK: Jessica Kingsley.

Thompson, J. (2003). *Applied theatre: Bewilderment and beyond.* New York, NY: Peter Lang.

Thompson, J. & A. Jackson. (2006). Applied theatre/Drama: An e-debate in 2004: Viewpoints. RIDE: *Research in Drama and Education, 11*(1), 90–95.

Times Colonist (2000). "New play teaches art of dealing with dying," December 11, D2.

van Erven, E. (2001). *Community theatre: Global perspectives.* New York, NY: Routledge.

Vine, C. (1993). TIE and the theatre of the oppressed. In A. Jackson (Ed.), *Learning through theatre* (2nd ed.) (pp. 109–130). London, UK and New York, NY: Routledge.

Wagner, B. J. (1976). *Dorothy Heathcote: Drama as a learning medium.* Washington, DC: National Education Association.

Willett, J. (Ed.) (1964). *Brecht on theatre* (J. Willet, Trans.). New York, NY: Farrar, Strauss & Giroux.

Zull, J. (2002). *The art of changing the brain: Enriching the practice of teaching by exploring the biology of learning.* Sterling, VA: Stylus.

AUTHOR INDEX

Ackroyd, J. 14
Afzal-Khan, F. 4, 116
Ahsan, N. 107-110
Allen, G. 204
Anouilh, J. 11
Arnold, R. 18
Arrabal, F. 9

Bailey, C.H. 165, 192
Balfour, M. 119-120, 131
Balfour, M. & Somers, J. 14, 102, 132
Ball, S. 88, 101, 103
Barnhart, C. 24
Basting, A.D. 169, 170, 182
Bates, R.A. 65
Beckerman, B. 13
Blau, H. 8
Boal, A. iv, vi, vii, 4, 10-11, 17, 21, 52,
    69-73, 75, 77-80, 81-83, 108, 120-
    121, 125-126, 131, 133, 145, 179,
    191, 199, 203
Bond, E. 23
Booth, E. 191, 203
Bornat, J. 180-182
Bowles, N. 44-47

Bradby, D. & McCormick, J. 14
Bray, E. 19, 26
Brecht, B. 7-8, 52, 149, 170, 177, 197
Brian, C. 146-151
Bridal, T. 153, 165
Brook, P. 9, 205
Bruner, J. 204
Burnaford, G., Aprill, A. & Weiss, C.
    196
Burton, B. & O'Toole, J. 81
Bury, A., Popple, K. & Barker, J. 87
Butsch, R. 189
Butterwick, S. & Selman, J. 52, 66

Carklin, M. 39-40
Carlson, M. 7-10
Cassidy, H. & Watts, V. 47, 151
Chinyowa, K. 105
Cocke, D. 135, 190
Cohen-Cruz, J. 151, 152
Cohen-Cruz, J. & Schutzman, M. 81
Coleridge, S.T. 12
Conquergood, D. 194
Coult, T. & Kershaw, B. 66

Cox, M. 119, 132
Croyden, M. 9

Dalrymple, L. 39, 194
Damasio, A. 188, 203
Delgado, & Heritage, P. 203
Denzin, N. 187, 194
Dewey, J. 204
Diamond, D. 81
Doll, W. 204, 205
Donelan, K. 198
Donelan K. & O'Brien, A. 57-62
Drennan, B. 66
Dugga, V.S. 89-92
Dutlinger, A. 119
Dwyer, P. 74-77

Eagleton, T. 188
Edson, M. 87
Eisner, E. 195, 199
Ellis, A. 22
Esslin, M. 8
Eyre, R. & Wright, N. 8, 197

Filewod, A. 19, 66
Foreman, R. 9
Fraden, R. 132
Freire, M. 23
Freire, P. 10, 52, 69, 71, 72, 205

Gallagher, K. 194
Gaskell, I. & Taylor, R. 116
Giannachi, G. & Luckurst, M. 19
Giesekam, G. 6

Gladwell, M. 205
Goleman, D. 18
Goodwin, J. 189
Gray, R. 88, 102
Gray, R., Fitch, M. I., LaBrecque, M. &
    Greenberg, M. 88
Gray, R. & Sinding, C. 23, 101
Greene, M. 188, 191, 195
Grotowski, J. 8, 9
Grow, M.L. 62-65

Haedicke, S. 191, 198
Haedicke, S. & Nellhaus, T. 151
Handke, P. 9
Hart, H. 193
Hayes, J. & Napp-Schindel, D. 165
Hennessy, J. 32-33
Heritage, P. 120, 128-131, 133, 198
Horitz, T. 137-142
Howard, L.A. 77-80
Hughes, C. 165
Hughes, C., Jackson, A. & Kidd, J. 153

Idoko, E.F. 132

Jackson, Adrian 70, 75, 79, 131
Jackson, Anthony 3, 31, 47, 187, 189,
    192, 197, 200
Jackson, A. & Leahy, H. 154, 166
Jellicoe, A. 141

Kelin, D.A. 182
Kidd, R. 66
King, N. 6

Kirby, M. 8, 10

Knowles, D. 10

Kostelanetz, R. 9

Kuftinec, S. & Alon, C. 121-124

Kumar, S. 116

Kuppers P. & Robertson, G. v

Kushner, T. 11, 51, 52, 198

Lamden, G. 20, 26

Landvik, T. 142-146

Leonard, R. H. & Kilkelly, A. 135, 136, 151, 152

Lev-Aladgen, S. 102

Little, E. 198

Maclean, N. 170

Magelssen, S. 155, 159-161, 166

Maiter, S., Simich, L., Jacobson, N. &Wise, J. 190, 194, 199

Malcolm-Davies, J. 154, 166

Maslow, A. 201

McAvinchey, C. 132

McConachie, B. 151

McDonnell, B. 11, 197

McKenzie, J. 24

McLauchlan, D. 155, 162-165

Meirelles, F. 109

Mienczakowski, J. & Morgan, S. 102

Mitchell, T. 125-128

Morell, A. 119

Morgan, N. & Saxton, J. 24, 192

Muiruri, S. 97-101

Mundrawala, A. 114-115

Munier, A. & Etherton, M. 106, 116

Mutnick, D. 70

Myerhoff, B. 170

Napp-Schindel, D. 153, 164, 165, 166

Neelands, J. 135

Neelands, J. & Goode, T. 191

Newman, P. 23, 195

Nicholson, H. v, vi, 13, 26, 174-178, 188, 193, 195

Noble, S. 102

Nogueira, M. P 151

Nogueira, M. P., Goncalves, R. M. & Scheibe, C. 151

O'Brien, B.C. 182

O'Connor, P., O'Connor, B. & Welsh-Morris, M. 94-97

Oddey, A. 19

Odhiambo, C. 89, 105, 106, 116, 117

Orenstein, C. 52

O'Sullivan, J. 102

O'Toole, J. 10-11, 21, 31, 47, 187, 188

O'Toole, J., Burton, B. & Plunkett, A. 47

Paterson, D. 198

Paulus, D. 189, 199

Pavis, P. 17

Pflanzer, H. 6, 178-180

Prendergast, M. 24, 189

Prentki, T. 105, 106, 116

Prentki, T. & Preston, S. v, 14

Prentki, T. & Selman, J. 10, 52, 66

Prior, R. 197

Riccio, T. 66

Robinson, K. 200

Rohd, M. 27

Saldaña, J. 119

Samson, F. 199

Salverson, J. 3, 66

Sato, S.M. 196

Saxton, J. 6

Saxton, J. & Burke, M. 155-158

Saxton, J, & Miller, C. 4, 23, 25, 102

Schechner, R. 6, 12, 21-22

Schechner, R., Chatterjee, S. & Boal, A.
    71-73

Schechter, J. 51-52

Schön, D. 205

Schweitzer, P. 48, 169-170, 180, 183

Schutzman, M. 81

Shank, T. 53-57

Shapiro, J. & Hunt, L. 92-94

Shaughnessy, N. 199, 200

Shaw, G.B. 7, 87

Shepherd, S. & Wallis, M. 13

Sills, P. 49

Sinclair, C. 152

Smillie, R. & Randall, J. 48

Somers, J. 120

Somers, J. & Roberts, G. 20

Stein, J. 198

Sternberg, P. 27

Strickling, C.A. 102

Strimling, A. 183

Sullivan, J. 17

Swartz, L. 49

Swortzell, L. 187, 191

Tan, J. 48

Tarlington, C. & Michaels, W. 9

Taylor, P. v, 6, 14, 132

Thompson, J. v, 12, 14, 120, 132

Thompson, J. & Jackson, A. 6

Van Erven, E. v, 151

Van Poppel, E. 116

Vine, C. 32

Wagner, B.J. 25

wa'Ndeda, M.P. 111-114

Wang, W. 171-173

Weigler, W. 27

Willett, J. 52, 170

Winston, J. 33, 41-44

Zull, J. 6